C000172759

Europe's path to crisis

MANCHESTER
1824
Manchester University Press

Europe's path to crisis

Disintegration via monetary union

Tom Gallagher

Manchester University Press

Copyright © Tom Gallagher 2014

The right of Tom Gallagher to be identified as the author of this work has been asserted by him in accordance with the Copyright, Designs and Patents Act 1988.

Published by Manchester University Press
Oxford Road, Manchester M13 9NR, UK
and Room 400, 175 Fifth Avenue, New York, NY 10010, USA
www.manchesteruniversitypress.co.uk

Distributed in the United States exclusively by
Palgrave Macmillan, 175 Fifth Avenue, New York,
NY 10010, USA

Distributed in Canada exclusively by
UBC Press, University of British Columbia, 2029 West Mall,
Vancouver, BC, Canada V6T 1Z2

British Library Cataloguing-in-Publication Data
A catalogue record for this book is available from the British Library

Library of Congress Cataloging-in-Publication Data applied for

ISBN   978 0 7190 9603 7   hardback
        978 0 7190 9604 4   paperback

First published 2014

The publisher has no responsibility for the persistence or accuracy of URLs for any external or third-party internet websites referred to in this book, and does not guarantee that any content on such websites is, or will remain, accurate or appropriate.

Typeset
by Action Publishing Technology Ltd, Gloucester
Printed in Great Britain
by Bell and Bain Ltd, Glasgow

For my mother and my
brothers and sisters

Contents

Preface

'Euroquake' is a vivid phrase that does not underplay the scale of the crisis facing the European Union today. Monetary union was meant to be the decisive stage in the 50-year march towards a European state run along post-national lines. Instead, it has plunged the EU into a crisis with calamitous effects not just for many of its members but for the entire global economy. Faulty design and implementation ensured that ideology took priority over practical measures in the affairs of the currency union. During nearly five years of continuous economic crisis the emphasis has been on shielding special interests and intensifying efforts to concentrate power in the hands of the very officials who have primary responsibility for the debacle. Advocates of a supra-national Europe now find it virtually impossible to point to common benefits arising from their preference for concentrating power at the apex of unaccountable power structures. They also increasingly disagree among themselves about how to move on from an impetuous experiment – the European single currency – that has created more ill-will in Europe than any event since the EU's formation.

This book shows how today's crisis is very much rooted in the decisions and mindset that have shaped the EU from its earliest years. A democratic partnership involving the nations of Europe and its citizens was rejected by its architects. Such a course could have created a stronger and more genuinely cooperative Europe able to avoid the acute errors committed by isolated elites convinced that destiny had entrusted them to totally re-order European societies.

The EU's decision-makers form an oligarchy with favoured economic interest groups and activist groups with social agendas that favour accelerated European integration. Like other closed elites, there is no willingness to review the failures, biases and broad choices taken by the EU. Top-down efforts to create a borderless Europe around an agenda which only vested interests desire continue, despite their impracticality and potential for serious strife.

The people whose taxes fund the EU's activities continue to be overlooked and often disparaged. Indeed, not just in Britain, they are seen as increasingly unreliable because of their refusal to abandon national loyalties for pan-

European and indeed global ones. Nationalism continues to be the official enemy which fully justifies the EU's existence, however much the policy failures accumulate. But there is a huge paradox to be found here.

Nationalism has flourished within the EU's very own power structures as France and, more recently, Angela Merkel's Germany seek to use the EU to project their own national influence and interests, and more recent members follow their examples. Pro-integration efforts by France and Germany have been handicapped because of the different political and economic conditions in both countries and their contrasting visions of how the EU should evolve. Both of them, first France and much later Germany, have been unafraid to use the power that they wield in the EU's institutions to buttress their own positions.

The EU, for many of its 500 million citizens, has become synonymous with centralisation and tight regulation, disconcerting levels of social change, numbness towards democracy and, finally, with a menacing economic crisis and low-grade efforts to solve it. The book argues that building Europe without Europeans will rob the EU of its remaining legitimacy and plunge the continent into renewed strife in the name of an unloved ideology whose failures easily outweigh its successes. It places the EU's current difficulties in a long-term explanatory framework and argues that peace and stability in Europe cannot endure if the people have such a meagre voice in its governing arrangements.

The traditional nation-state has often been ill-equipped to handle globalised economic forces. But in the marathon post-2009 crisis the European Union has demonstrated that it lacks the necessary skills and resources to an even greater degree. Furthermore, it has been ready to tear up the social contract between citizens and their rulers with more alacrity than is usually the case with national decision-makers. The need for the EU to re-design itself as an entity concerned to identify and defend a European common good has never been more pressing. The prevailing posture for almost half a decade has been to defend, with startling rigidity, a failed blueprint for European convergence that benefits only a tiny proportion of a fast-diminishing pro-integration constituency in Europe.

There is now a need to discard the elite evangelicalism about 'more Europe' in all seasons and instead have a transparent debate about what models of economic coordination are viable for increasingly daunting times. No shortage of precedents reveal the harm that can be caused by doggedly persisting with strategies or models which leave a daunting human casualty level as their goals slip ever further out of reach.

Abbreviations

CAP	Common Agricultural Policy
CDU	Christian Democratic Union (Germany)
EC	European Community
ECB	European Central Bank
ECJ	European Court of Justice
ECSC	European Coal and Steel Community
EDC	European Defence Community
EEC	European Economic Community
EFSF	European Financial Stability Facility
EMU	European Monetary Union
EP	European Parliament
EPU	European Payments Union
ERM	Exchange Rate Mechanism
EU	European Union
LTRO	Long-Term Re-Financing Operation
MEP	Member of the European Parliament
NATO	North Atlantic Treaty Organization
OECD	Organization for Economic Cooperation and Development
OMT	Outright Market Transactions
SEA	Single European Act
SPD	Social Democratic Party (Germany)

Chronology

1950s

9 May 1950: Declaration of the Schuman plan.
18 April 1951: European Coal and Steel Community treaty signed by six founder members of the Common Market.
1952: European Court of Justice established.
1–2 June 1955: Messina conference to draw up plans for an economic community.
25 March 1957: Treaty of Rome signed by the six.
7 January 1958: European Commission begins work.

1960s

1963: The ECJ gives precedence to Community law when in conflict with national law.
22 January 1963: Franco-German pact of friendship signed.
6 July 1965: Empty Chair crisis begins, France boycotts community institutions.
28–29 January 1966: Luxembourg compromise ends French boycott.

1970s

7–8 October 1970: Werner Report on monetary union adopted.
1 January 1973: The UK, Denmark and Ireland join the EC.
9–10 December 1974: European Council formed at summit of EC leaders.
13 March 1979: European Monetary System begins.

1980s

1 January 1981: Greece becomes the tenth EC member.
1 January 1986: Spain and Portugal join the EC.
17 and 28 February 1986: Single European Act signed.

20 September 1988: Bruges speech, Margaret Thatcher warns about a European 'super-state'.
10 November 1989: The Berlin Wall comes down.

1990s

7 February 1992: The Maastricht Treaty is signed.
1 November 1993: The name of the European Community is changed to the European Union.
1 January 1995: Austria, Finland and Sweden join the EU.
2 October 1997: Treaty of Amsterdam is signed.
1 June 1998: European Central Bank is instituted.
1 January 1999: Participating countries in the eurozone establish their exchange rates.
15 March 1999: The European Commission resigns following a report identifying severe shortcomings.

2000–2009

12 May 2000: Joschka Fischer delivers 'Humboldt speech' in which he calls for the EU to become an inter-governmental federation with core states taking the lead.
14–15 December 2001: Laeken European Council launches a Convention which soon becomes an effort to formalise the various EU treaties in a new European Constitution.
1 January 2002: Euro currency begins to circulate in most of the EU.
29 October 2004: The treaty establishing a Constitution of Europe is signed in Rome.
29 May 2005: Constitution rejected by French voters.
1 June 2005: Constitution rejected by Dutch voters.
1 January 2007: Romania and Bulgaria join the EU.
1 January 2008: Cyprus and Malta adopt the euro.
1 December 2009: The Lisbon Treaty (successor to the Constitution) comes into effect.
December 2009: Following a change of government, Greece is revealed to have a massive budget deficit; its credit rating slumps in subsequent months.

2010

7 March 2010: President Sarkozy states that he doesn't believe Greece will need financial help.
6 April 2010: Greek financial emergency as bond yields soar over the country's ability to fund its budget deficit without outside help.

22 April 2010: The EU's official statistics agency says that it has doubts about the accuracy of Greek budget data.

2 May 2010: Greece agrees to a bail-out involving the EU, ECB and the IMF (the troika), a first for the countries using the euro.

7 May 2010: The US urges bolder action by EU to stem the crisis.

10 May 2010: The EU agrees to set up a €750 billion bail-out fund that would be available to assist troubled eurozone economies. It will be known as the European Financial Stability Facility (EFSF) and later it emerges that a permanent agency, the European Stability Mechanism, will supersede it.

23 July 2010: The EU releases 'comprehensive and rigorous' bank stress tests. The exercise 'confirms the resilience of EU and euro area banking systems to major economic and financial shocks' according to the ECB.

18 October 2010: France and Germany briefly agree at Deauville that a future permanent bail-out fund can require sacrifices from bondholders. Turmoil on the bond markets follows.

28 November 2010: Ireland signs up to a €68 billion bail-out which will be supervised by the troika. A separate agreement with the ECB requires the investment of unsecured and unguaranteed bondholders in bust banks to be met in full by the state.

2011

1 January 2011: Estonia adopts the euro.

4 February 2011: Bad response at EU summit to Franco-German call for 'competiveness pact' .

March 2011: EU leaders agree on rules for a permanent bail-out fund worth €500 billion, to operate from 2013, but later subject to successive changes.

6 March 2011: Portugal asks for and in May receives a financial bail-out of €78 billion.

25 March 2011: A watered-down version of the competitiveness pact called the 'Euro-Plus' pact agreed by EU leaders.

October 2011: Second bail-out to Greece with tougher terms offered by the troika as economic decline accelerates.

10 November 2011: Greek Prime Minister Papandreou resigns after strong EU resistance to his plan for a referendum on a new tougher bail-out.

12 November 2011: Italian Prime Minister Silvio Berlusconi resigns following dismay among EU decision-makers about his handling of a worsening financial crisis.

December 2011: The ECB launches a Long-Term Re-Financing Operation (LTRO) to pump credit into ailing European banks.

December 2011: All EU countries except the UK agree on a new inter-governmental treaty meant to lead to a fiscal stability union. A primary aim is to agree rules for restraining state spending and borrowing and tougher penalties for whoever breaks them.

2012

January 2012: Standard and Poor's, a leading credit rating agency, strips France of its triple A status and classifies the debts of Portugal and Cyprus as junk.

February 2012: Greece is the focus of the world's biggest ever debt restructuring deal. Its debt level falls from €350 billion to €240 billion (destabilising the financial sector in Cyprus).

May 2012: François Hollande elected President of France and soon emphasises growth rather than austerity as a response to the crisis.

June 2012: Spain accepts €100 billion to prop up its banks with protracted negotiations over the conditions to be attached to additional EU and IMF assistance.

June 2012: Cyprus makes an application for a bail-out package.

25 July 2012: ECB chief Mario Draghi indicates that it is prepared to launch an 'unlimited bond-buying plan' to preserve the euro.

6 September 2012: Unlimited bond-buying scheme called Outright Market Transactions (OMT) is launched to assist struggling eurozone members; the chief condition is a programme of budgetary reforms.

October 2012: The European Stability Mechanism (ESM), a permanent rescue fund, is launched after amendments to the Lisbon Treaty in late 2011. Its purpose is to act as a 'financial firewall' preventing financial contagion across the eurozone.

2013

March 2013: The Netherlands admits that it is unable to meet the EU's target of keeping budget deficits under 3 per cent of GDP.

16 March 2013: EU bail-out of Cyprus announced, initially with plan to tax small savers in its banks. Jeroen Dijsselbloem, the new head of the eurogroup of finance ministers, announces that such a 'haircut' of savers could shape future rescue plans in the eurozone.

April 2013: Figures show the USA returning to pre-crisis levels of growth while the eurozone economy stagnates.

June 2013: Youth unemployment in Italy, Portugal, Spain and Greece stands at between 45 and 65 per cent of their working populations.

14 June 2013: After the IMF criticises the troika's approach to the Greek crisis, Klaus Regling, the head of the eurozone's bailout funds, says that the IMF should not play a role in future eurozone rescue packages.

July 2013: Mounting evidence that Germany is dragging its feet over a proposed eurozone banking union.

20 August 2013: In the face of growing evidence that its debt burden is unsustainable, Wolfgang Schäuble, German Finance Minister, predicts that Greece will require a third bail-out.

22 September 2013: Angela Merkel is re-elected as German Chancellor.

September 2013: Figures show that 70 per cent of young people in the Greek labour force are unemployed.

November 2013: The Irish government announces that it will pay down massive loans without securing the precautionary line of credit urged by independent advisers. To fund its liabilities, Ireland requires surpluses to average above 4 per cent for the next decade or more. Its GDP fell by nearly 17 per cent between 2008 and 2013.

18 December 2013: A shell banking union was announced at the latest EU summit. The timing was driven by the conclusion of talks between the CDU and SPD parties in Germany prior to the formation of a grand coalition. There was widespread agreement in published analyses that a much-delayed initiative would be unable to address systematic weaknesses in the European financial sector. A theoretical back-stop for banks in difficulties of €55 billion will only be in place by 2026. Germany managed to veto risk-sharing with states continuing to bail out banks. The process for closing down banks is extremely complex. States like Germany also retain a national veto on bank closures. The Commission and the ECB (which criticised the absence of a central credit fund) were sidelined in what will be an inter-governmental initiative. Coordination between national governments failed in the past and the new package is seen as a disincentive for foreign creditors to return to the EU investment field. The largely presentational banking union increases the possibility that states in the future will use large amounts of public money to salvage badly run banks.

31 December 2013: Latvia joins the eurozone, despite one poll showing that only two out of ten of its citizen supported accession.

Biographies

ADENAUER, Konrad (1876–1967), Chancellor of West Germany 1949–1963.

BALL, George (1909–1994), United States Under-Secretary of State 1961–1966.

BARNIER, Michel (1951–), Commissioner for the Internal Market and Services 2009–.

BARROSO, José Manuel (1956–), President of the European Commission 2004– ; previously Foreign Minister of Portugal 1992–1995; Prime Minister 2002–2004.

BERLUSCONI, Silvio (1936–), Prime Minister of Italy 1996, 2001–2006, 2008–2011.

BLAIR, Tony (1953–), Prime Minister of Great Britain 1997–2007.

BONDE, Jens-Peter (1948–), Danish MEP 1979–2008 and tenacious critic of EU's approach to democracy.

BRANDT, Willy (1913–1992), Chancellor of West Germany 1969–1974.

CHIRAC, Jacques (1932–), President of France 1995–2007.

CHURCHILL, Winston (1874–1965), Prime Minister of Great Britain 1940–1945, 1951–1955.

COHN-BENDIT, Daniel (1945–), Euro-Federalist and Green MEP since 1994.

DE GASPERI, Alcide (1881–1954), Prime Minister of Italy 1945–1953.

DE GAULLE, Charles (1890–1970), President of France 1944–1946, 1958–1969.

DELORS, Jacques (1925–), President of the European Commission 1984–1994.

DE MAN, Hendrik (1885–1953), leading pre-1940 Belgian Socialist active in promoting European cooperation on the left.

DRAGHI, Mario (1947–), President of the European Central Bank 2011– .

ERHARD, Ludwig (1897–1977), West German Minister of Economics 1949–1963; Chancellor 1963–1966.

FISCHER, Joschka (1948–), German Foreign Minister 1998–2005.

GISCARD D'ESTAING, Valéry (1926–), President of France 1974–1981; Chairman of the Convention on the Future of Europe 2002–2003.

HALLSTEIN, Walter (1901–1982), President of the European Commission 1958–1967.

HOLLANDE, François (1954–), President of France 2012– .

JUNCKER, Jean-Claude (1954–), Prime Minister of Luxembourg 1995– ; Head of Ecofin 2005–2013.

KINNOCK, Neil (1942–), Commissioner for Transport 1994–1999; Vice-President of the EU Commission 1999–2004.

KLAUS, Václav (1941–), Eurosceptic; President of the Czech Republic 2003–2013.

KOHL, Helmut (1930–), Chancellor of West Germany and later a united Germany 1982–1998.

LAMY, Pascal (1947–), Chef de cabinet of Jacques Delors 1984–1994; Commissioner for Trade 1999–2004; Director-General of the World Trade Organization 2005–2013.

MACSHARRY, Ray (1938–), EU Trade Commissioner 1989–1994.

MERKEL, Angela (1954–), Chancellor of Germany 2005– .

MITTERRAND, François (1916–1996), President of France 1981–1995.

MONNET, Jean (1888–1979), the leading early architect of European integration. He held numerous posts in French and European governance designed to further that goal.

MONTI, Mario (1943–), Commissioner for the Internal Market and Services 1995–1999; for Competition 1999–2004; Prime Minister of Italy 2011–2013.

NOEL, Emile (1922–1996), Secretary-General of the European Commission 1957–1987.

PAPANDREOU, Andreas (1919–1996), Prime Minister of Greece 1981–1989, 1993–1996.

POMPIDOU, Georges (1911–1974), President of France 1969–1974.

PRODI, Romano (1939–), President of the European Commission 1999–2004, later Prime Minister of Italy.

RAJOY, Mariano (1955–), Prime Minister of Spain 2011– .

REDING, Viviane (1951–), Commissioner for Education and Culture 1999–2004; for Information Society and Media 2005–2009; for Justice, Fundamental Rights and Citizenship 2010– .

REHN, Olli (1962–), Commissioner for Enlargement 2004–2009; for Economic and Monetary Affairs 2010 – .

SANTER, Jacques (1937–), President of the European Commission 1994–1999; Prime Minister of Luxembourg 1984–1994. From 2012, chief EU fund-raiser for the permanent bail-out fund.

SARKOZY, Nicolas (1955–), President of France 2007–2012.

SCHÄUBLE, Wolfgang (1942–), Head of West German Chancellery 1984–1989, Minister of the Interior 1989–1991, 2005–2009; Minister of Finance 2009– .

SCHMIDT, Helmut (1918–), Chancellor of West Germany 1974–1982.

SCHRÖDER, Gerhard (1944–), Chancellor of Germany 1998–2005.

SCHUMAN, Robert (1886–1963), a decisive figure in launching European integration, Prime Minister of France 1947–1948; Foreign Minister 1948–1952.

SPAAK, Paul-Henri (1899–1972), a pivotal figure in the rise of the European Community, Prime Minister of Belgium 1938–1939, 1946, 1947–1949; Secretary-General of NATO 1957–1961; chairman of the team that drafted the Treaty of Rome in 1967.

SPINELLI, Altiero (1907–1986), veteran Italian champion of European federalism whose Spinelli Report in 1984 influenced later integrationist developments.

THATCHER, Margaret (1925–2013), Prime Minister of Great Britain 1979–1990.

TRICHET, Jean-Claude (1942–), Governor of the Bank of France 1994–2003; President of the European Central Bank 2003–2012.

VAN ROMPUY, Herman (1947–), President of the European Council 2009– .

VERHEUGEN, Günther (1944–), Commissioner for Enlargement 2004–2009; Commissioner for Enterprise and Industry 2005–2009.

VERHOFSTADT, Guy (1953–), Prime Minister of Belgium 1999–2007, 2007–2008; a leading Euro-federalist.

WEIDMANN, Jens (1968–), President of the Bundesbank 2011– .

WERNER, Pierre (1913–2002), Prime Minister of Luxembourg 1959–1974, 1979–1984; author of the 1970 Werner Report.

Introduction

The idea of a common currency union is a big mistake, an adventurous, reckless and mistaken goal which will not unite Europe but, instead, divide it.
Professor Ralf Dahrendorf, 1995[1]

On 12 October 2012, the committee allocating the Nobel Peace Prize announced that the award was going to the European Union. The jury, headed by Thorbjon Jagland, a Norwegian who also held a key position in the Council of Europe, singled out 'the Union and its forerunners' due to it having 'contributed to the advancement of peace and reconciliation, democracy and human rights in Europe'.[2]

The announcement surprised most observers commenting on the decision in major publications. This was not least owing to the huge difficulties that the EU was having in finding the means to overcome Europe's deepest post-war economic crisis by far.

Cooperation and trust were increasingly scarce commodities in the inner councils of the EU. A sense of equality uniting countries supposedly resolved to build a common European home had given way to simmering resentments and open rivalries. Weaker members found themselves effectively under the direction of stronger members which had done well out of the creation and management of the single currency. Germany had done particularly well, something that was down to its own efforts, according to most of its own policy-makers as well as admirers of the country's system of political economy. Others argued that its economic profile enabled it to build up a massive trading surplus thanks to a fixed exchange rate mechanism which soon became a straitjacket for weaker members.

A monetary union encompassing seventeen disparate economies had opened up a new North–South fault-line in Europe less than a generation after the East–West one had been greatly diminished. Three days before the award had been announced in Oslo, the depth of the rupture had been highlighted when the German Chancellor, Angela Merkel, arrived in Greece for a six-hour visit. It was hard to see what prompted her to make such a lightning trip other than photo opportunities bound to show her as a courageous and resolute leader ready to enter the lion's den to preach the necessity that nations must live within their means.

The entire EU was being violently shaken by the clash of rival economic moralities. Within Germany, there was an impressive united front publicly affirming that fiscal consolidation or belt-tightening was the only remedy for economic competitiveness. Other creditor countries in Northern Europe endorsed such a view. But public opinion in countries across the north Mediterranean, from Portugal to Greece, challenged policies which seemed designed to plunge them into a downward spiral of depression. Many economists, watching how the debt of the eurozone periphery continued to grow in proportion to national output despite draconian austerity measures, backed the apparent victims, however profligate some of their governments had been in the past. It seemed difficult to avoid frightening levels of economic contraction and unemployment in a growing list of countries which from 2010 had reluctantly accepted that they must extricate themselves from difficulties largely through their own painful efforts.

In Athens on 9 October 2012 Merkel was confronted by enraged demonstrators whom 7,000 police struggled to keep under control. The slogans, some of which assailed Germany for imposing a new 'Fourth Reich', indicated that many no longer believed that, within a eurozone where key financial decisions were made by the European Central Bank (ECB), their country enjoyed meaningful independence. One group of protesters sat atop a jeep dressed in Nazi uniforms, while another, clutching the Greek flag, lay underneath the wheels of the vehicle.[3] By contrast, when Merkel's predecessor, Konrad Adenauer, had paid an official visit to Athens in 1954, only a decade after the wartime German occupation, he had been greeted as a friendly head of state.

Under Adenauer and his successors, Germany had developed into one of the most impressive democracies in the history of modern Europe. But Greece, thirty years after it joined the EU in 1981, was awash with extremism: Golden Dawn, a neo-fascist party, enjoyed growing influence among state officials and approval in the wider society as the conventional parties faced mounting rejection.[4]

Greece had joined the European Union in the hope that membership of the world's most successful regional entity could enable this strategically placed Balkan country to put poverty and instability permanently behind it. But the changes and improvements which Greece experienced as a member were, in many ways, superficial. The EU turned out not to be an agent for overdue modernisation. Decision-makers in Brussels proved to be false friends to the wider society by allowing transfer funds to be wasted by incompetent or even venal local elites. A pattern of 'corruption with favours ... distributed by the "party–state"' was entrenched by a relationship which thwarted genuine development.[5]

Greece, in 2001, was even allowed to join the single currency although it was meant for countries with far sounder finances. It was not alone. Spain, Portugal and Italy had become founder members in 1999. A borderless financial system, far from leading the way towards economic and political convergence, instead plunged the EU into a crisis. A decade or more of the currency union ensured that national financial problems were transferred across much of the seventeen-member eurozone. The intensity of cross-border financial activity, often in the form of investment by creditor countries in Northern Europe in indebted but fast-growing Southern European ones, removed the defences which nation-states normally have against economic calamity elsewhere.

State indebtedness in Greece and Portugal and private indebtedness in Spain and Ireland, due in large part to a runaway property boom, would tip each of these countries into crisis. One after another from early 2010 onwards, states on the periphery of the eurozone found it difficult to borrow in the financial markets in order to raise the revenue even to provide normal services. A financial crisis in the United States had led to a sharp curtailment of borrowing worldwide, especially to countries which looked to be credit risks. The EU was forced to intervene in one eurozone member after another to prevent a collapse of financial institutions. The European Central Bank, the body overseeing the financial affairs of the eurozone, bailed out insolvent banks and governments in return for tough austerity measures.

In Greece, no corner was turned. Deficit levels and debt ratios rose relentlessly. A second bail-out was required in the autumn of 2011. But by the following spring unemployment had topped 20 per cent and nearly 50 per cent of young people were out of work. The EU had become a pitiless austerity union in the eyes of many casualties of the financial emergency. In the autumn of 2012, polls showed that the far-left Syriza party and the neo-fascist Golden Dawn party were in second and third place, with Pasok, in charge of the country for most of the years of EU membership, reduced to 8 per cent.

One incident which revealed the depth of the rupture between many Greeks and the EU occurred on 6 September 2012. In the centre of Athens, members of the security forces set up mock triple gallows on an open-top van, with a sign reading 'Troika' – in reference to the austerity inspectors from the European Union, the IMF and the European Central Bank. An officer from each of the services – police, coast guard and firefighters – then stood with his head in a noose.[6]

This book explores why the boldest initiative in the sixty-year quest to achieve a borderless Europe has exploded in the face of the EU. A close examination of each stage of the EU financial emergency offers evidence that the European values that are supposed to provide solidarity within the twenty-eight-member EU in good times and bad are flimsy and thinly distributed.

The EU's claims to be an averter of conflicts, an effective crisis manager, a guardian of representative democracy, an institution capable of restraining national enmities, and one that invariably shows compassion to members in difficulties have now been tested and found wanting in many eyes. But it would be wrong to assume that the EU's difficulties are mostly recent in origin. This book aims to show that it is possible to view the current difficulties of the EU as rooted in much longer-term decision-making. Conscious choices were made by the architects of the EU which prevented a genuine European partnership developing, one firmly grounded in democratic values and a desire to co-exist with a national outlook. A number of undoubted achievements, not least the creation of an arena enabling France and Germany to evolve from being deadly enemies to usually cooperative neighbours, have been eclipsed by long-term failures. Instead of harnessing national energies, by working with and not against national parliaments, the EU has waged an unnecessary and costly battle to subdue the nation-state and delegitimise all forms of nationalism. It has kept the people at arm's length, preferring to rule through unwieldy, overlapping and sometimes clashing structures which lack a proper mandate. By contrast it has entered into increasingly close relations with corporate and banking interests, especially in the last two decades, often absorbing their priorities and worldview. In the process, a quasi-state in which bureaucrats interact closely with these economic forces, as well as lobbies promoting particular social and environmental agendas, has taken shape. Meanwhile, there is little room for individuals, small and medium-sized businesses, and communities lacking strong advocates in Brussels, to have their voices heard.

Left-wing and even *avant-garde* in many of its cultural and social policies, the EU has been devoted to a form of capitalism which benefits major transnational corporations as well as leading countries where the state is a powerful economic actor; new members, whose entry after 2004 almost doubled the size of the EU, were required to undergo economic shock therapy in order to gain admission. Many have found it hard to hold their own against core states with stronger firms able to flood their domestic markets and marginalise national firms.

Convergence of the economies of Western and Eastern Europe will be slow to occur, if it ever does. More likely is a repeat of the dominant power relations seen in the Americas for much of the past century where the United States has been able to impose its economic preferences on weaker countries located in its shadow.

The crisis of the eurozone has widened the gulf between the economies of Northern and Southern Europe to an ominous degree. The EU is reluctant to review its failures, its biases, and the broad choices which drive forward its policies except in contrived exercises whose outcome is often pre-determined. That is why a book that aims to place its current difficulties in a long-term explanatory framework is necessary, perhaps even overdue.

By 2012, it was impossible to mask the scale of the financial crisis and the questions it raised about the viability of the European project. With the eruption of the Cyprus crisis in the spring of 2013, it was becoming almost impossible to present the EU as a union standing for European solidarity. A European 'general interest' was hard to invoke as shown by the evasive and cliché-ridden terms in which top EU figures often spoke at dramatic moments in the extended crisis.

A carelessly constructed and poorly managed currency union had revealed ominous cracks in the common European home of twenty-eighty states – between North and South, creditor and debtor countries, between countries inside and outside the eurozone, and even between core eurozone states over the extent to which national sacrifices should be made by them in order to keep the euro afloat.

Bilateral relations have also suffered, none more so than the ones between Germany and Greece. Germany has been the most prominent advocate of strict austerity measures in return for EU financial help that will come disproportionately from its own funds. In February 2012, the country's Finance Minister, Wolfgang Schäuble, said he wanted to 'help' Greece but would not 'pour money into a bottomless pit'. He recommended the postponement of impending elections and the continuation of a technocratic government for a year. This brought a retort from the elderly Greek President, Karolos Papoulias, who had fought against German military occupiers after 1941: 'I do not accept having my country taunted by Mr Schäuble, as a Greek I do not accept it. Who is Mr Schäuble to taunt Greece?'[7] By September 2012, only a quarter of Germans thought that Greece should stay in the eurozone or receive further help.[8]

Not only had the deep and complex financial emergency shattered the EU's image as a competent manager of Europe's economic affairs but it had also damaged reputational pillars upon which it rested its claims to be one of the most progressive forces seen in European history. National enmities had returned to the foreground of European affairs, creating antagonism between different peoples and parts of their governing elites. The seductive claim that the EU is an essential guarantor of democracy in countries susceptible to authoritarian rule has also been badly undermined. This is not only due to the revival of illiberal and extremist parties but to the EU's own readiness to foist unelected technocrats on crisis-ridden countries. Democratic procedures have been side-stepped in order to drive forward what are viewed as essential structural reforms, ones whose worth is hotly disputed among world economists and reviled by millions bearing their impact. If and when the EU emerges from this crisis, it will have a huge amount of work to do in order to restore the reputation of its political and economic brand.

But EU rhetoric depicts the crisis as a manageable one, and for several years problems were viewed as temporary, or else rooted in global structures or

North American events.[9] Each new initiative is usually described as one leading the union towards a solution of its difficulties. Officially, it is still the EU goal to have, by 2020, 75 per cent employment in a union of twenty-eight states whose population is just over 500 million.[10] This will mean creating 17 million new jobs even though it is not since the 1970s that the EU has seen growth rates capable of generating such levels of employment.

The EU has a tangled form of decision-making in which power is shared between an administrative corps, the European Commission, the European Council in which the interests of major states are reflected, and the European Parliament, still lacking the competences taken for granted by parliaments in most democracies; much energy is used up in turf wars between these bodies, as the present crisis has shown, and the institutional tussles have only intensified with the arrival on the scene of the European Central Bank in the last fifteen years.

There is no agreement on how the political and economic structures of the EU can be re-balanced in order to respond effectively to the crisis. For two years, Germany promoted austerity measures which would be accompanied by central oversight of budget deficits, but it was opposed to economic transfers from North to South to rescue indebted countries. A change of government in France in mid-2012 saw the balance of power briefly shift at European level: a desire for greater centralisation was matched by a willingness to muster enormous sums to extend a lifeline to countries in crisis and retain market confidence in the ones seen to be next in line. The ECB, on the board of which Latin states enjoy a majority, became a central player and it was the turn of Germany to experience isolation and harbour growing doubts about what its role in the EU should be. But without effective answers for daunting economic problems at home, France's President Hollande was incapable of replacing Germany as a crisis manager.

Calls for creating a more integrated EU bloc have accompanied each stage of the crisis. Plans for a banking union with a single supervisor authorised to intervene in the affairs of troubled banks were agreed in December 2012. But it soon became clear that Germany, the main advocate of pan-European solutions, was dragging its feet because it wished to exempt many of its own banks from such a regime.[11] EU anti-crisis measures have lacked substance. Often their purpose appears to be to provide sound-bites for the crisis summits held at regular intervals since the spring of 2010, or else position beleaguered leaders to overcome electoral challenges (such as the contest Angela Merkel faced in September 2013). Plans for economic governance of the EU contain bold intentions but they are invariably vague on detail. There is no architecture in place that can bind an unworldly union closer together in practical ways. Nor is there a groundswell of popular support. But at each previous great leap forward for EU integration, what the voters think or want has not mattered very much.

Resistance has been overcome by various stratagems. But this time, the lives of millions of citizens have been seriously affected because the single currency, billed as the most ambitious step taken to unite Europe, has turned into a practical fiasco. Top-down efforts at unification will be harder to accomplish because of a sullen populace and inter-elite rivalries. The view that integration efforts are bound to succeed because of their own inherent virtues is also losing its appeal. The cheerful evangelicalism, summed up in the remark of Spanish Eurocrat Javier Solana to a British journalist, 'Our philosophy in Europe is, jump in the pool, there is always water there', practically vanished after 2008.[12]

It was this absence of a cautious or critical perspective that led to the ill-fated adoption of the single currency. Eurocrats continue to plan and scheme for the future. But they lack an understanding of what is needed to give new projects a sense of permanence. The importance of having genuine legitimacy among those who pay the EU's bills is still not appreciated. Nor is the necessity to punish failure among office-holders as well as reward success. Nor is the need to have objectives which do not merely satisfy particular vested interests but also strengthen the values which are supposed to be at the heart of the European project.

The single currency debacle could be described as a failure of character and judgement at the top of the EU. But it exemplified long-term weaknesses. The misbegotten enterprise had been driven forward by a narrow range of forces: France, always keen to find ways to project its influence through new European initiatives; and, increasingly, Germany, no longer preoccupied with restoring its reputation, but grappling with the immense challenge of re-unifying the country following the collapse of Soviet-backed communism.

There had been no critical mass of opinion in favour of adopting the euro. Nor indeed had there been for embarking on the integration journey nearly fifty years earlier. The original Common Market had been formed to no small degree to erect stronger defences against a predatory Soviet Union. The desire to supplant the US dollar as the premier global currency was an important motive for amalgamating the currencies of fifteen countries and forming the euro in 1999. Deception was practised about the exact motives for embarking upon integration: political unification was the aim, as Jean Monnet would occasionally publicly reveal. Thus when speaking to the Council of Europe on 28 March 1953, he stated that 'Our Community is not an association of producers of coal and steel; it is the beginning of Europe'.[13] In order to placate wary populations in countries like Britain, the measures of accelerating economic coordination were what was often depicted as the end point.

The European Central Bank was deliberately created to be insulated from the will of the electorate as indeed was the European Commission before it. Institutions which lack democratic accountability are at risk of being captured by special interests. The concern with the welfare of a reckless and covetous financial sector appears to have preoccupied the ECB far more than the needs of pensioners, savers, non-unionised workers, small business owners or vulnerable younger citizens who, across the northern Mediterranean, are in danger of becoming 'a lost generation'.

The EU's policy-making record has been one of growing failure and the single currency crisis is just the most spectacular of a string of recent crises. But there has never been any enthusiasm among the interlocking political and bureaucratic elites to step back and take stock, especially to see how best to ensure that national democracy is reconciled with European administrative centralism.

Bureaucrats, and the heterogeneous interest groups which orbit the EU's power structures, continue to wield more power than they could ever hope to enjoy in most national democracies. The most popular justification for this benign absolutism is the need to keep evil incarnate, political nationalism, at bay. Voters in the EU are still treated with reserve by Eurocrats because they appear susceptible to the dangerous charms of identifying with a particular nation's fate. The example of one toxic brand of nationalism which had devastating consequences for much of Europe in the second quarter of the last century is seen as clinching evidence that this political concept is a tainted one. Yet effective government in which the voice of citizens counts at least to a meaningful extent appears capable of flourishing only within the context of nation-states. Reckless nationalism may indeed be a danger when the mood of citizens grows intransigent or the concept is manipulated by unscrupulous figures. However, nationalism cannot be dis-invented. It will remain in contention as long as the EU is unable to devise institutions which successfully represent the general and particular interests of European citizens.

There is also an even greater paradox. Nationalism has flourished within the EU's very own power structures due to the fact that resources and advantages are unevenly distributed. Its resources come from its national members but the way they are allocated often depends on the national influence that members can bring to bear in top-level EU decision-making. Small countries can prove surprisingly strong in obtaining structural funds (Ireland before 2008) or else in evading sanctions for doubtful behaviour (Greece in the same period). But one country stands out in terms of its ability to bend EU institutions to its will.

It may not be unreasonable to claim that France has wanted the EU to turn into the power it could not be on its own and, from de Gaulle's time onwards, has used the EU to project its own national influence and interests. But France failed to supply effective champions for its inter-governmental vision of a strong Europe. Germany had a more genuinely federal vision: much of the architecture of European integration resulted from joint Franco-German efforts. Synergies arising from certain political partnerships (Schmidt and Giscard and later Kohl and Delors) drove the integration agenda forward. But ultimately France and Germany were an odd couple. The different economies and political systems of both the EU's continental giants failed to provide a common basis for moving towards establishing a European state. France proved a neurotic and self-absorbed actor in the EU drama for long periods; indeed the damage done in the 1960s and 1995–2005 period to the supranational agenda by France was arguably much greater than the harm caused to the project by outright Eurosceptics like Margaret Thatcher.

Perhaps unavoidably Chapter 1 begins with an exploration of the long-term preparations that were made to create a single currency encompassing a large part of the European Union. It shows how the impetus was essentially political, to erode the power of the nation-state and speed up the installation of a supra-national alternative through hurtling towards monetary union. Reordering the financial landscape of a large part of Europe was finally embarked upon in the 1990s with little care or long-term planning. There was an astonishing degree of complacency that nations with different economic needs and conditions could make a viable combination in the absence of fiscal and political unity. Poor-quality management meant that countries and banks across Europe became loaded down with debt on the assumption that they would be supported by the financial firepower of the eurozone as a whole. The evangelical fervour with which the single currency was promoted and the refusal to cast aside complacency and heed warnings about the dangers which it posed for European cooperation reveal a strongly dysfunctional side to the EU – an entity confident and assured in its planning role but often hopelessly inept in managing and implementing some of its key projects.

Chapter 2 examines the different ways in which the European Union seized the initiative from the European nation-state, from the formation of the Coal and Steel Community to the Maastricht Treaty. Not only was a Europe without powerful nations a primary goal but there was a growing willingness to remove the project from any real democratic oversight. This meant that democratic validation was never a crucial requirement, one of the early failures which has undermined the credibility of the EU during its years of crises. Another was a tendency to promote policies that benefited vested interests rather than European citizens as a whole. The Common Agricultural Policy is probably the most glaring example. It could be viewed as a forerunner of the single currency, since the motivation for its adoption and survival in the face of numerous criticisms has been strategically placed European elites in the agricultural sector.

Chapter 3 concentrates on the role of France and Germany in the EU. Both states have often exercised dominance at key moments and have collaborated to drive the integration project forward. But, as this chapter argues, their pro-integration endeavours have often, in practice, been ineffective ones. France found it easier to come to terms with a previously implacable enemy, Germany, than to submerge its destiny completely within the EU. Germany was willing to allow France to use the EU for its own national purposes. It was often too indulgent when presented with the evidence that France desired a strong Europe with weak institutions, one more easily directed by France. Even during the high tide of supra-nationalism coinciding with Jacques Delors's decade at the head of the European Commission, France pursued a policy of extracting maximum national advantage from the EU. Overall, its role as a promoter of European integration has been erratic, being unable to balance French and wider European priorities. Germany's leadership usually lacked the persuasive skills to encourage France down a more consistent European path. Arguably, it bears major responsibility for the low-grade planning that preceded the launch of the single currency and for its faulty implementation.

Chapter 4 examines the difficulties that have arisen for the EU as it has tried to foster a new European consciousness. Educational and media strategies as well as a set of symbols have been devised to establish a coherent European identity and promote common values and attachments. But opinion polls and other evidence indicate that they have not had a significant effect on popular awareness in many member states. Citizens often evaluate the EU in terms of its impact on their lives and conditions. Instead of improvements and widening opportunities, European integration has been increasingly linked with disruption, greater centralised oversight and now a complex and menacing economic crisis that leaves few unaffected. Complaints have mounted about over-regulation and irritation has grown about efforts to supplant national values with an international set in which group rights have been privileged over individual ones. The chief beneficiaries of this attempt to promote a European mosaic identity often appear to be social and ethnic groups with influential advocates in the EU institutions. Moreover, the emphasis on financial concerns has resulted in a clearcut alliance between key elite forces at the top of the EU and some of the EU's leading economic and financial sectors.

These various alliances have been the foundation of new trans-national initiatives in the economic and legal spheres. Further centralisation has resulted and it has been justified by the need to marginalise nationalism. But the visionaries advocating post-national governance too often have refused to confront the shortcomings of the EU. They assume the sharp rivalries between states and EU institutions over influence can be accommodated by more centralised direction (of a benign kind of course). There is an absorption with redesigning and expanding institutions and creating new ones rather than questioning the effectiveness of the bureaucratic and highly regulated way in which a common Europe has been reconstructed.

With such an inflexible and patronising approach, it is hardly surprising that European integration has failed to capture the imagination. The obsession with building a Europe in which Europeans continue to have little say appears undiminished in the face of spectacular policy failures. It is therefore unsurprising that the EU faces a mounting crisis of legitimacy. This is likely to continue as long as the EU's multi-level institutions persist in having an interior conversation with carefully selected partners while proclaiming themselves to be the legitimate representatives of over 500 million Europeans.

Chapter 5 examines the increasingly strained relationship between the EU and the democratic process. EU institution-building has been a sixty-year experiment that increasingly keeps democracy at arm's length. The distrust of voters is increasingly on display from those in charge of the EU and elections are seen as a major distraction that interrupts EU business. The preference for post-democratic arrangements has been fuelled by stinging referendum defeats for the constitution-building exercise begun in 2002. The autocratic way in which the process was handled by Valéry Giscard d'Estaing provided ample evidence that deepening integration was taking place at the expense of democracy. After 2005, in the face of popular rejection, EU institution-builders were determined to persist and the 2009 Lisbon Treaty was the result. This chapter argues that ethical standards and competent decision-making are becoming casualties of the democratic deficit. Arguably, the absence of democratic scrutiny and approval contributed greatly to the low-grade design and implementation of the single currency. The absence of democratic safeguards has allowed it and other unpopular innovations to be retained, due solely to the backing that they enjoy in influential quarters of the EU .

The EU was viewed as an effective sponsor of democracy in Southern and Eastern Europe in the final quarter of the twentieth century. But the euro crisis has seen its reputation as a democratising agent rapidly fade. Democracy is being rationed and withheld from indebted countries. Few decision-makers in the EU seem to realise the harm that can arise from the retreat towards rule by a combination of well-placed oligarchies. It can only hope to enjoy popular legitimacy if it rehabilitates democracy. Unless enabling citizens to influence its affairs becomes a priority, complete rejection by alienated citizens in voiceless nation-states will be its probable fate.

The focus of Chapter 6 is on the evolution of the crisis in the eurozone and the shortcomings which have impeded the EU from bringing it under control. It examines how certain long-term EU traits – procrastination, a desire to safeguard vested interests, a readiness to modify supposedly inviolable EU rules, and a refusal to allow a radical re-think in the face of acute policy failures – have shaped its response to the post-2009 financial crisis. This chapter shows that despite plans for fiscal centralisation, the commitment to integration is fading in different parts of Europe and monetary union is itself starting to break down as capital is repatriated to home countries in vast amounts.

Remarkably, sweeping proposals for 'more Europe' continued to be unveiled right through the crisis. But leading national and institutional players were unable, or unwilling, to close ranks and find common and agreed answers to the long-running emergency. A defiance of economic reality meant that the EU's reputation crumbled among former admirers and evoked mounting fury among citizens in places where policy failures resulted in accelerating social hardship.

Chapter 7 offers a portrait of a European Union in 2013 wracked by mutual suspicions. Elites in that year dropped the pretence that further integration efforts could produce common benefits. The EU had devised such defective processes for managing high-level responsibilities that it remained paralysed when these low-grade forms of management spun large areas of the eurozone into crisis. The absence of any momentum behind fiscal or banking union showed how the entity had simply run out of road, producing a widening chasm between victims of the single currency and a shrinking number of countries still sheltered from its malign effects.

Compared with the likely massive losses across the entire eurozone banking sector deriving from faulty investment decisions, the proposed amounts set aside to try and clean bank balance sheets are paltry. Years of 'kicking the can down the road' with low-grade crisis management appear to lie ahead, leading to the unravelling of much of the social and economic progress seen in post-1945 western Europe. That is unless citizens cry 'enough', and European cooperation is re-launched on a more just and sensible basis.

Notes

1 Klaus Kastner, 'Prof Ralf Dahrendorf – a visionary', Observing Greece, 27 April 2013.
2 *The Times*, 12 October 2012.
3 Alkman Granitsas, 'Merkel sees hope as Greeks protest cuts', *Wall Street Journal*, 10 October 2012.
4 Helena Smith, 'Greek police send crime victims to neo-Nazi "protectors"', *Guardian*, 28 September 2012.
5 Kevin Featherstone, 'The Greek sovereign debt crisis and EMU: a failing state in a skewed regime', *Journal of Common Market Studies*, 49, 2, March 2011, p. 196.
6 Olga Kazan, 'Thousands of Greek police join anti-austerity protests as June unemployment hits 24.4 percent', *Washington Post*, 6 September 2012.
7 Louise Armistead, 'Germany is "playing with fire" on Greece, warns finance minister', *Daily Telegraph*, 16 February 2012.
8 *Financial Times*, 3 September 2012.
9 See Wolfgang Münchau, 'The dangers of Europe's technocratic busybodies', *Financial Times*, 14 July 2013.
10 *EUObserver* (Brussels), 7 September 2012.
11 Clive Crook, 'In Cyprus, Europe sets a new standard for stupidity', Bloomberg News, 19 March 2013.
12 Gideon Rachman, 'Europe's zero-sum dilemma', *The National Interest*, May–June 2012.
13 F. Roy Willis, *France, Germany and the New Europe 1945–1967* (Stanford, CA Stanford University Press, 1968), p. 85.

1

Creating the single currency: the triumph of ideology over good sense

Scholars of integration have paid insufficient attention to the prospect of disintegration, ranging from fragmentation to system failure ...

The collapse of the euro would represent major system failure with incalculable repercussions for the member states, the EU and the global economy. It cannot be ruled out because the euro status quo is neither stable nor sustainable.

Professor Brigid Laffan, European University Institute[1]

But it is a dangerous error to believe that monetary and economic union can precede a political union or that it will act (in the words of the Werner report) 'as a leaven for the evolvement of a political union which in the long run it will in any case be unable to do without'. For if the creation of a monetary union and Community control over national budgets generates pressures which lead to a breakdown of the whole system, it will prevent the development of a political union, not promote it.

Professor Nicholas Kaldor, 1971[2]

Monetary union: dreams and warnings

Among some of its most fervent advocates, European Monetary Union (EMU) was meant to bring about the final merging of European destinies into a common political entity. The assumption was that, perhaps quite quickly, governments would harmonise their economic arrangements, ushering in a united continent. In retrospect, it is striking that so many politicians and many financial specialists were prepared to believe that a common currency and fixed exchange rates could drive forward an integration agenda in the face of volatile markets and trading cycles.

The insipid appearance of the coinage and banknotes raised little alarm. Their designs avoided all trace of national symbols. There were no portraits of kings and queens or of past champions of culture or heroism. The designers used architecture for inspiration: gates, bridges, archways and rose windows.

The Commission had also designed a new logo for the currency, a curved 'E' for Europe, but with a double horizontal bar.[3] Absent were any inspiring symbols denoting a human being whose special qualities correspond to an ideal European community. Peasants or fishermen, responsible for keeping the people fed in their epic struggle with nature, could have been invoked but weren't, despite the importance of the Common Agricultural Policy; the mother as the home-maker nurturing a new generation of young people whose endeavours would enable Europa to renew itself was probably too nationalist a motif to play with. Probably, there was insufficient agreement to ensure that it was those politicians from the 1950s who had begun the march towards European fusion whose heads decorated the notes and coinage.

Many observers were surprised when, through much manoeuvring and deployment of political will, eleven of the then sixteen members of the European Union were accepted into the euro area as founder members and the European Central Bank opened for business on 1 January 1999. Two years later, on 31 December 2001, the euro ceased to be a virtual currency with the arrival of 15 million banknotes and 51 billion coins that were soon to be the only legal tender for 306 million people in twelve countries.

Sheltering under the umbrella of the single European currency were nations with disparate economies that were reliant on different areas of business, industry and commerce. Economists on the political left and right expressed misgivings. Wynne Godley, a longstanding critic of Margaret Thatcher's free market economics, had asked as early as 1992 'what happens if a whole country ... suffers a structural setback. As long as it is a sovereign state, it can devalue its currency ... With an economic and monetary union, this recourse is obviously barred.' The Cambridge economist endorsed the warning of Professor Martin Feldstein that in the absence of a system of fiscal equalisation, 'then there is nothing to stop it suffering a process of cumulative and terminal decline leading, in the end to emigration as the only alternative to poverty or starvation'.[4]

On the political right, Nobel Prize-winning economist Milton Friedman also warned that the single currency would ultimately cause major problems. 'The euro was really adopted for political and not economic purposes, as a step towards the myth of the United States of Europe,' Friedman declared in September 1997. 'I believe its effect will be exactly the opposite.'[5]

Currency unions had risen and fallen in Europe in previous centuries, leaving abundant evidence that when problems arose in one country, it was hard to prevent severe fall-out in others that were participating. By 2009 sixteen countries were sharing a currency during an era of accelerating globalisation which had already led to the intensification of mutual activities. But they were still far short of enjoying a common political identity which, hitherto, had been seen as a necessary bulwark for a common currency. Nevertheless, the *Financial Times*, the voice of the European business world, was unperturbed. It was euphoric when the currency began to circulate: 'The new currency is a triumph of political will over practical objections. Its physical launch is a testament to a generation of visionary leaders who pursued a dream, often against the grain of public opinion ... That the Euro has arrived is also a tribute to the dedication and common sense of central bankers and treasury officials across Europe.'[6]

The explicit assumption from most political, academic and media commentators was that the new currency would exercise a strong gravitational pull. Europe would be propelled into a new epoch of heightened cooperation. There would be a gradual convergence of economies, institutions, banking laws, fiscal policies and national cultures.

A serene economic future was thought to be much likelier inside the eurozone than outside. This is why countries which struggled to meet the fiscal requirements for entry were nevertheless keen to join. They were prepared to surrender powers which modern states had always used to extricate themselves from economic crises – control of interest rates and the ability to devalue their national currencies in order to boost economic competitiveness. The supervision of the new currency was given to the ECB with its headquarters in Frankfurt.

In practice, the ECB's management would be an unhappy compromise meant to reconcile the contrasting approaches to banking supervision of its two chief national guardians, France and Germany. Warnings that the currency union could only be a safe alternative if the tax and budgetary arrangements of its members were to be subject to tight central oversight were brushed aside. Eleven states with different conditions, needs and levels of development formed the Economic and Monetary Union in 1999 with Greece joining in 2001, Slovenia in 2007, Cyprus and Malta in 2008, Slovakia in 2009 and Estonia as late as 2011.

The currency had a bank but 'no government and no laws except for allegedly binding fiscal rules emanating from the Maastricht Treaty signed in 1992'.[7] There was no desire to proceed cautiously by experimenting with incremental change. It would have been possible to retain an exchange rate mechanism, with wide bands that could have enabled countries hit by the types of crises that overwhelmed them after 2008 to make the adjustments needed to return to competitiveness. Instead, the function of exchange rates appeared to have been forgotten: they moved upwards and downwards so as to stimulate the necessary economic adjustments, allowing countries to stay competitive.

The euro did not stimulate productive growth knitting the sinews of the currency union together in a single economic entity. Instead, long-term growth was confined to specific countries, most notably Germany but also the Netherlands, Finland and Austria. Contrasting outcomes would become hard to overlook by its tenth anniversary: enormous trade surpluses in Germany;

uncontrollable credit booms in Spain and Ireland; a plundering of the public finances in Greece under the eyes of a self-satisfied ECB.

Crashing to earth

Far from laying the foundations for a common European economy, the single currency had instead opened up ominous new centrifugal tendencies. Low interest rates encouraged a productivity gap in the eurozone, confirming Germany as the dominant industrial nation in Europe. It was able to export massively to the rest of the eurozone, receiving payment in borrowed money, much of which had emanated from Germany, or at least from its careful savers.

Sharpening economic divergences between creditor nations of the North and increasingly indebted nations on the periphery of the eurozone sparked off an extended crisis in 2010. At the time of writing it rages on, with no agreement over how it should be resolved. Instead, ever more costly temporary measures are adopted to contain the crisis as centrifugal tendencies emerge which could eventually rival those seen in other unions that burst apart because of fundamental policy disagreements. In 1997, the already-quoted Milton Friedman had warned that 'The euro will aggravate the political tensions to the extent that economic shocks ... which could until now be facilitated through exchange rate adjustments, will change into political controversies.'[8]

At the start of the crisis in 2010, the eurozone's gross domestic product, at $12.2 trillion, had been more than twice as big as that of China and its income per capita more than four times as high.[9] But from Brazil to Turkey, countries which had once seen the EU as an entity worthy of emulation began to revise their judgements about its performance.[10] Pascal Lamy, who had played a key role in expanding the EU's powers in the 1980s, went as far as to say in 2013 that 'For the first time in 60 years, the rest of the world is starting to have serious doubts about the solidity of the European project. This has led to an unprecedented process of "re-nationalisation" in the area of international relations. It is as if diplomats in foreign capitals were hedging their position in case there is a break-up of the European Union.'[11]

Europe's mishandling of the crisis has even caused the Pentagon to express public alarm: 'We are extraordinarily concerned by the health and viability of the euro because in some ways we're exposed literally to contracts but also because of the potential of civil unrest and break-up of the union,' declared General Martin Dempsey, chair of the US Joint Chiefs of Staff in 2011.[12]

In January 2012, the IMF marked down global growth in 2012 by 1.2 percentage points compared with its forecast in April 2011. This has been largely attributed to mismanagement of the euro crisis.[13] The growth gap in 2012 between the US (+2.2) and the eurozone (−0.4), standing at 2.6 per cent, was the biggest since 1993. It was no one-off. Professor Willem Buiter, Citi-bank's chief economist, predicted the differential would widen to 3.4 per cent in 2014 and continue at abnormal levels through the latter part of the decade.[14]

Journey towards monetary destiny

For most of the existence of the European Union, the push towards integration has involved political leaders trying to achieve common ground around a uniform monetary policy for Europe. The catalyst had been the collapse of the Bretton Woods system of fixed exchange rates based on the US dollar in the early 1970s. The EU's response was to create fixed but adjustable exchange rates (the 'currency snake') aimed at minimising exchange rate fluctuations between the member states. These fluctuations impeded the strengthening of trading links which were seen as vital for a primary EU objective, economic convergence, to work. However, by 1974 the West was confronted by a major increase in the price of oil. The performances of EU economies rapidly began to diverge. The governments of several of the struggling EU economies – first the UK, Italy and Ireland, then later France as well – were forced to leave the 'snake'. It shrank to include Germany, Denmark and the Benelux states, in practice a sub-zone of the EU where the Deutschmark prevailed.[15]

The real forerunner of the euro was the Exchange Rate Mechanism (ERM), which was pioneered by Germany's Chancellor Helmut Schmidt and Valéry Giscard d'Estaing, President of France, in 1978–79. A shifting cast of Franco-German leaders would, for the next two decades, provide vital ballast for monetary union. The ERM was the foundation of a European Monetary System (EMS) which has been described as 'the single most important move in a supranational direction since the signing of the Treaty of Rome in 1957'.[16] Not only did the ERM bring to life the concept of a European zone of monetary stability, but it enabled the Deutschmark to become its anchor currency. The conviction of a pro-integration French economist, Jacques Rueff, expressed in 1950 that 'Europe shall be made through the currency or it shall not be made' was one shared by a powerful set of decision-makers in the decades to come.[17]

The opportunity for a breakthrough occurred at the very end of the 1980s. The ending of the Cold War enabled the issue of German unification to explode on to the political agenda in 1989–90. France had motives for wishing to lock Germany into a European currency. François Mitterrand and other powerful figures in Paris were keen to break what was perceived to be German domination of European monetary policy under the EMS. Helmut Kohl was receptive. In 1988, he had told a sceptical board of the German state bank, the Bundesbank, that Germany had to accept the single currency for France as it had to 'accept the weather'.[18]

It was Kohl's dominating concern to stabilise the Franco-German relationship and offer concrete proof of his government's commitment to closer European integration. Unsurprisingly, the unification process would become a major preoccupation for several of Germany's EU partners as Soviet power retreated eastwards. In December 1989, Mitterrand had warned the German Foreign Minister, Hans-Dietrich Genscher, that if Germany turned its back on the integration process because of unification, this would provoke a return of traditional balance-of-power politics in Europe.[19] It would be at the European Council meeting held in Strasbourg three weeks after the fall of the Berlin Wall that Kohl gave his public backing for the single currency.

But the most energetic proponent of European Monetary Union (EMU) located at the heart of European politics was not Kohl but Jacques Delors, who ran the European Commission, the EU's administrative corps, from 1984 to 1994. He was the most powerful figure ever to occupy that post and the Delors Report, published on 17 April 1989, proposed a three-stage passage to EMU.

In August 1990, the European Commission published a formal opinion on EMU, written largely by Delors. It displayed an evangelical faith in the inherent viability of the project by dropping the idea of sanctions to be imposed on countries which over-borrowed.[20] It showed, in some eyes, how blind faith had supplanted careful pragmatism about how to ensure that still-divergent economies combined in a realistic common framework. The evangelism of the powerful French technocrat produced an angry counterblast from Hans Otto Pohl, head of Germany's national bank, the Bundesbank. In Munich on 3 September 1990, he stated that 'in losing the Deutschmark we would be sacrificing a hard currency on the European altar without knowing what we would get in return'.[21] On 23–24 September 1992, the pitfalls arising from countries with divergent economic needs being squeezed into a single financial entity were shown when Britain and Italy crashed out of the ERM. Pohl's successor, Helmut Schlesinger, had been hesitant about the path of monetary union ever since the appearance of the ERM in 1978. According to Bernard Connolly, head of the European Commission's monetary affairs unit in the early 1990s, he had been appalled by the events of that September. The fear that had haunted him ever since the ERM was imposed on a reluctant Bundesbank in 1978 had been realised: 'The Bundesbank had lost control of the money market.'[22] He even made these thoughts very public shortly afterwards when he launched a withering attack 'on the whole concept of the ERM, describing it as, in essence, a machine for enriching speculators that would create wave after wave of instability in foreign exchange markets'.[23]

But a determined set of Franco-German politicians felt they had the wind of history behind them. They were able to stare down warnings about impracticality and hubris from independent-minded officials even though they rarely engaged with their arguments. True believers like Delors and Kohl were not restrained by the vast differences in basic economic conditions across EU countries that were bound to affect the workings of a currency union, and how such divergences could be narrowed and eventually 'harmonised'; public and private sectors varied in size, as did the degree of government regulation and subsidy, the role of corporatist institutions versus free markets, and the scope and direction of social security systems.

However, by the 1990s, a critical mass of elite support was evolving for the goal of speeding up the completion of the European construction that would supplant the national governments. Delors was the principal evangelist. In 1990, he publicly advocated 'a Europe of concentric circles, with at the centre those who want to go the furthest, that is to say to political union'. He also conceded that there could be 'a second circle open to those who don't want to go as far as political union'.[24]

The main backing came from Germany where inhibitions were fewest in the EU about moving towards a post-national future. In 1994, the then ruling Christian Democratic Union released the Schäuble-Lamers Paper written by two top politicians, one of whom would later play a key role in the crisis of the euro. Wolfgang Schäuble publicly endorsed the formation of a 'hard-core' of members to accelerate or deepen the integration process.[25] The idea of a two-speed Europe obtained further endorsement in 2000 when Joschka Fischer, leader of the German Greens and his country's Foreign Minister, advocated 'a treaty within a treaty'. Like Schäuble, he saw the euro as a bridgehead for a supra-national Europe.

In France, backing for a union based around inter-governmentalism was stronger than for outright European federalism and after 2000 the next stage in building 'more Europe' would be the quest for a European constitution. Some countries, though, remained impervious to the charms of a united Europe. In December 1992, the people of Switzerland voted against their country's incorporation into the European Economic Area, widely viewed as a halting place before a country became a full member. Far from suffering, the Swiss franc appreciated in value and consumer confidence started to improve, more than a year ahead of any rally elsewhere in continental Europe.[26] Switzerland and Sweden were the two main economies of mainland Northern Europe which kept their freely floating currencies. They performed well during the single currency era against Germany and the Netherlands whose growth rates slowed down for much of this period.[27]

Cutting corners to build the monetary house

If economic criteria had applied, the currency union would have been confined to no more than five countries with sound finances and not dissimilar economic profiles. Such a bloc might or might not have proven dynamic and disciplined enough to evolve into a coherent economic entity. But owing to the overtly political character of the project and its careless design, it failed to be a catalyst for advancing European integration to a decisive stage. Its failings sprang in large part from its political nature. Politics would continue to be national in their main focus which meant that even in the lead EU states, there was often a reluctance to put Union interests above national ones (that were often electoral in character).

Admitting Italy would prove to be the key miscalculation. It showed that, armed with new powers and responsibilities, the EU was not prudent and alert as it began the most intricate and audacious stage in the European project. Instead, more than ever, it was acting more like a club with informal rules allowing an astonishing degree of indulgence for feckless but influential members.

Italy's national debt was around 120 per cent of GDP. But the Maastricht rules for membership of the single currency required national debt to be below 60 per cent. Then as now, many senior German officials were apprehensive about abandoning rules designed to stabilise a high-risk economic experiment. German government documents, newly released in 2012, revealed that many in Helmut Kohl's Chancellery had deep doubts about a European common currency when it was unfurled in 1998.[28] Experts did not hesitate to point to Italy as being the euro's weak link.

But Chancellor Kohl was uncomfortable at the likelihood that one of the six founder members of the European Community would be left on the sidelines. He had good inter-personal relations with Romano Prodi, Italy's Prime Minister who, though on the moderate left, shared Kohl's Roman Catholic formation. Carlo Ciampi, who had been governor of the Italian Central Bank for many years, also enjoyed the Catholic links valued by Kohl, having been educated at a Jesuit boarding school. 'Without Ciampi, Italy would never have managed to be on board at the beginning of the monetary union,' according to former Finance Minister Theo Waigel. His advocacy of a euro encompassing a small number of compatible countries was swept aside by Kohl's missionary zeal.[29]

But the byzantine methods used to hustle Italy into the eurozone were costly ones that would come back to haunt EU decision-makers at perhaps the worst possible moment. The Italian government used derivatives to bring Italy's deficit to below the 3 per cent required to gain admission to the single currency. Debts were offloaded to obliging banks on very unfavourable terms. In June 2013, as Italy was struggling to avoid a bail-out that would place it under the supervision of the EU and the IMF, the scale of the losses incurred by this financial alchemy started to leak out. Italy had managed to lose €8.1 billion on derivatives contracts of €31.7 billion (and this was only a quarter of the total amount). Worse, Italy was struggling against the odds to make a strategy of fiscal austerity work. It was one of the key plans of the ECB's chief since 2011, Mario Draghi, to contain the eurozone crisis – the same individual who had been director of the Italian treasury at the end of the 1990s when the Faustian pact had been made.[30]

If Chancellor Kohl, Italy's sponsor, was aware of such reckless manoeuvres, he only displayed nonchalance. At a European Union special summit in Brussels in early May 1998, he declared that he felt the 'weight of history' and, without further ado, provided his unreserved support for Italy's application. 'Not without the Italians, please. That was the political motto,' according to Joachim Bitterlich, Kohl's foreign policy adviser. Kohl consoled himself that problems with Italy were manageable because of the nature of Italy's debt. Bitterlich recalled that 'It was atypical because 80 per cent of what Italy owed was to its own people. So people said that under these circumstances, we can accept the Italians.'[31]

The concern of German officials that austerity measures in Rome were accounting tricks or short-term palliatives that would be cast aside when political pressure subsided failed to act as a reality check. Sir John Kerr, a former British ambassador to the EU, closely involved with expanding the role of the EU, stated in 2012: 'Think back 20 years when we were working all this out. My view was that it would be five, possibly six countries that would start. It never occurred to me that Italy or Spain, let alone Greece, would qualify.'[32]

Kohl, a key power-broker launching one of the most audacious plans seen in modern European history, was content to block out inconvenient economic information about its viability. History may well judge him no more kindly than communist rulers in the former East Germany who ploughed on until 1989 with a disfunctional economic system. He failed to take seriously those who warned that Italy's lax habits could debauch the new currency. Italy became a stark example of the stubborn belief of a self-righteous politician that economic development was bound to conform to the generous visions of leaders building a new Europe.

Gerhard Schröder, Kohl's successor as German Chancellor, called the euro a 'sickly premature baby'. But that was when he was leader of the Social Democratic opposition. Once installed as leader of the EU's lead nation, he soon conquered these inhibitions. Because of its large deficit, Greece didn't qualify to join the single currency but it lobbied energetically and was able to storm the EU's defences based on the supposedly inviolable Maastricht criteria. Once again a political decision was taken, enabling an errant member to circumvent rules because of its agility in pulling strings and persuading EU grandees to throw away their own rule book. A former senior adviser to Schröder, Wolfgang Nowak, recalled in 2011: 'We were told by Gerhard Schröder that he would make an "honest" currency out of the euro. But his first official act was to admit Greece, a country that had been blatantly falsifying budget figures.'[33] On 5 June 2000, eurozone finance ministers agreed on Greece joining the eurozone. According to Austria's Karl-Heinz Grasse, 'Greece will become a member for sure. It meets all the requirements.'[34]

How Greece got away with it emerged in January 2010 when the then Greek Finance Minister, George Papaconstantinou, revealed how the investment bankers Goldman Sachs helped the Greek government to mask the true

extent of its deficit with the help of a derivatives deal that legally circumvented the EU Maastricht deficit rules. Goldman Sachs was just the best
known of a series of investment banks willing to offer complex financial
products which would enable a reckless government like that of Greece to
push part of its liabilities into the future. The deal centred on so-called cross-
currency swaps in which government debt issued in dollars and yen was
swapped for euro debt for a certain period – to be exchanged back into the
original currencies at a later date. The rules governing the EU's statistical
branch, Eurostat, meant it was not required to comprehensively record transactions involving financial derivatives. 'The Maastricht rules can be
circumvented quite legally through swaps,' a German derivatives dealer was
quoted as saying. In 2002, the Greek deficit amounted to 1.2 per cent of GDP.
After Eurostat reviewed the data in September 2004, the ratio had to be
revised up to 3.7 per cent.[35]

Regarding the charge that Greece had cooked the books in order to gain
entry to the euro, George Papandreou, Greece's Prime Minister, was
disarming. In an interview with *El Pais* in 2010, he admitted that 'the
Commission was provided with incorrect figures for six years', but went on to
say that 'part of the responsibility was on Greece, but the Eurozone also
lacked the tools to notice that'.[36] Papandreou's refrain, 'yes we cheated but
you should have noticed', acquires more credibility when figures on the extent
of corruption in Greece prior to the crisis are kept in mind.

Later in 2010, Karel de Gucht, the EU's Trade Commissioner, claimed that
the Greek problems were no surprise to Brussels; EU leaders were aware of the
fact that the Greek government had been providing false data from the very
beginning of the country's euro-membership.[37] In perhaps most political
entities possessing some degree of democratic accountability, this would have
resulted in a political storm. It is hard to imagine top officials *not* being forced
to explain their actions to a legislative body. But no storm ensued and it was
soon the turn of a far more important figure, Jean-Claude Juncker, head of the
group of EU finance ministers, Ecofin (Economic and Financial Affairs
Council), to be even more outspoken. He confessed in late 2010 that:

> It was obvious that one day Greece would have to face these kind of problems,
> and I knew that problems would arise because we – the French, the Germans,
> ECB President Trichet, the Commission and myself – had been discussing the
> perspectives of what was not at that time known as the so-called Greek crisis
> ... The Greek crisis could have been avoided, but not starting last year,
> starting two or three decades ago.[38]

These were admissions from leading EU decision-makers that Greece had been
allowed to cheat on its accounts in order to comply with the Maastricht
criteria and therefore join the euro. France and Germany had shown no willingness to thoroughly vet Greece once its creative accounting and outright

deception about its economic condition had grown in boldness.[39] The two national drivers of European integration did not think two or three steps ahead and ask what could happen to the ECB if the financial house of cards in Greece toppled.[40] This is worth recalling at a time when the same governments are urging a gigantic leap of faith towards different forms of European fiscal convergence.

With the guardians of the European project behaving with such negligence, it is too convenient to simply brand Greece as the dominant villain. In 2004, Peter Doukas, the Budget Minister in a new, centre-right government, wished to begin cleaning out the Augean stables. He discovered that the difference between the published deficit and the real one was huge. 'The budget said the deficit was 1.5pc. The real shortfall was 8.3 per cent,' Doukas recalled. 'I said we should start chopping down the budget. But the answer I got at the time was: "We have the Olympic Games in a few months and we cannot upset the whole population and have strikes."' Instead, Greece stepped up its borrowing and top European banks 'queued up to lend'. The markets could see no risk of default because Greece's currency was locked into that of Germany's.[41]

Carlo Ciampi, the veteran governor of the Italian Central Bank, used the prestige he enjoyed in Berlin to be arguably more reckless than the undisciplined Greeks. He carried out a neat accounting trick, which involved selling national gold reserves to the Central Bank and imposing a tax on the profits. The budget deficit shrank accordingly. Under a former leading communist, Massimo d'Alema, the Italian centre-left government appointed in 1998 became even more adventurous. D'Alema proposed financing a European economic stimulus programme through euro bonds and not factoring the associated expenditures into the national deficits. Gerhard Schröder in Berlin proved resistant. Yet the German ambassador in Rome cabled home that members of the Italian government were demanding that the budget consolidation be spread out, the stability pact be interpreted more flexibly and Italy be freed 'from the shackles of the Maastricht Treaty'. Such a stance would hardly be altered when Silvio Berlusconi began a lengthy period in government in 2001.[42]

Expediency triumphs over good management

Perhaps if the German ambassador's candour had broken through customary political restraints, an even starker truth would have been recognised. Greek financial chicanery and Italian weakness for creative accounting appeared to underline an enduring North–South economic fault-line in Europe. Almost 150 years ago, when the influential English economic thinker Walter Bagehot was pondering the problem of European monetary integration in the *Economist*, he ruled out a single European currency. But with Italy and Germany in the process of forming two large states, he thought two currencies might be possible. According to Matthew Yglesias, 'he looked forward to a future in which there would be one Teutonic money and one Latin money and posited that "looking to the commercial activity of the Teutonic races, and the comparative torpor of the Latin races, no doubt the Teutonic money would be most frequently preferred."'[43]

In the euro's first decade of life, the growing economic divergences on a North–South basis lent credence to Bagehot's strictures on the cultural basis of economic behaviour. Tight wage restraint was imposed in Germany and the Netherlands which enhanced the competitiveness of their goods. Exports to Mediterranean Europe surged, exacerbating inflation there. Lower wages in Northern Europe, meanwhile, ensured weak demand for imports from the Mediterranean EU states. But, as Charles Dumas relates, that's where Teutonic and Dutch prowess ended: 'The resulting trade surpluses enjoyed by Germany and the Netherlands were imprudently invested in such assets as U.S. subprime-mortgage paper and Greek government bonds.'[44]

Perhaps the key act of short-term irresponsibility which placed the euro on a disastrous trajectory was the one emanating from Paris and Berlin in 2004 following a period in which the French and German economies had over-heated. France and Germany proceeded to defy the terms of the Stability and Growth Pact, requiring fiscal discipline in order to maintain the stability of the EMU.[45] They had both overspent, and their budget deficits exceeded the 3 per cent limit to which they were bound. The Commission, then led by Romano Prodi (under whom Italy had joined the euro), had the power to fine them. But EU finance ministers, grouped in Ecofin, voted not to enforce the rules, ones which were designed to protect the stability of the euro. 'Clearly,' Prodi said, 'I had not enough power. I tried and they [the finance ministers] told me to shut up.'[46] Technocrats from the European Commission working on the currency project knew a central mechanism was needed to ensure member governments complied with the rules. But according to Jacques Lafitte, one of the architects of the single currency, they had already been overruled. Speaking to the BBC in 2012, he recalled that 'We made suggestions to the member states at the time but these were rejected because they would have involved transferring sovereignty from national governments to Brussels or maybe Frankfurt ... We knew deep inside. Again, we could not say so publicly. We were mere technocrats.'[47]

Jean-Pierre Raffarin, France's Prime Minister in 2002, had already put tax cuts above the Stability Pact, stating that the pact 'was not written in stone'.[48] This remark well illustrates how the workings of the most ambitious of the EU's post-national initiatives have been shaped by informal actions, often by the stronger players. De Gaulle had memorably stated in 1963 that 'treaties are like maidens and roses, they each have their day'.[49] The prevalence of this opportunistic mindset in the world of European politics, when new institutions were being constructed which could ill-afford design faults and poor maintenance if they were to survive, was ominous. It showed how far leadership fell short of the minimum requirements needed to drive the project onwards towards its goal of a complete continental union. Western Europe's post-Cold War politicians were very lucky compared to their predecessors during a century marked by war, occupation and violent extremism. But Chirac, Major, Blair and Schröder were, arguably, less gifted and courageous than figures like Gustav Stresseman, Leon Blum and Jan Masaryk, operating in a more dangerous and unforgiving environment.

It was assumed that clever political artisanship could master and contain economic problems. The European economic order was sufficiently robust, after sixty years of recovery and prosperity, to withstand regular interference by politicians with the task of winning elections and raising campaign finance often the primary things on their mind.

Franco-German defiance of what were seen as inconvenient rules, ones actually designed to maintain monetary stability, were only likely to encourage weaker EMU states to fill the gap between tax receipts and spending by large-scale borrowing – and this is what happened.[50] Germany was perhaps the main culprit. (Britain, outside the euro, should not be excused since it voted in Ecofin to waive sanctions.) Berlin, having long insisted that macro-economic decision-making in the EU must be free of subjective political considerations, had in fact surrendered to the worldview of its partner in building the European project: France. The French elite had long been prone to shaping major economic decisions, meant to create an integrated economy, around political criteria. By now, Berlin enjoyed the authority to point out to Paris that such days were over since too much was at stake with the euro. But it failed to do so.

Countries in the wrong currency

In 2007, before the outbreak of the global financial crisis, the gross general government debt of Greece was 105 per cent of GDP, essentially the same level as Italy's. The figures for Germany and France were 65 and 64 per cent respectively, but above the 60 per cent target that was laid down in the Maastricht criteria for joining the euro area.[51]

The Greek current account had actually been in near balance in the mid-1990s before Greece had pledged its destiny to the single currency, but by 2008 the budget deficit was 15 per cent of GDP. 'The massive mis-alignment was the direct result of EMU,' according to the London-based financial journalist Ambrose Evans-Pritchard. Large parts of Greek manufacturing, as well as the shipping industry, had been badly damaged by currency over-valuation. Cheap foreign imports displaced Greek-made goods due to the euro being valued at a disadvantageous rate for Greek exports. The verdict of the *Daily Telegraph*'s international business editor is harsh: 'Greece was not an economic basket case in 1995. It became one as a result of joining the wrong currency.'[52]

Membership of the euro also proved dysfunctional for Portugal as it struggled to cope with vast capital inflows that had a destabilising impact on the economy.[53] Large chunks of its light manufacturing industry were wiped out by Chinese imports, flooding Portugal at an unrealistic exchange rate. The country's 'low-tech, low-cost manufacturing exports, including textiles, garments, shoes and furniture, were hit hard by globalisation, when the EU opened up to the east and China joined the World Trade Organization'.[54] To cling on to its textile and footwear industries, Portugal needed a 50 per cent devaluation against China.[55]

The Portuguese political scene was dominated by two unimpressive parties, the Socialists on the mild left and the Social Democrats, further to the right. Their only real differences sprang from cultural divisions to do with Portugal's deep cleavage between clericalism and secularism as well as controversies continuing to flow from the short-lived revolution of 1974–75 which followed the collapse of a lengthy far-right dictatorship. Both these ideologically opaque parties were absorbed with placing their clients in advantageous positions inside a bloated state. EU transfer funds were used to replenish party coffers and boost the fortunes of politically adept business moguls. Under Anibal Cavaco Silva, Prime Minister from 1986 to 1995, and at the time of writing Portugal's elected President, EU funds were mainly poured into grandiose infrastructure projects whose upkeep it is now hard to maintain. Into the new century, cheap overseas credit fuelled poor investment choices: 'we invested in non-tradable, non-competitive sectors like public infrastructure, construction, telecoms, energy, banks and retail distribution' according to the Portuguese economist, Pedro Santa-Clara.[56] By contrast, broader technical advances were neglected in the educational field. During the post-2011 crisis forces deeply embedded in the state and with a presence across the party system would continue to fiercely defend their privileges.

Greece: countdown to disaster

Of all the Mediterranean eurozone countries, it was Greece where bad governance produced the most calamitous effects. Andreas Papandreou was the chief architect of a patronage-dominated state which he adapted to absorb the bounty of EU funds that started to flow in 1981 when he came to power and Greece joined the EU. He was an economist who had taught in the USA for many years, conveying the air of an erudite and cosmopolitan figure, but this skilful populist turned out to be a cunning old-style chieftain with no interest in any project of long-term modernisation. His message, based on Third World rhetoric, was that Greece was an 'underdog' society which had been exploited by foreigners and their domestic accomplices.[57]

He soon made his peace with the Greek upper class and crushed those in his Panhellenic Socialist Movement (Pasok) who clung to hopes that it could be a

Western-style pluralist party.[58] He thrived in the 1980s by turning patronage politics into a fine art. The civil service and proliferating ancillary bodies were packed with supporters. The civil service doubled in size in the 1980s even though the population only grew by 10 per cent.[59] An OECD report in 2011 found that the administration lacked the habit of keeping records or the ability to extract information from data (where available), and generally of managing organisational knowledge. The problems found in Greece's central administration, says the OECD, were the result of decades of clientelism and the sheer volume of laws and regulations that governed competencies within the ministries. The report found 17,000 such laws, decrees and edicts.[60]

The performance of the EU's own institutions, notably the European Commission, showed that under the influence of the French administrative norms which had also shaped the Greek civil service, rules had proliferated. The German social scientist, Max Haller, in his 2008 study of the EU, argued that the 'more rules and prohibitions exist, the higher the number of possibilities for breaking some of them'.[61] Tax evasion became endemic in Greece, as shown by a massive parallel economy, one most clearly visible in tourism and construction. Various sources estimate this subterranean economy to be worth over 30 per cent of GDP. Transfer funds from the EU played a crucial role in keeping a rickety economic edifice standing.

For many years, data from Transparency International had usually shown Greece to be the most corrupt country in the EU. The 2009 Corruption Perception Index, measuring the degree to which corruption is perceived to exist among public officials and politicians, saw Greece share last place with Bulgaria and Romania. Greece was the largest recipient of Community money in 2008: Athens received roughly €6.3 billion, far ahead of Poland, in second place, with €4.4 billion. Out of the €5.9 of billion of agricultural aid recovered by the EU Commission between 2000 and 2010, €1.3 billion was clawed back from Greece. On regional funds, the EU recovered €842 million from Athens in 2000–06. In 2009, the Commission reduced by €26 million regional aid for Greece due to serious weaknesses in management and control systems.[62]

However, there were never strong voices to be heard in the EU halls of power calling for Greece's serious flouting of rules to be ended for the sake of the well-being of the European project. Greece disrupted EU initiatives meant to stabilise the troubled post-communist Balkans because of outrage that Macedonia had adopted a name and state symbols which were felt to belong to Greece. Papandreou was the black sheep of the EU until ill-health and scandal ended his political career in 1996, but Pasok belonged to one of the influential political groupings, the Party of European Socialists, which meant that it could pull strings in high places. Its chief rival, New Democracy, enjoyed prominence in the rival European Popular Party. During Pasok's stints in office, it inherited the bloated state and simply found room for its own people. Kostas Karamanlis, Prime Minister from 2004 to 2009, was the nephew of Konstantin Karamanlis who led the country in the years immediately after the removal of the Greek military junta in 1974. Roy Jenkins, President of the European Commission from 1977 to 1981, found the most insistent sponsor of Greece was President Giscard. Many years later, Giscard remarked to Helmut Schmidt:

> To be perfectly frank, it was a mistake to accept Greece. Greece simply wasn't ready. Greece is basically an Oriental country. Helmut, I recall that you expressed scepticism before Greece was accepted into the European Community in 1981. You were wiser than me.[63]

Giscard had exhibited utopian faith about Greece despite the impediments in the way of it becoming a member able to pull its weight in the EU for the benefit of its citizens and the wider project.[64]

A stern moralist discourse has emanated from Berlin as the extent of Greek malfeasance and its damage to Europe has become grimly clear since 2009, but official German shock about the Levantine excesses of their Greek partners is overdone. It has been claimed in the *Financial Times* that top German companies, household names in fact, paid billions of dollars of bribes during the years of easy money and all-round excess. This was the bill of fare in order to secure lucrative but over-priced industrial contracts.[65] Later, when the financial crisis was affecting Greece, Germany was one of several EU states which, in total, sold it over €1 billion of arms. France was by far the biggest seller, with a €794 million aircraft deal, according to European Council data on arms licences granted by member states.[66] In 2011, 10 per cent of OTE, the Greek telecoms provider, was sold to Deutsche Telekom for around €7 a share, down 75 per cent on its price three years earlier.[67]

Ignoring the warning signs

The air was full of self-congratulation when the tenth birthday of the European Central Bank was celebrated in Frankfurt in February 2008. Speaking in front of Chancellor Merkel and the finance ministers of all fifteen members of the eurozone, the European Commission's President, José Manuel Barroso, said that the bank and the euro had been invaluable for Europe. They had helped to protect the economies of member states from the series of shocks that the global economy had suffered over the decade, from the dotcom bubble and the fall-out from the terrorist attacks on the US on 2001 through to the turmoil triggered by poor-quality mortgage lending.[68]

Leading Eurocrats appeared mindful of the place that might await them in history as a result of managing a common currency for nearly 300 million European citizens. But there was no appetite for taking precautions involving checking the soundness of the banks and the borrowing practices of weaker members to try to stave off danger from a volatile global financial scene. Nor was there any admission that far from economic convergence occurring, a two-tier eurozone had sprung up. Export-orientated creditor nations which had done well from low interest rates co-existed uneasily with debtor states which relied on service industries, combined with a volatile property market and uninterrupted credit flows, to remain afloat. As Charles Dumas observed: 'Hope that such imbalances would be evened out by the ready mobility of labor was always flawed: in the absence of a common language, tax structure and social-security entitlements, workers were never likely to cross borders to take up job opportunities in sufficient numbers.'[69]

Supposedly the engine powering Europe towards further integration, the eurozone had, by its tenth anniversary, increasingly partitioned much of the continent into two zones whose conditions were starting to be as contrasting as the mutually reliant American and Chinese economies. In what seemed to be a perfect marriage of convenience, Germany thrived off exports sold to peripheral economies that borrowed money at low-risk rates, often from its banks. The chief market for Germany's manufactured goods became the Southern European members of the eurozone. In the thirty months from the end of 2008, Germany ran a current account surplus of around €335 billion, two-thirds of which (€220 billion) originated in the trade surplus the country ran with its eurozone partners.[70]

The cash surpluses earned from selling to the 'Club Med' countries were offered back to them in the form of cheap credit. The low interest rates which the ECB insisted on maintaining made it possible for members such as Greece to obtain credit and then to issue sovereign bonds at almost the same interest rate as German bonds. This low rate had been set to help Germany when it was grappling with integrating the former communist East Germany.[71] The resultant weakness of the euro greatly assisted its exports in non-EMU countries. By 2012, many economists agreed that Germany's real exchange rate was about 40 per cent below what it would have been if the Deutschmark had still been in use. This conferred enormous advantages to its exporters, with 40 per cent of German exports going to the eurozone and 20 per cent to the rest of the European Union.[72] The artificially low cost of credit set off a credit boom in the peripheral eurozone states which stoked inflation, further benefiting Germany's price competitiveness.[73]

McKinsey management consultants attributed two-thirds of German growth in the 2002–12 period to the euro's introduction.[74] So there was unlikely to be overmuch angst in Frankfurt or Berlin about the speed at which the European money carousel was whizzing around, although it was thought in some influential quarters that the ECB had a duty of care.

On 7 March 2011, a former Irish Prime Minister who later represented the EU in Washington, DC, John Bruton, delivered a lecture at the London School of Economics in which he openly criticised the ECB for failing to rein in

speculative bubbles in member countries. He argued that under the statutes of
the European System of Central Banks, the ECB was indeed empowered to
intervene to correct such problems. He complained that a blind eye was
turned to 'irresponsible lending' by German, French, Belgian and British
banks.[75]

The convenience of selective memory

The ECB President, Jean-Claude Trichet, and his officials displayed no
outward concern about large capital flows from the core to the periphery.
Ireland, where bank borrowings massively exceeded the size of their balance
sheets, was praised in EU and IMF reports right up until the beginning of its
financial crisis in the autumn of 2008. Cyprus was admitted to the eurozone in
2008 despite the Commission knowing that the country had a bloated
banking system, making it dependent on continued large capital inflows. The
ECB made reference to its skewed economic model in a 2007 report: 'Much of
the financing of the deficits in the combined current and capital account over
the past two years has also come from capital inflows in the form of "other
investment," comprising non-resident deposits and loans.'[76]

Six years later, German Finance Minister Wolfgang Schäuble would
declare: 'The banking sector in Cyprus simply has no future in its current
form. Everyone in the Eurogroup agreed on this.' Jeroen Dijsselbloem, the
head of Ecofin, chimed in, declaring that Cypriot banks 'have to be downsized
and rebuilt on a healthy and sustainable business model'.[77] Yet Cyprus was
hustled into the eurozone when it was already clear that its economic profile
stood in the way of economic convergence in the eurozone and when it ought
to have been more widely obvious (not just in Cyprus) that its membership
could place it in serious harm's way.

Political complacency and banking excess

Klaus Regling is one of the few European officials to admit that the international bodies which had an oversight role over smaller economies had failed in
their job. He had been head of the Commission's Directorate General for
Economic Affairs (2001 to 2008) and was then the head of the European
Financial Stability Facility (EFSF: the bail-out fund). Speaking in Dublin on 27
April 2011, he admitted that the frenetic policies of economic expansion being
pursued In Ireland 'were not criticised really by outside bodies, who were in
charge of doing this, of supervising the economy – the IMF, the OECD, the
European Union, including me, myself in my job'.[78]

One analyst has found that the tone of 'Commission assessments and
Council opinions published on Ireland between 2002 and 2007 ... became
less critical and more approving over time'.[79] In 2006, the Council and the

Commission concurred that 'the fiscal position can be considered as sound and the budgetary strategy provides a good example of fiscal policies conducted in compliance with the Stability Pact'. In 2007, the German ambassador to Ireland, Christian Pauls, had publicly criticised excessive labour costs in Ireland and a bloated public sector when speaking to a group of potential German investors who were visiting. Naturally, the government did not like any home truths being told about a country heavily promoted as a bastion of free market economics; he received a reprimand from his hosts, and it was rare to hear similar candour in the last years of optimism about the prospects of the eurozone.[80]

At no level of EU decision-making was any will discernible to scale down the credit splurge. Those officials who had successfully argued that national sovereignty should be transferred to the ECB and the European Commission showed few qualms about how it was being used in the economic and financial realms. Nobody of any standing wished to take a hard look at the conduct of European banking or face up to the need to rationalise banking strategy if Europe was to come through deteriorating world economic conditions unscathed. The sheer weight of the banks in the European economy was striking. Europe's banking system is three and a half times Europe's GDP, while the US banking system is 80 per cent of US GDP.[81]

Only later, when the eurozone confronted a full-scale emergency, would there be frantic calls to move towards fiscal union by harmonising taxes and spending policy. Germany's Wolfgang Schäuble, a devotee of supra-nationalism, asserted the need for a full-scale political union if resources were to be transferred from one region to another in the way that happens in the US federal system. But such calls lacked credibility due to the clear improvisation behind them and the fact that some of their main advocates had not been reliable stewards of the eurozone during the years of apparent plenty.

The German banking and regulatory establishments persisted in underwriting 'Club Med' debts even as the signs that it was feeding a large, unstable asset bubble accumulated.[82] When the subprime crisis started to rock the US financial world in 2007, European banks believed salvation lay in turning even more to European sovereign debt, especially from those countries with the best returns. Data from the Bank of International Settlements shows that between the second quarter of 2007 and the third quarter of 2009, when the crisis in Greece first became visible, bank lending to the governments of Portugal, Ireland, Italy, Greece and Spain, largely through bond purchases, rose faster than usual, by 24.2 per cent, to $827 billion.[83] Some regulators realised that elementary prudence was being flouted.

Alarm at the sight of most banks setting aside no capital for sovereign defaults led in 2006 to a financial accord known as Basel 2. It was meant to create an international standard for banking laws and create early warning systems to guard against unconventional banking practices, but nobody with clout at the top of the EU was willing to enforce a stiffer regulatory regime. The Single European Act, since its introduction in 1986, had boosted the influence of the financial sector in the European arena. While European officials always seemed to have time and energy to whittle away at the powers of nation-states, there was no equivalent will to tame banks and investment companies behaving in predatory or downright reckless ways.

Complacency reigned among regulators both at national and European level due to the fact that for the first decade of the euro's existence, bond yields among Germany, Greece, Portugal, Ireland, Italy and Spain had stayed close together (despite growing economic convergences between them). This meant that 'investors buying and selling those bonds acted as if the countries were almost equally safe simply because they were members of the euro zone, despite shaky finances in Greece, real estate bubbles in Ireland and Spain and high debt in Italy'.[84] In 2005, banks, national treasuries and the European Commission held internal discussions on why the spreads between Germany and other countries did not seem to reflect the differing risks, according to a senior Brussels official involved with bank regulation, but no decisive corrective action ensued.[85]

The mentality that there was no need to repair the instruments for European financial management if they were not demonstrably broken appeared to prevail. Fund managers snapped up higher-yield bonds, ignoring the fiscal fragility of countries on the eurozone periphery. Liz Alderman and Susanne Craig relate that 'Société Générale went from issuing no Greek debt in 2005 to being the world's eighth-largest underwriter just a year later. The bank has made $61.5 million in fees from underwriting debt for euro zone countries since 2005, according to Thomson Reuters. Deutsche Bank, the top underwriter of euro zone debt in that period, took in $87 million in fees.' There were huge corporate and individual returns to be made from banishing any doubts about the soundness of sovereign debt even in disorderly states like Greece.

States could be even more impervious to reason than financial adventurers. Alderman and Craig relate the experience of Marc Flandreau who, in 2005, was a senior adviser in Paris at Lehman Brothers, one of several banks selling sovereign bonds for the French government:

> he suddenly wondered whether France's finances were solid enough to merit the low interest rates at which it and the other members of the euro zone were selling their bonds. He wrote a memo to the French Treasury expressing his concerns. 'They went totally ballistic,' Mr. Flandreau recalled. 'They said, "You guys should shut up, you're selling our stuff."'[86]

Low-grade response to European financial crisis

From 2009 onwards, the limitations of the euro were cruelly exposed by a deepening financial crisis. It was first described by EU leaders as a liquidity crisis confined to a small tier of delinquent members which had borrowed and spent beyond their means. Only in 2011 was Chancellor Merkel prepared to concede that much of the European banking sector was in crisis. Reckless lending to unstable parts of the eurozone had coincided with a global financial crisis and soon would be the chief engine intensifying it.

The eurozone had turned into a meeting place for nation-states with different economic agendas. As Edwin M. Truman pointed out it was 'a halfway house' that had not served its members well. Exporters had made considerable savings on transaction costs associated with separate national currencies. Internal nominal exchange rate stability had been maintained, but 'internal and external deficits and debts expanded, imbalances grew, leverage increased, and asset bubbles emerged and burst' during the euro's increasingly fraught twenty-first-century debut.[87]

Credit conditions tightened as investors belatedly compensated for unwise risk management in the past. Countries on the periphery of the eurozone found themselves with large amounts of short-term debt that they could no longer roll over at low cost. First Greece, then Ireland, next Portugal and later Spain saw their debt levels become unbearable between 2009 and 2011.

As late as 2012, the head of the EU Commission, José Manuel Barroso, was prepared to convey 'a message of confidence' to the world that the EU was 'on the right track'. Speaking at the UN General Assembly on 17 May, he was 'fully confident' that the seventeen countries using the euro and all European institutions would do whatever was necessary to overcome the financial crisis: 'We are doing a root-and-branch reform of our budgetary and economic policies ... and we are making good progress in laying firm foundations for strong economic recovery and sustainable growth.' But Nobel economics laureate Joseph Stiglitz told the assembly 'the best that can be said for Europe and the United States is that they look forward to a long malaise, slow growth or stagnation'.[88]

ECB officials, and the senior-level EU bureaucracy in general, were reluctant to engage with experts like Stiglitz.[89] Even such an energetic champion of European integration as George Soros was kept at arm's length. The preference for avoiding transparent debate about the purpose and direction of the single currency was noticeable from the years of its genesis. Today, it seems axiomatic that a lot of pain could have been avoided by renouncing secrecy more suited to the Kremlin or the Vatican and discussing models of best practice and sound ways of managing difficulties.

In too many policy areas, however, EU officials have preferred experts and analysts who already share their own ideological commitments. Their caution is understandable, if only up to a point. The birth of the euro was messy and sometimes confused. Momentum derived not from the project's logical and timely appearance but from the personal agenda of key politicians and the need to consolidate long-term policies like maintaining progress in Franco-German relations and keeping a reinvigorated Germany within the European fold. The euro was a leap into the unknown and there was always nervousness about whether the Maastricht Treaty had provided a secure enough foundation for its operational effectiveness.

Above all, there was a tension between the clashing imperatives of sovereignty and integration that troubled its architects and supervisors. Kenneth Dyson has summed up some of the central dilemmas, describing it as a project that was

> characterized by two main asymmetries: between centralized monetary policy and decentralized banking and financial market supervision; and between a supra-national monetary pillar and an economic pillar in which the states retained the central attributes of sovereignty, not least in fiscal and economic reform policies.[90]

He pointed out potential pitfalls and dangers but appeared supportive towards its aspirations. In 1999 he wrote that 'Its great strengths are power-sharing in the Council and the ECB [and] a shared culture of capitalism based on an ascendant liberal revolution.'[91]

In time, it would emerge that it was less liberal capitalism and more a corporatist form of governance shaped by entrenched interest groups which defined its operations. Even in the years of promise, decisions were made in opaque and secretive ways. There was no encouragement for public deliberation about what comprised best practice for building up the vitality of the single currency. So it is not surprising that academics, even sympathetic ones, were kept at arm's length by the decision-makers and their advisers. It is clear, at least from the references in the books of authoritative observers like Dyson and other academics, that direct engagement between them and EU decision-makers was rather sparse.

Jean-Claude Trichet shielded attention from the eurozone's weak spots. He preferred instead 'to concentrate on positive statements and downplayed the negative news or left it out of his speeches altogether'.[92] But the evasive monetary technocrat at the helm of the ECB from 2003 to 2011 could not cover up the improvisation and outright disregard for treaty rules; the degree of academic attention devoted to the breaching of the Stability Pact in 2004 by France and Germany or the admission of unsuitable countries like Italy and Greece into the single currency in the first place was incredibly sparse. In retrospect, these were moves that had a fateful impact on the evolution of the single currency. They were performed by well-placed insiders and ought to have punctured a number of assumptions about the essentially rational and forward-looking nature of EU decision-making. Such unsettling events undermined the view that a Europe seemingly locked in a path towards integration was a predictable and rule-based entity which avoided the crude power politics of previous centuries.

The reluctance to provide information about the euro or stimulate debates on how it ought to best advance meant that it failed to become a central issue of research in the burgeoning field of EU studies. It is perhaps no coincidence that the books that garnered most attention were written by the veteran economics journalist David Marsh or the disaffected EU official Bernard Connolly, who had been one of the chief planners for the single currency at its inception.[93]

Remarkably, even after four years of continuous crisis, the euro appears to still be the Cinderella of European studies. No major academic publisher has launched a new journal of 'Single Currency Studies'. Incisive articles on the currency crisis and some of its wider ramifications have appeared in the *Journal of Common Market Studies Annual Review of the European Union* but, more often than not, they are written by non-academics. In the first half of 2013, it was the issues of European regionalism and Euroscepticism which dominated the contents of the *Journal of Common Market Studies*. There were ten articles in Volume 51, No. 1, Special issue 'Confronting Euroscepticism' but none were on the financial crisis as a trigger for renewed hostility to the EU.

The *Journal of European Public Policy*, published eight times a year, was also preoccupied by other themes in EU studies whose importance may not pass the test of time. In 2011 the crisis of the eurozone was overlooked. Volume 18, No. 4, 2011, was a special issue mainly devoted to 'The politics of the Lisbon Agenda', increasingly seen in the world beyond as an obsolete waste of time and resources, however elaborate the rhetoric and spin emanating from Brussels. The crisis had no more success in reaching the pages of this journal in 2012. Of the four issues consulted in 2013, there were two special issues. One, Volume 20, No. 2, was on 'The representative turn in EU studies' (dealing with legislative themes). No. 3 was a special issue devoted to 'Morality policies in Europe: concepts theories, and empirical evidence'. However, there was nothing on the moral dimension of the eurozone crisis, an issue remarked upon with mounting frequency by financial analysts and national commentators as social distress accelerated across much of the twenty-eight-member union.

David Marsh wrote in 2010: 'A project that was often (rightly) said to be mainly political rather than economic in inspiration was ill-served by Europe's 21st century leaders, who displayed enormous incompetence in operating and safeguarding it.'[94] Arguably, such incompetence would have been harder to get away with if the European studies community (on both sides of the Atlantic) had displayed far more tenacity and vigilance in tracking the affairs of the single currency.

Three years into the crisis, European decision-makers had no agreed or credible roadmap for tackling it. Austerity programmes were failing to tackle the structural aspects of the crisis. There was no growth programme and the likelihood of one that could save most of Europe from long-term recession appeared extremely low. Structural reforms, above all relating to the ill-managed financial sector, were belated and hesitant.[95]

Across the whole of the euro area, government debt, not supposed to exceed 60 per cent of GDP, rose from 85.3 per cent in 2010 to 87.2 per cent in 2011.[96] Internal divergences grew about who deserved the chief blame for the collapse of a project that not long before had seemed destined to give Europe the foundations that it needed to remain a major world economic force. It was starting to be belatedly recognised even by previously ardent defenders of the currency union that what it lacked amounted to potentially fatal flaws.

The eurozone did not coincide with a nation or even to an intermediate zone with a common culture and language. The obstacles in moving towards a fiscal union that would facilitate intra-regional financial transfers to mitigate localised difficulties were formidable ones. The euro was exposed as an essentially top-down political project in the hands of politicians, functionaries and lobbyists who had lost touch with some essential aspects of political reality. They had forgotten that the eurozone remained a confederation of different economies. It was one where, by 2012, countries sharing a currency were increasingly fearful of holding each other's assets even as their leaders were contemplating the leap towards a full fiscal union.[97]

Notes

1 Brigid Laffan, 'No easy options on horizon as crisis raises spectre of euro area fragmentation', *Irish Times*, 5 September 2013.
2 Nicholas Kaldor, 'The dynamic effects of the Common Market', *New Statesman*, 12 March 1971.
3 Julius W. Friend, *Unequal Partners: French–German Relations 1989–2000* (Washington, DC: Praeger, 2001), p. 67.
4 Wynne Godley, 'Maastricht and all that', *London Review of Books*, 8 October 1992.
5 Open Europe, 'They said it: how the EU elite got it wrong on the euro', June 2010.
6 'Small change, giant leap', *Financial Times*, 2 January 2002.
7 John Lanchester, 'Once Greece goes', *London Review of Books*, 8 July 2011.
8 Agence France Press, 10 September 1997.
9 *Daily Telegraph*, 28 October 2011.
10 Two contrasting views about the impact of the EU's difficulties on Turkey are: Abigail R. Esman, 'Will the new Turkey become the model for a new Europe?', *Forbes Magazine*, 12 February 2011; Leon Hader, 'The rest won't overwhelm the west', *Realclearworld*, 1 July 2011.
11 Pascal Lamy, 'European leaders must lead from the front', World Trade Organization, Geneva, 21 June 2013: www.wto.org.

12 Ambrose Evans-Pritchard, 'Merkel's Teutonic summit enshrines Hooverism in EU treaty law', *Daily Telegraph*, 12 December 2011.
13 Ambrose Evans-Pritchard and Louise Armistead, 'IMF slashes global growth over euro woes', *Daily Telegraph*, 20 January 2012.
14 *Daily Telegraph*, 29 November 2012.
15 Loukas Tsoukalis, *The New European Economy Revisited* (Oxford: Oxford University Press, 1997), pp. 141–2.
16 Martin Holmes, *From Single Market to Single Currency: Evaluating Europe's Economic Experiment* (London: Bruges Group, 1995), electronic version, no page number.
17 'A tortuous path: From Bretton Woods to euro', *Economist*, 11 June 2009.
18 Douglas Webber, 'Successful and genuine failures: France, Germany, and the others in the history of "multi-speed" European political integration', Fourth Pan-European Conference on EU Politics, Riga, 24 September 2008: http://jhubc.it/ecpr-riga/virtual-paperroom/125.pdf.
19 Stephen Wall, *A Stranger in Europe: Britain and the EU from Thatcher to Blair* (Oxford: Oxford University Press, 2008), pp. 117–22.
20 Charles Grant, *Delors, Inside the House that Jacques Built* (London: Nicolas Brealey, 1994), p. 146.
21 Grant, *Delors, Inside the House*, p. 146.
22 Bernard Connolly, *The Rotten Heart of Europe* (London: Faber, 1995), p. 204.
23 Connolly, *The Rotten Heart of Europe*, p. 206.
24 Grant, *Delors, Inside the House*, p. 125.
25 Friend, *Unequal Partners: French–German Relations*, pp. 63–4.
26 Connolly, *The Rotten Heart of Europe*, p. 394.
27 Charles Dumas, 'Euro was flawed at birth and should break apart now', Bloomberg News, 1 April 2012.
28 Sven Böll, Christian Reiermann, Michael Sauga and Klaus Wiegrefe, 'Euro struggles can be traced to origins of common currency', *Der Spiegel Online*, 7–8 May 2012.
29 Böll et al., 'Euro struggles can be traced'.
30 *Financial Times*, 26 June 2013.
31 Böll et al., 'Euro struggles can be traced'.
32 'Euro fault lines evident from day one', *Irish Independent*, 30 January 2012.
33 Wolfgang Nowak, 'Germans don't want a Europe of broken promises and big bail-outs', *Daily Telegraph*, 6 September 2011.
34 BBC News, 5 June 2000.
35 Beat Balzli, 'Greek debt crisis: how Goldman Sachs helped Greece to mask its true debt', *Der Spiegel Online*, 2 August 2010.
36 *El Pais*, 23 May 2010.
37 Open Europe, 'The truth about EMU conditions', 6 May 2010.
38 Open Europe, 'Europe's worst kept secret', 11 October 2010.
39 Takis S. Pappas, 'The causes of the Greek crisis are in Greek politics', *Open Democracy*, 29 November 2010.
40 Ferry Batzoglu et al., 'Generations of pork: how Greece's elite ruined the country', *Der Spiegel*, International Edition, 7 July 2011.
41 'Euro fault lines evident from day one'.
42 'Euro fault lines evident from day one'.
43 Matthew Yglesias, 'Are Greeks lazy?', *Slate*, 19 December 2011.
44 Dumas, 'Euro was flawed at birth'.

45 Gaby Umbach and Wolfgang Wessels, 'The changing European context of monetary union: "deepening", "widening" and stability', in Kenneth Dyson (ed.), *The Euro at Ten: Europeanization, Power and Convergence* (Oxford: Oxford University Press, 2008), p. 65.
46 Christopher Booker and Richard North, *The Great Deception: Can the European Union Survive?* (London: Continuum, 2006), p. 492.
47 'Euro fault lines evident from day one'.
48 Booker and North, *The Great Deception*, p. 492, from *Daily Telegraph*, 20 June 2002.
49 Booker and North, *The Great Deception*, p. 151.
50 Sebastian Dellepiane Avellaneda and Niamh Hardiman, 'The European context of Ireland's economic crisis', *The Economic and Social Review*, 41, 4, Winter 2010, p. 247.
51 Edwin M. Truman, 'Unraveling the euro crisis', speech delivered at the National Economists Club, 26 January 2012, Petersen Institute for International Economics: www.piie,com/publications/paper/paper.cfm?ResearchID=2035.
52 Ambrose Evans-Pritchard, 'Europe's nuclear brinkmanship with Greece is a lethal game', *Daily Telegraph*, 10 May 2012.
53 See Ricardo Reis, 'The Portuguese slump-crash and the euro crisis', paper delivered at the Brookings Panel on Economic Activity, Washington, DC, 21–22 March 2013.
54 Peter Wise, 'Portugal: waiting it out', *Financial Times*, 26 May 2013.
55 Ambrose Evans-Pritchard, 'Europe, free speech, and the sinister repression of the rating agencies', *Daily Telegraph*, 7 July 2011.
56 Wise, 'Portugal: waiting it out'.
57 Pappas, 'The causes of the Greek crisis'.
58 See Michalis Spourdalakis, *The Rise of the Greek Socialist Party* (London: Routledge, 1988).
59 Takis S. Pappas, 'Why Greece failed', *Journal of Democracy*, 24, 2, April 2013, p. 38.
60 See 'Greece: Review of the Central Administration', OECD Public Governance Review, Paris 2011, www.oecd.org/gov/49264931.pdf.
61 Max Haller, *European Integration as an Elite Process: The Failure of a Dream?* (London: Routledge, 2008), p. 189.
62 Valentina Pop, 'Greece scores worst in corruption ranking', *EUObserver*, 17 October 2010.
63 Maurice Weiss, 'Interview with Helmut Schmidt and Valéry Giscard d'Estaing', *Der Spiegel Online*, 11 September 2012.
64 See Susannah Verney, 'Justifying the second enlargement', in Helene Sjursen (ed.), *Questioning Enlargement: Europe in Search of Identity* (London: Routledge, 2006), p. 26.
65 Misha Glenny, 'The real Greek tragedy – its rapacious oligarchs', *Financial Times*, 8 November 2011.
66 Martin Wolf, 'The "grand bargain" is just a start', *Financial Times*, 29 March 2011.
67 Glenny, 'The real Greek tragedy'.
68 'ECB feted on tenth anniversary', *European Voice*, 6 February 2008.
69 Dumas, 'Euro was flawed at birth'.
70 Derek Thompson, 'Fiscal union cannot save the euro', *The Atlantic*, 28 November 2011.
71 Jeremy Warner, 'Time to put the doomed euro out of its misery', *Daily Telegraph*, 13 April 2012.

72 Matt Cooper, 'Germany can't make Germans out of us because of euro crisis', *Irish Examiner*, 18 May 2012.

73 Gisela Stuart, *Die Welt*, 6 May 2010, quoted in Open Europe, 28 May 2010.

74 Cooper, 'Germany can't make Germans'.

75 Leigh Phillips, 'ECB turned blind eye to predatory lending', *EUObserver*, 8 March 2011.

76 Valentina Pop, 'Cyprus "business model" was no mystery to EU', *EUObserver*, 23 March 2013.

77 Pop, 'Cyprus "business model"'.

78 *Sunday Independent*, 1 May 2011.

79 Jim O'Leary, 'External surveillance of Irish fiscal policy during the boom', Irish Economy Note, 11 July 2010: www.irisheconomy.ie/Notes/IrishEconomyNote 11.pdf, p. 11.

80 'Reprimand for German envoy over his "coarse" Irish speech', *Irish Independent*, 17 September 2007.

81 Phillips, 'ECB turned blind eye'.

82 Walter Russell Mead, 'Will German politicians wreck Europe to save their own skins?' *Via Meadia*, 28 January 2012. www.blogs.the-american-interest.com/wrm.

83 Liz Alderman and Susanne Craig, 'Sovereign debt turns sour in euro zone', *New York Times*, 10 November 2011.

84 Alderman and Craig, 'Sovereign debt turns sour in euro zone'.

85 Alderman and Craig, 'Sovereign debt turns sour in euro zone'.

86 Alderman and Craig, 'Sovereign debt turns sour in euro zone'.

87 Truman, 'Unraveling the euro crisis'.

88 Edith M. Lederer, 'EU confident Europe will overcome crisis', *Jakarta Post*, 18 May 2012.

89 See Wolfgang Münchau, 'The dangers of Europe's technocratic busybodies', *Financial Times*, 14 July 2013.

90 Kenneth Dyson, 'The first decade: credibility, identity and institutional fuzziness', in Dyson (ed.), *The Euro at Ten*, pp. 6–7.

91 Kenneth Dyson, *The Politics of the Euro-Zone: Stability or Breakdown?* (Oxford: Oxford University Press 1999), p. 206.

92 David Marsh, 'Faltering ambitions and unrequited hopes: the battle for the euro intensifies', in Nathaniel Copsey and Tim Haughton (eds), *JCMS Annual Review of the European Union 2010*, 49, p. 54.

93 See David Marsh, *The Euro: The Politics of the New Global Currency* (London and New Haven: Yale University Press, 2009) which was re-issued (in an expanded version) in 2011 with the more sobering title *The Euro: The Battle for the New Global Currency*; also Connolly, *The Rotten Heart of Europe*.

94 Marsh, 'Faltering ambitions', p. 46.

95 Constantin Gurdgiev, True Economics, 21 May 2012: www.trueeconomics. blogspot.com, quoting 'Euro area crisis – no growth in sight', *Sunday Times*, 20 May 2012.

96 Valentina Pop, 'European finances still in bad shape, statistics show', *EUObserver*, 16 May 2012.

97 Ralph Atkins, 'Convergence in reverse', *Financial Times*, 4 September 2012.

2

The builders of the European Union and their project: 1950–1992

We are clearly confronted with a tension within the system, the dilemma of being a monetary union and not a fully-fledged economic and political union. The tension has been there since the single currency was created. However, the general public was not really made aware of it.[1]

Herman von Rompuy, 26 May 2010

The President of the European Council delivered these remarks when the seriousness of the financial crisis that first revealed itself in Greece became evident across the rest of the eurozone. He was, no doubt reluctantly, drawing attention to one of the chief features of the European integration project since its inception over fifty years earlier – namely that the political character of the project needed to be shielded from a populace which in most places remained unconverted to the idea of creating of a single European state. Commitment to a political union was expressed in the founding documents of the entity which, from 1993, was known as the European Union. But early resistance from politicians in some of the founding states prompted the architects of European convergence to focus their energies instead on economic and monetary union. The hope was that if an economically integrated Europe began to take shape, the momentum behind the need to create the common political system needed to run a United States of Europe would simply become unstoppable.

Europe's very practical visionary

The chief architect of this astoundingly bold project was a cosmopolitan French businessman, Jean Monnet, who gained much experience in diplomacy, banking and administration during his long life, stretching from 1888 to 1979. Thanks to enjoying high standing among American policymakers who were involved in the economic reconstruction of Western Europe after 1945, he was able to promote economic cooperation in the production of coal and steel among former combatant countries. Transfer of economic sovereignty to supra-national authorities like the European Coal and Steel Community, launched in 1953 with Monnet as its first head, had to proceed with caution. He became aware that political nationalism, though discredited by the uses that it had been put to in Europe between 1914 and 1945, had far from exhausted its credibility. The hankering for a single political order spanning much of the continent remained only a minority taste – indeed, who was to say it might not vanish as a goal if the emergency conditions flowing from wartime devastation and the threat of further advances by Soviet communism receded in importance?

Opposition to replacing the conventional nation-state with a European construction remained in place even decades after the drive towards European integration began. By the last quarter of the twentieth century, this project had real achievements to its credit. Common rules for trade, for investment and for services, and a European common market, had been agreed with beneficial economic results. The effort of binding the economies and the societies of a continent more closely together transformed the atmosphere between previously antagonistic neighbours. These historically fierce enemies, among whom the return of war seemed increasingly unthinkable, became partners at many different levels. Building on their common European perspectives rather than their national specificity no longer just appealed to utopian intellectuals or politicians with a cosmopolitan background. The European Community had been an astounding success in economic and political terms compared to the coercive union that existed east of the rivers Elbe and Danube in Soviet-dominated Eastern Europe. From the 1970s onwards, it enjoyed fresh renown by becoming a democratic home for countries in Southern Europe escaping from stifling right-wing dictatorships. In the 1990s, it crowned its success as an agency strengthening a sometimes very weak democratic impulse in authoritarian Europe, when it opened the way for the former communist states of Central and Eastern Europe to become full members. It established its geopolitical importance in a Europe transformed by the end of the Cold War just as it was pressing ahead with bold internal measures designed to seize the power of initiative from nation-states in crucial aspects of economic and social affairs.

The chief architect of this Europe without nationalism was a true internationalist who, ironically, might have struggled to obtain a place in the project he laboured to build when it reached maturity at the turn of this century. Jean Monnet has countless academic centres for the study of European integration named after him but he never went to university. The son of a wealthy brandy-maker from the Cognac region of France, he left school in 1904, at the age of 16, to work in his father's firm, and spent more time representing the firm abroad than in France. He demonstrated the ability to keep a cool head in a crisis very early in his life, becoming a senior administrator responsible for France's overseas supply during the First World War before he had even reached the age of thirty. Such an experience enabled him to understand the meaning of global interdependence.[2] But he abandoned a career in the League of Nations, where he was deputy head for a time, to plunge into the world of international finance. Today, there are few European decision-makers (Eurocrats) who can claim to have even a fraction of Monnet's experience of practical challenges. Too often, they exercise their political or bureaucratic roles behind an iron curtain shielding them from contact with the public.

The summer of 1940 found Monnet in Europe, involved in the doomed effort to keep alive Franco-British resistance on mainland Europe to the Nazi German military juggernaut. On 2 July 1940, he wrote to Winston Churchill, the British Prime Minister, stating that he would like to serve the British government as the best way to 'serve the true interests of my country'.[3] The British Prime Minister asked Monnet to 'proceed to the United States of America and there continue ... those services in connection with supplies from North America which have been so valuable to us'.[4] By the end of the 1930s, according to a French aide, Jean-Louis Mandereau, Monnet 'wrote French poorly [having] completely abandoned the French milieu ... Frankly, when I was working with Monnet in the United States, he was an American who was defending the interests of France. We only spoke English. He was more at ease among Americans than Frenchmen.'[5]

Monnet's immersion in the Anglophone world until he had almost reached the age of sixty is not something which those burnishing the legacy of the founder of modern European federalism usually wish to emphasise. But it was of immense help in enabling his federalist agenda to shape European policy. He was an unabashed Anglophile who had helped prepare the text on Anglo-French union agreed by the British war cabinet in May 1940 (a reference to Britain and France adopting a common currency being struck out).[6] But Britain ceased to be a major factor in his plans once it became clear that the British appetite for common European moves hardly extended beyond a genuine wish to see the nations of Europe cooperating more closely on an inter-governmental basis.

This was the position revealed at a large European Congress that convened at The Hague in May 1948. 713 delegates, more than half from Britain and France, met. They were sharply divided into two camps: the federalists who wanted a 'European assembly' with governmental powers and the 'confederal-ists' like Winston Churchill (himself in attendance) who retained an attachment to the national dimension.[7] By now Monnet was head of the French planning commission. In early 1946, he had engineered a coup in Washington, managing to secure half of the loan the USA was allocating to France, 'the Blum loan', for the French industrial plan which he controlled.[8] Against a background of difficult US relations with French allied figures, not least Charles de Gaulle, Monnet had acquired the reputation of 'the Frenchman that Washington trusted most' by the close of the world conflict.[9]

He won the confidence of top US officials in the administration and across the political spectrum in Washington, DC.

America obliges

In 1953, Monnet demonstrated the strength of these ties by opening an office for the European Coal and Steel Community in Washington, DC, next door to the law firm of his close American ally, George Ball, a senior Democratic policy-maker through the 1960s. He also succeeded in maintaining close links with the Republicans, not least his friend of many years, John Foster Dulles, who was US Secretary of State from 1953 to 1959.[10] His commitment to functional integration, involving the transfer of more and more governmental functions from national to a European-level administration, made plenty of sense to leading Americans. Monnet was active at a time when the US federal government had acquired almost unprecedented power over the individual states of the union due to the way in which America had mobilised in the world emergency from 1941 onwards. American officials with responsibilities to help rebuild war-shattered Europe were unwilling to become dragged into national rivalries, which was the fate of President Woodrow Wilson's ill-starred American bid to stabilise Europe after the First World War. They made clear their aversion to US funds being swallowed up in competing national schemes. Washington insisted that a large portion of its reconstruction and relief funds should be allocated according to pan-European criteria and in the service of a pan-European plan. In October 1949 Paul Hoffman, who headed the important European Cooperation Agency, made a major speech in which he called repeatedly for 'integration' as the price for a continued, generous level of dollar aid.[11] For both Hoffman and his political chief, US Secretary of State Dean Acheson, the desired ultimate goal was a Europe that resembled far more closely than before the political model of a United States of America.[12]

What the Schuman Plan achieved

The decisive breakthrough for Monnet's post-national thinking was the proclamation of the Schuman Plan in May 1950. Robert Schuman, the French Foreign Minister, unveiled a plan to modernise coal and steel production and form an economic 'community' to that effect, one which embraced Germany. The plan had been draw up in secret by Monnet's staff in the planning commission.[13] He knew it would appeal to Schuman, who hailed from the disputed Alsace-Lorraine province and had fought in the German Army nearly forty years earlier. Schuman was gripped by the need to replace Franco-German rivalry with cooperation. The plan was pushed past a suspicious governing coalition as well as unenthusiastic economic interest groups,[14] its most startling feature being the establishment of a supra-national body of independent persons who were primarily responsible to the community.[15] This High Authority's goal was to make the modernisation of coal and steel production the basis for common economic development. It was hoped that the creation of common internal and external markets would ensure that regions which had been devoted to manufacturing the weapons of war could open a new chapter in their histories based on peaceful cooperation. Once the Benelux countries and Italy agreed to be part of a European Coal and Steel Community (ECSC), it was ratified by the Treaty of Paris in March 1951 and came into effect in July 1952.[16]

Trade between the six members expanded rapidly and paved the way for the establishment of an outright customs union with the signing of the Treaty of Rome in 1957, establishing the European Economic Community (EEC). A European economy was planned through piecemeal integration sector by sector and the next area where cooperation was agreed was in the field of nuclear energy. With the formation of Euratom (the European Atomic Energy Community) in 1955, Monnet stated baldly that: 'The United States of Europe means: a federal power linked to the peaceful exploitation of Atomic Energy.'[17] Such a view would be regarded as tantamount to career suicide in today's EU where the green environmental cause has almost become an article of faith. Indeed, if a re-incarnated Monnet hoped to win the obligatory approval of the European Parliament to go forward as a commissioner, it is almost certain that he would be comprehensively turned down.

What helped Monnet's vision to prosper was that he himself did not have political ambitions. He was not seeking to acquire an ascendancy which would force longer-established political figures to defer to him.[18] He was uninterested in launching a crusade in the democratic arena for his idea and displayed a detachment towards the necessity of democratic assemblies.[19] He preferred to use his persuasive skills on men of influence and elites in the public sphere and in various economic sectors. He would quite possibly have applauded José Manuel Barroso, a future EU Commission President, when he declared in 2010 at the start of the eurozone crisis: 'Governments are not always right. If governments were always right we would not have the situation that we have today. Decisions taken by the most democratic institutions in the world are very often wrong.'[20] A cardinal virtue of the EU according to supporters was that it avoided, unlike so many governments, becoming the slave of public opinion. Executive power would be in the hands of unelected bureaucrats who could keep a healthy distance from elections and voters.

In retrospect, it is not surprising that Monnet had little time for Altiero Spinelli, an ardent federalist from Italy, imprisoned by Mussolini for his communism and throughout his life an adherent of the radical left. He may have regarded his strong radical leftist sympathies as inconvenient at a time when Monnet's emphasis was on winning over people in powerful places through emphasising the practicality of the EU vision for Europe. After 1945 Spinelli campaigned for a centralised United States of Europe with its own constitution and armed forces but the idea only acquired real popular appeal in his native Italy. Monnet preferred as a close accomplice the Belgian Paul-Henri Spaak, also with a long pedigree in his country's far-left politics, but who preferred to realise goals by lobbying and bureaucratic warfare. Monnet had no identifiable successor capable of infusing the European idea with fresh enthusiasm. Jacques Delors, whose integration record matches Monnet's, was chiefly a gifted manager of officials. Despite Tony Blair's damaging association with the post-2003 Iraq conflict, Monnet would possibly have been far *less* reluctant than his successors at the forefront of the European project to harness the British politician's talents as a publicist and give him a position as the standard-bearer of integration. Blair's credibility, however, was a shadow of what it used to be when the time came to appoint a President of the European Council in 2009.

It had been a sensitive military issue, the arming of Germany, which, in the early 1950s, had frustrated the federalist ambitions of Monnet and his followers. 1954 witnessed a concerted attempt to set up a European Defence community. It was quickly followed by a proposal from Spaak for setting up a European Political Community (EPC). It would act as a 'common political roof' over both the Coal and Steel and the Defence Communities, 'creating an indissoluble supranational political community based on the union of peoples'.[21] The heads of government in Germany and Italy were vocal advocates. At a meeting of the six in Paris in August 1954, Spaak pleaded with a sceptical French Prime Minister, Pierre Mendes-France, to support the defence initiative: 'what matters is the integration of Europe. EDC is only the first step in that direction, but if there is no EDC, then everything falls to the ground.'[22] Similar fervour was on display during crunch talks preceding the decision to build a common currency. Hoary clichés beloved of Eurocrats such as 'it is now or never, the train is leaving the station', were invoked. Mendes-France was chastised for not being 'a good European'. Ideological fervour cast aside elementary questions of common sense about how a united army, amalgamating recent aggressors, could function effectively at the height of the Cold War. A scornful de Gaulle, then in opposition, had declared in November 1953: 'Since a victorious France has an army and defeated Germany has none, let us suppress the French army ... After that, we shall make a stateless army of Frenchmen and Germans, and since there must be a government above this army, we shall make a stateless government, a technocracy.'[23] The French national assembly threw out the proposal in 1954, and a chastened Monnet quit as head of the European Coal and Steel Community. The use in public declarations of phrases like 'supra-nationalism' and 'European government', previously used by Monnet to give the integration cause a high profile, was curtailed or scaled back.²⁴ Emphasis instead was placed on removing tariffs and moving towards a fully fledged customs union among the original six.

Despite such a stinging reverse, the European movement retained strong momentum. The idea of a common European future appeared to be an inspiring one enabling the main democratic states of Western Europe to acquire a legitimacy in concert which simply was not to be found in the totalitarian states of East-Central Europe or the right-wing despotisms in the Iberian peninsula and later Greece. The six belonging to the ECSC were starting to experience economic recovery. The widely perceived shortcomings of government in the hands of a corps of bureaucrats who enjoyed little real supervision from elected institutions would be some distance in the future. There was still a trust in experts such as the nine members of the High Authority 'responsible for initiating and framing most of the measures needed to administer the common market'.²⁵

Monnet never showed much sign of deep religious attachments but Roman Catholic political backing was essential for his European strategy in its formative years (if not really in later ones). It was Christian Democratic parties which were leading both Germany and Italy back to respectability. Robert Schuman was a practising Catholic, who followed a monastic way of life in his later years, dedicated to reading and praying.²⁶ He became a symbol of the idealism behind the attempt to bury Franco-German rivalry.

It has been little commented subsequently that the retreat of Catholic values and disappearance of public figures conspicuously shaped by them may have diminished European awareness, making the movement not just more secular but also more technocratic and consumer-orientated. It was noticeable that when the Church acquired a high-profile Pope, John Paul II, after 1978, relations between the Vatican and the EU failed to come alive. It has been claimed that this Polish pope distrusted Jacques Delors's left-wing Catholic ties and relations between these two European pace-setters of the 1980s remained distant, with Christianity failing to become a major driver of post-1989 European identity.²⁷

The United States would, in turn, diminish in importance as a backer of European unity and indeed there were times when it would be seen as a threatening 'other' against which Europe was urged to define itself. But during the Republican presidency of Dwight Eisenhower from 1953 to 1961, constant encouragement for accelerating the integration drive came from the United States. Major funding for trans-national initiatives continued to be available and backing for European trade liberalisation continued despite its harmful effects on American steel exports to Europe. The USA facilitated the creation of Euratom against the interest of its own atomic energy industry.²⁸

No account of European integration in the 1950s is complete without recalling the extent to which the European efforts to achieve greater integration were nurtured and encouraged by the Eisenhower administration. The United States funded the European Payments Union (EPU) at the start of the 1950s in order to liberalise trade. It also pressed for trade liberalisation through the Organisation of European Economic Cooperation (OEEC) and backed the ECSC despite its detrimental effect on American steel exports. It committed itself almost aggressively to the notion of a Defence Community, and the contribution of the anti-Soviet hawk, Secretary of State John Foster Dulles, to the cause of European unification was so substantial that a case can easily be made for a building in the European quarter of Brussels to be named in his honour.[29] Perhaps his most crucial contribution was his refusal to back the Anglo-French military adventure in Egypt in 1956. The Suez affair, in particular, caused the British administrative elite to reassess its hitherto detached attitude to the Common Market. In France, it was another painful episode in the country's search for a new post-imperial role.

Countless post-war European academics in the European social sciences and humanities were numb to the concept of nationalism, if not actively hostile to it. They believed, like the nineteenth-century French radical Proudhon, that nationalism was the supreme enemy that led inevitably to war. He articulated such a view in his book *The Federal Principle* (1863), arguing that 'not only nation states should be welded together in a European federation, but that the states themselves should be broken up into regional governments'.[30] But the building-block for the new Europe still had to be existing nation-states. Initially, Monnet had invested much hope in a transnational Europe led by France and Britain. But Britain, through being detached from European institution-building, dashed these hopes. Instead, he began to view Franco-German cooperation as being capable of promoting the synergy for a new European political framework.[31]

France and Germany: a blossoming partnership

Partitioned and confronted by destroyed cities and a huge refugee population from central and Eastern Europe, Germany did not immediately appear capable of playing such a pivotal role, but a politically stable and economically robust German state was taking shape under Chancellor Konrad Adenauer as the 1950s progressed. It stood in marked contrast to France, polarised ideologically, with a weak political centre, and convulsed by civil–military tensions flowing from the attempt to retain Algeria as an integral part of France. A Common Market appeared to provide a golden bridge enabling France to make a semi-dignified retreat from these assorted troubles. A crucial turning-point was the return to the political helm of Charles de Gaulle in 1958 and the establishment of a Fifth Republic in which the fulcrum of power lay not in a fractious national assembly but in an executive presidency. De Gaulle concluded, while extricating France from

Algeria, that the EU need not be a curb on the French nationalism which defined his own ruling philosophy. Highly placed decision-makers became convinced that supra-nationalism could serve French interests. The coordination of economic activity by bureaucrats and planners had been a longstanding French speciality; the French economy was directed by the state to a degree unusual in a democratic capitalist country. So the creation of a common European economy which would be the brainchild of technocrats and business leaders closely enmeshed with the political world did not involve huge adjustments on the part of France.

There were numerous signs that West Germany would assent to French leadership in the European project. It ardently wished to see an initiative superseding nationalism progressing as it appeared to open the way for Germany to return as a legitimate actor in European affairs.[32] It is not surprising that in 1966, even against a backdrop of strife between de Gaulle and the EU, Altiero Spinelli could write:

> Characteristically, Community allegiance is especially evident among the French ... whose European Community officials are generally among the firmest and most intelligent exponents of a united Europe. They bring to their work in Brussels the kind of preparation and zeal for efficient administration they previously had in Paris, a factor which makes them generally superior to their colleagues from other countries.[33]

For West Germany, an unambiguous European destiny was the means of erasing guilt for the sins which the Nazi rulers of the Third Reich had brought down on German heads between 1933 and 1945. Of all the Allied states, it had been the USA which had stood out for rehabilitating Germany and not imposing a punitive peace. So West Germany might conceivably have established itself as a large strategically placed American bridgehead in Europe, but the appeal of a cohesive and internationally minded Europe was stronger. This vision prevailed even if had a pronounced Gallic colouring.

German cultural identity was strong, as were social and economic bonds which had contributed to post-war recovery along with external help. Its position in the heart of the continent was pivotal. So Germany was bound to count for a great deal indeed, even in a Europe of regions and provinces. Adenauer's republic, with its capital in the sleepy town of Bonn, hastened its exit from purgatory by being willing to pay the largest share of the bills for the measures of economic coordination that took shape in the 1950s.[34] The cost of preserving employment in the Belgian coal mines was subsidies amounting to $US 141.42 million between 1953 and 1958, with Germany the biggest contributor.[35]

The most ambitious subsidy for an economic producer group was the Common Agricultural Policy (CAP). The aims behind it were to keep agricultural prices high, impose barriers against non-EU farmers, and send substantial subsidies to domestic farmers who were disproportionately to be found in France. It has been described by the historian Mark Gilbert as 'at bottom a bargain between France and Germany'.[36] France was prepared to hold up further measures of economic integration, to the disadvantage of German industry, unless the cost of subsidising French agriculture came to be borne by the Community as a whole; France was 'largely un-competitive on the world market yet competitive within Europe'.[37]

The smaller partners

For Italy's post-fascist leadership, the emerging European community was a means for a country, which had been a source of aggression far and near under Mussolini, to renew itself and convince neighbours that it had put militarism and territorial expansion firmly behind it. Alcide de Gasperi, Prime Minister from 1948 to 1954, had been the strongest backer in public of Spaak's 1954 attempt to move swiftly ahead towards the stage of building a supra-national political community. He even advocated the drawing up of a European Constitution. But Italy was not a major player in the early construction of the Common Market. A fragile democratic order was shown by a succession of short-lived governments and an outbreak of political terrorism from the late 1960s onwards. The Christian Democratic party enjoyed an uneasy ascendancy and its European preoccupations rarely extended beyond ensuring that Italy benefited from the allocation of EU subsidies and enjoyed high representation in a European bureaucracy growing in size from the 1960s. But at least the two implacable rivals from 1948 to 1990, the Christian Democrats and the Communists, were able to close ranks in their shared adherence to a strong European entity.

Belgium, like Italy, was an internally fragmented state (along linguistic and ethnic lines) and European integration was viewed as a possible escape from a burdensome internal political scene. Belgium derived an unmistakable advantage from the decision to make Brussels the headquarters of most of the European institutions. Paul-Henri Spaak was the only left-winger who was in the leadership of the integrationists. He began on the Trotskyite far left and ended up as the beneficiary of significant amounts of funding from the US Central Intelligence Agency once he became head of the European Movement.[38] Belgium had been a pioneer of the politics of deal-making and brokerage among established group interests that the EU would come to stand for. Spaak's patron before 1940 was Hendrik de Man who dominated the Belgian Socialist Party from 1934 until the German takeover of Belgium in 1940.[39] He championed the ideal of 'planism' in the 1930s in order to acquire broad political consensus for economic recovery, and he organised numerous conferences with participation from across Europe to promote this idea.[40] By 1938, de Man was recommending that the time had arrived for 'authoritarian democracy'.[41] After the Nazi occupation of Belgium, he drew up the Socialist response. One clause of the document released in July 1940 stated: 'Peace has not been able to develop from the free understanding of sovereign nations and rival imperialisms: it will be able to emerge from a Europe united by arms, wherein the economic frontiers have been leveled.'[42] He could have been one of the architects of a new post-war Europe if, like Spaak (whose ideas were not different from his in 1940), he had found himself in Allied territory by the time Hitler had completed his western conquests.

It would be Spaak who urged Monnet to conceal the project's overtly political goal and to proclaim instead that it was a desire to harvest the fruits of economic cooperation that drove on the builders of a new Europe. This Machiavellian approach to politics exemplified Spaak during his contrasting political experiences. For most of his public career, he had been drawn to a form of elitist politics without an active democratic component.

Belgium and the other 'Benelux states', the Netherlands as well as tiny Luxembourg, favoured European cooperation because of the desire to avoid further collisions with a powerful Germany which nobody could anticipate was about to embark on an era of peace and progress lasting over sixty years. The Netherlands stood somewhat apart though. The Dutch position on Europe in the 1950s was close to that of Britain: it was hostile to international institutions which supplanted the nation-state, ready to lift controls on the German economy, and keen to explore functional cooperation starting with coal and steel.[43] But the Dutch leadership subjected plans for integration to rigorous examination. Dutch hardheadedness was frustrating for a passionate Latin Europhile like Spinelli. He wrote in 1966:

> Dutch public opinion ... their more spontaneous sympathies remain not towards their southern neighbours but towards those of the north, above all the British. In the abstract they are generally favourable to solutions which imply real transfers of authority to united European organisations, but in the concrete they always demand long and minute preliminary intergovernmental negotiations, which inevitably help to strengthen that Europe of the nations which, as a matter of principle, they say they abhor.[44]

The Dutch had strongly opposed Monnet's bid in 1950 to place the High Authority for Coal and Steel beyond the reach of inter-governmental oversight. He gave way in the face of insistence from Dirk Spierenburg, the Dutch chief negotiator, for an inter-governmental 'watchdog'. Monnet's price was for majority voting rather than unanimity to apply. The Council of Ministers from the six founders could also take part in decision-making but without instructing the High Authority. In this way, the Council of Ministers came into existence.[45]

Contending national and European agendas

Dutch objections to centralisation were followed by a much more formidable challenge from France. De Gaulle was determined to exploit France's primacy in the Community to safeguard French agriculture and the Common Agricultural Policy was his chief instrument. On 9 December 1961, France's partners were warned that de Gaulle would block the next round of tariff cuts on manufactured goods if the CAP deadline set by the Treaty of Rome was breached. The deadline was 31 December 1961: in the end, an accord was only reached on 14 January 1962 after the six EU members 'stopped the clock' and carried on bargaining.[46] Under the CAP, high domestic prices and subsidised exports were guaranteed and for almost the next half century no less than 40 per cent of the EU budget would be spent on agriculture. Less than 5 per cent of the labour force was employed in agriculture, but the farming sector was politically influential, no more so than in France. Serious rioting in Brussels in 1971 led to the Agriculture Commissioner Sicco Mansholt ditching plans for a shakeout that would have seen the disappearance of perhaps half of the EU's ten million farms.[47] A cheap food policy would have boosted the EU's popularity but decision-makers preferred to appease an influential and determined mobilised producer interest. Inevitably, 'the mismatch between the priorities of the EU budget and those of the great majority of citizens' damaged the EU's standing and the CAP became a symbol of the gulf between vested interests well-looked-after in Brussels and the ordinary citizenry of Europe.[48]

France was reeling from national humiliation in Algeria and it may have been too much to expect that national advantage would be set aside to strengthen the prospects of an untested project groping towards continental unity. De Gaulle was regularly at loggerheads with Walter Hallstein, who had headed the European Commission since 1957. Europe's civil service was meant to be a vanguard of committed de-nationalised Europeans who would turn the European idea into a living reality as their powers of decision-making expanded.[49] It was unfortunate that its first head was a dry and inflexible bureaucrat rather than a politically skilled salesman able to popularise the challenge to the primacy of the nation-state. Hallstein had led German negotiations at the 1951 Treaty of Paris and it was appropriate that a top German policy-maker became the first head of a body meant to bring the European vision to life. But he appeared to be a prototype for 'the arrogant gray men who believe they can engineer society, oblivious to history, language, culture, values and place'.[50] David Brooks, the author of these words, had served in Brussels in the 1980s before becoming a leading American commentator and he had observed how the domination of 'the technocratic mind-set' had led the EU badly astray. Hallstein, a professor of comparative law at Frankfurt university, had been a prisoner-of-war in the USA during 1944–45 and he was a beneficiary of the inter-university exchange programmes between the USA and Germany into which the Americans had invested much energy from 1945 onwards.[51] Hallstein remained a pedantic central European professor who insisted on being addressed as 'Professor Hallstein', as a bemused British politician recalled after an encounter with him in the 1960s.[52] Max Haller, a German academic from a later era, accused him of violating 'the spirit of the Treaty of Rome by creating corporatist and centralized bureaucracies outside its framework'. Under the 1957 Treaty, the Commission enjoyed considerable autonomy. It is not a secretariat taking orders from governments or parliaments.[53] It has the exclusive right to initiate legislation, 'a privilege which has never been granted to any other bureaucracy'.[54]

De Gaulle was affronted by Hallstein's efforts to further expand the authority of the Commission. He ordered French officials to boycott the European Community's institutions through the second half of 1966. De Gaulle at this time was trying to win European support for his vision of a French-led Europe independent of the 'Anglo-Saxons'. The Dutch and most German policy-makers refused to abandon an Atlanticist perspective, relying on American leadership in the still perilous Cold War. But political opinion in the national parliaments of the six and in the European Parliament (which had evolved from the ECSC's Assembly) was broadly with de Gaulle in his bid to hold back a federalist agenda. He proclaimed that 'we are no longer in the era when M. Monnet gave the orders' and Hallstein's desire to extend his period as Commission head was vetoed by France in 1967.[55] The British authors of an influential work critical of the EU's accumulation of power concluded: 'De Gaulle's lasting achievement in the context of European integration was that he ensured that the member states kept their central role in the process of supra-national decision-making'.[56]

But after the closing of the de Gaulle era in 1969, power struggles continued over whether common European initiatives should be shaped by inter-governmental cooperation or by an agenda of post-national centralism. Sometimes, the outcomes appeared ambiguous and it was often the interplay of personalities and particular domestic political contexts which shaped developments.

The European Council, composed of the heads of state and government of all the member states, became increasingly prominent after de Gaulle's time. But it was not given formal status until the passing of the Single European Act in 1986, the first major treaty revision since the Treaty of Rome. The European Community had appeared rudderless due not least to the slowdown in growth which had resulted from the sharp increase of world oil prices in the mid-1970s. But long-term trends were boosting the authority of those who wished to make the Commission a springboard for fully fledged federalism. Here the role of the European Court of Justice (ECJ) becomes crucial. It is supposed to guarantee the maintenance of the balance among European institutions, and respect for the rule of law. An appraisal of its judgments shows that it was strongly inclined not only to reinforce the independence of the Commission but to boost its authority. Treaty law was interpreted in a series of judgments to give laws 'their fullest and most efficient effect, with consequences often not obvious in the original texts'.[57] The ECJ widened the scope of EC law and extended the competences of the Commission. This was 'probably the most important single-factor in keeping the sense of the "Community" alive in an era of inter-governmentalism'.[58]

Perhaps the most crucial judgment took place in 1962 in the van Gend en Loos case when a court judgment established the principle of direct applicability of Community law in the member states.[59] This was decided by the narrowest of margins, four to three votes, and the outcome sprang from the arrival at the court of the federalist Robert Lecourt. Wolfram Kaiser has described how de Gaulle underestimated the ability of trans-national networks to foil his inter-governmental vision:

> Lecourt was extremely well-networked across the EEC both as a leading French politician from the strongly pro-integration ... MRP [French Christian Democrats] and as a constitutional lawyer. Ironically, he was nominated for the ECJ by the greatest champion of member state sovereignty ... de Gaulle – most likely as a result of a deal with the MRP in advance of the parliamentary elections in the autumn of 1962. Clearly, de Gaulle, who had not the slightest interest in the ECJ, was out-manoeuvred by the partly overlapping Christian democratic-federalist and the European law networks ... with fundamental long-term consequences for the supranationalization of the present-day EU.[60]

In 1964 the ECJ delivered a landmark ruling when it declared that where there is a conflict between Community law and national law, EC law must prevail. This had not been explicitly spelled out in the treaties but the ECJ ruled that member states had intended that EC law should be supreme in the application of the EC treaties. Jens-Peter Bonde, a veteran Danish politician at European level, described this ruling as 'a coup d'état'. Proposals for the supremacy of EC law over national law had been rejected in the final drafting of the Treaty of Rome but once the principle had been affirmed by the ECJ, it proved to be 'the foundation on which the whole edifice of supranational government could be built'.[61]

The European Parliament's debut

From de Gaulle onwards, politicians keen to uphold national prerogatives in the new Europe of overlapping political authority were slow to recognise the in-built advantages enjoyed by the Commission even when it was poorly led, as was the case for much of the period between 1967 and 1984. Instead, much of the attention was focused on the role of the European Parliament and whether the relevance of national parliaments could be preserved if the EU enjoyed a steady increase in power and influence.

An assembly had in fact existed since 1952 as a body nominated by national parliaments to watch over the work of the ECSC. In 1976, EC foreign ministers approved the European Elections Act, allowing direct elections to the European Parliament (EP). Starting from 1979, the Assembly was enlarged from 198 members to 410, and a five-year term between elections was agreed. Direct elections were supposed to give the integration process a new legitimacy. A respectable 60 per cent of eligible European citizens turned out to vote. In countries with political systems that enjoyed low prestige the turnout was high, over 90 per cent in Belgium and well over 80 per cent in Italy. But, at the other extreme, turnout in Britain was just 33 per cent.[62]

The EP evolved from being a merely consultative body to one which in the 1970s acquired powers of co-decision in European budgetary matters and increasing powers of appointment to the commission. But as crises like those of the Yugoslav conflict of the early 1990s or the post-2009 European financial emergency have shown, the EP has been reluctant to play a leading role in EU affairs even where there is paralysis in other decision-making centres. In 2009, when its powers vastly exceeded those it had started out with in 1952, one strongly pro-EU journalist wrote: 'One uncomfortable truth is that the parliament has earned a reputation over the years as a talking shop for political has-beens and never-weres, with a special talent ... for exploiting loose expenses rules.'[63]

Consolidating the elitist approach to Europe

Voters increasingly proved numb to the EP's existence. The biggest drop in electoral turnout occurred during the period when the EU saw an unprecedented growth in its powers following the 1991 Maastricht Treaty; down from 56.8 per cent in 1994 to 49.8 per cent in 1999. But the voters may not have been terribly missed. The authors of the first social-scientific study of the integration process – Ernst Haas and his neo-functionalist school – thought the challenge for those building a common Europe was how to make 'Europe without Europeans'.[64] Unlike new states where the need to create national citizens from inhabitants who often possessed a local consciousness was seen as paramount, Commission bureaucrats preferred to interact with other elites. There was no decisive change under Delors despite some populist attempts to reach out to trade unions and regional sectors.

Lobbyists were often the only external pressure which EP members felt. It was noticed in the early 1990s that French companies in the defence sector maintained an exceptionally wide range of links on a permanent basis with Strasbourg committees as well as several Commission Directorates.[65] Strasbourg was the official seat of the European Parliament even though most of its activity occurred in Brussels. French insistence that the EP retain a French base meant that it operated as a two-centred assembly. This further inhibited its acquisition of a legitimising role for the institutions of the new Europe. The slightly pejorative term 'Eurocrats' appeared to apply equally to EP members (of whom there were 750 by 2005) and Commission officials. The French academic, Philippe Nemo, complained in 2010 of a European caste divorced from public opinion:

> Their blindness is aggravated by their tendency to live and socialize only among themselves, influencing and reassuring one another in the politically correct ideology that they absorb from the equally superficial media. [This is] the explanation [why] lobbies – for example, industrial interests which wish to gain access to cheap labour and keep wages low – wield disproportionate ... influence in Brussels.[66]

Only between 1985 and 1994 did it appear possible that a strong lead from European institutions might eclipse the role of the lead member states and enable decisive progress to be made towards the goal of European integration. These were the years when Jacques Delors, an iron-willed and well-connected former French politician, served as President of the Commission. In January 1990 Delors told the European Parliament that a European 'federation' should come into existence before the century ended.[67]

He had already been responsible for the 1986 Single European Act (SEA) which liberalised the internal market by removing many remaining trade barriers. But the SEA also greatly increased the supervisory role of the Commission in the economic sphere. Delors had admitted to the European Parliament on 6 July 1988 that most parliaments in member states had not yet woken up to the extent to which the freeing of the internal market 'would involve a seepage of their sovereignty to the Community'.[68] Margaret Thatcher, who had succeeded de Gaulle as the main opponent of supra-nationalism, felt that she had been hoodwinked. In her memoirs she noted that Delors 'had altogether slipped his leash as a *functionnaire* and become a full-fledged spokesman for federalism'.[69]

The conversion of the left

Delors was able to make real headway along the twisting path to a sovereign European state because of the growing influence of the political left. This influence was often reflected far more in terms of the weight Social Democrats and Marxists exercised in institutions such as the law and academia. These were spheres of influence which often counted for more in the European arena than in individual nation-states. The Europhile leanings of the political left also marked a break from the situation that had persisted until at least the

1960s. Michael Palliser, a civil servant who had helped steer Britain into the EC in 1973, recalled:

> One of the paradoxes of history is that in the early days of the European Community it was seen, for example by the Labour Party in this country and all the Scandinavian Labour Parties ... as a kind of right-wing Catholic cabal intent on forcing right-wing policies on a reluctant Europe.[70]

Emile Noel, Secretary-General of the Commission for nearly thirty years, had worked to reduce opposition in the German Social Democratic Party to European integration when he had been the adviser on Europe to Guy Mollet.[71] Mollet was the French left-winger who, as Prime Minister in the mid-1950s, had enabled Monnet's project to overcome important obstacles. By the 1980s, with the left increasingly unable to promote state control of the economy within the national context, the EU appeared to offer a desirable substitute. Delors greatly enhanced the EU's role as a regulator of state and private activity and as a distributor of a growing amount of public funds. It almost goes without saying that an EU fast transcending its original role as a customs union to standardise and supervise activities across the continent greatly appealed to many across the European left.

Appropriately, it is on the left of politics that the most enthusiastic advocacy of the integration cause is usually to be heard. Rarely has anyone written with such enthusiasm about the bureaucratic leviathan that the EU was turning into than Mark Leonard, the son of a British EU official who was educated at an international school in Brussels and who heads the European Council on Foreign Relations. He wrote in 2005:

> Over the last fifty years Europe's leaders have agreed to thousands of common standards, laws, and regulations. Together they fill thirty-one volumes and some 80,000 pages of text that regulate every facet of daily life ... They are known as the acquis communautaire – which literally means 'acquired fortune' or 'accepted fact' of the community.[72]

He went on to observe that 'What Monnet created was a machine of political alchemy. Each country would follow its national interest, but once the different national interests were put into the black box of European integration, a European project would emerge at the other end.'[73]

The institutions of a hopefully converging Europe appealed to many Social Democrats growing disconnected from their working-class base and possessing an increasingly international outlook. The EU's glamour was obvious. It was a seat of real power, with vast powers of supervision and control. Its rhetoric and imagery were progressive but it was not accountable to voters who had a tendency to remove Socialists from power via the ballot box after a limited period in office. The appeal of the emerging European Union even disarmed Neil Kinnock, the British Labour leader twice defeated by Margaret Thatcher, after having been a prominent critic of the EU for most of his parliamentary career. He ended his active career as a Vice-President of the European Commission from 1999 to 2004, entrusted with combating fraud.

To become the director and motivator asserting the power of the Commission across the European Community political system, Delors needed an equally forceful chief of staff. That man was Pascal Lamy, like Delors from a left Catholic background. At the *École Nationale d'Administration*, the academic preparatory school for top French bureaucrats, he had finished second in his year. A long stint as an inspector in the Ministry of Finance followed before he accompanied Delors into Mitterrand's government as Finance Minister before going on to Brussels in 1984. Lamy shook up the leisurely administrative regime inherited from Gaston Thorn, Commission head from 1981 to 1984. He was highly interventionist and hyper-active, ready to sweep aside conventions in order to ensure his chief's agenda was implemented at a rapid pace. The pliable Secretary-General of the Commission after 1987, David Williamson, even allowed Lamy to rewrite the minutes of Commission meetings. He installed pro-Delors loyalists in key posts but he himself periodically took up assignments in French politics and business.[74] This exceptionally forceful bureaucratic manager ended up as head of the World Trade Organization from 2005 onwards. But midway through Delors's decade of power in Brussels, events disrupted his plans for an EU that would acquire several of the features of a state. The fall of the Berlin Wall was followed by German unification and pressures to absorb former communist states into the EU which he was powerless to resist. Jean-Pierre Chevenement, an influential Socialist who remained unenthused by the new European faith, remarked in November 1989: 'the Berlin wall has fallen, one casualty: Jacques Delors'.[75]

Delors quit in 1994 with the ferocious wars in Yugoslavia a standing rebuke to the claim of Europhiles that it was thanks to the movement for European integration that flagrant nationalism had been tamed. As his successor, France and Germany both pushed for the Belgian, Jean-Luc Dehaene, Prime Minister of the country hosting most of the EU institutions whose politics, more than ever, were dominated by brokerage, factionalism and political clientelism. Britain's John Major may have done the European cause a favour by vetoing his appointment, though it would be the colourless Jacques Santer from Luxembourg who emerged as a compromise choice for Commission President. None of the structural weaknesses in the Commission identified in the 1979 report by the realistic Dutch Eurocrat, Dirk Spierenburg, had been rectified under Delors as was shown when the Santer commission collapsed in disgrace in 1999.[76] The report had painted a bleak picture of poor motivation, incompetence, clientelism and other maladies which most bureaucracies find it difficult to shake off.[77]

The triumph of bureaucracy and the retreat of statesmanship

Many officials, perhaps ones mainly from non-Latin countries, became detached from national influences. But it was a harder process to be socialised into the norms and values of 'Europeanness'. The evidence was weak from 1958 onwards that in Brussels the dedicated builder of the common European Home, *Homo Europeanus,* was being created, one as committed to advancing the EU's cause as bureaucrats in Vienna, Moscow or London had been in pursuing the objectives of the Austro-Hungarian, Soviet or British empires.[78] A bureaucracy wedded to the cause of European unification would only have become visible if it had been backed by high-quality political leadership. Usually the standard of leadership provided by national leaders was variable as they struggled to satisfy increasingly restive electorates. A series of political alliances in the late 1970s between Valéry Giscard d'Estaing of France and Helmut Schmidt of West Germany, and later between Germany's Helmut Kohl and François Mitterrand of France, put important momentum behind integration, especially in the financial realm. But President Giscard, despite his longstanding commitment to European federalism, was an elitist and autocratic figure, an unlikely initiator of a movement for Europe extending beyond established elites. Schmidt and Kohl, though wholehearted in their European vocations, had plenty of other preoccupations. European integration has suffered from the absence of charismatic and effective German advocates despite committed Europhiles being visible on nearly all points of the political spectrum.

Kohl and Mitterrand were replaced by Schröder and Chirac, essentially tactical politicians who never displayed long-term fidelity to the European cause (especially the Frenchman). By the 1990s, the quality of ambitious recruits to the political process across Europe was in decline. This meant there was a shortage of leading politicians with a firm grasp of economics or who possessed a policy agenda that extended much beyond winning the next election.

Monnet had declined to place too much faith in the electoral process when politicians were recruited from a deeper pool of talent. Instead, he had placed his emphasis on the transformative role of institutions and elites in building the new European order.[79] Nor had he probably set out to construct the elephantine bureaucracies that would be in charge of much European policy-making by the 1990s. The planning agencies that he set up in France and later the incipient EU were small by continental standards. But it had been a conscious decision of the builders of the European political and administrative house to make it a top-down construction. An enterprise of such audacity, seeking to sweep aside centuries of identification with the nation-state, needed top-quality people. Altruistic and disciplined officials, strongly committed to Monnet's European vision of a supra-national Europe, have never been absent from the Commission. However, as will be shown later, they have often been eclipsed by very routine people whose material ambitions and desire for enhanced personal status often gets in the way of realising the EU's chief objectives.

Monnet had few worthy successors and, as has been remarked already, he might have found it difficult to advance very far in the bureaucratic empire which he had laid the foundations for in the late 1940s. But sweeping new powers were vested in the Commission despite the fact that its credibility had already been weakened by the form its evolution had taken when the EU was confined to less than ten members. The decisive watershed was the treaty, adopted at the end of 1991, in the Dutch town of Maastricht. It re-worked the supra-national and inter-governmental balance in favour of greater central direction over a much broader policy range. A Common Foreign and Security Policy was unfurled. Every state except Britain acknowledged that it would abide by common Community standards in the field of social policy. Cooperation was institutionalised in sensitive policy areas like justice, policing and immigration.

Perhaps the key departure was that, under Maastricht, every member state, except Britain and Denmark, in principle relinquished its long-term right to make its own monetary policy.[80] It was agreed to create a European Central Bank to take the lead in managing a new single currency that would replace national currencies. The ECB's power was to be greater than that of central banks in most other democracies. There was no legislature able to amend its statutory powers. The European Parliament was therefore unable to call it to account after 2009 when it flouted the Maastricht Treaty by organising successive bail-outs of insolvent banks. As Mark Gilbert relates: 'The only nod in the direction of accountability was a requirement that the ECB should publish quarterly reports and send an annual report on its activities to the European parliament, which could then debate it.'[81] Key macro-economic decision-making was contracted out to cabals of bankers whose training and personal convictions predisposed them to making monetary stability a priority over growth and employment. It was an astonishing step for heads of government to take when they knew there was mounting unhappiness about the 'democratic deficit' in the European Community.

On 29 October 1993, the heads of government were summoned to an 'Extraordinary European Council' to affirm that, as from 1 November, the European Community would now be known as 'the European Union'. The communiqué proclaimed:

> The citizens of Europe know that the Community has brought them an end of bloody wars, a higher level of prosperity and greater influence ... they must also realize that the European Union will help them cope with industrial and social transformation, external challenges and a number of scourges of our society, starting with unemployment.[82]

The didactic and self-congratulatory nature of the statement highlighted the increasingly autocratic mood that gripped a Brussels bureaucracy where Jacques Delors was approaching a decade of being in charge. It is not surprising that in his wake, French officials were over-represented (16.8 per cent of officials were French compared with 12 per cent from the UK, and 10 per cent from Germany).[83] A biographer of Delors found that 'any official who is French, socialist and competent, with a useful area of expertise, is almost certain to be invited into the Delors network'.[84] Delors did not even permit the commissioners, usually politicians nominated by member states, to see the draft report for European Monetary Union.[85]

Beyond the army of career bureaucrats, there were few prominent Europeans committed to the supra-national ideal who enjoyed a popular appeal. Few intellectuals were committed to the goal of a single, unified Europe in comparison with the countless number who had placed a belief in socialism at the centre of their work for over a century. Nor were there many business people with a talent for self-publicity, one of the types of influential Europeans whom Monnet had courted in the 1950s. Probably, the financier George Soros is the only one of any prominence.

After 1989, Soros had formed the Open Society Foundation; it promoted social liberalism and mounted opposition to residual communist structures in post-Soviet states. In 2008, Soros money enabled the Council for European Foreign Relations to be established – a body which is ardent in its commitment to European integration. On 2 June 2012, Soros delivered a speech in the Italian city of Trento in which he described the Maastricht Treaty as ' fundamentally flawed' from the outset since 'it established a monetary union without a political union'. He pointed out, at what many saw as a moment of dire peril for Europe, that 'the architects believed, however, that when the need arose the political will could be generated to take the necessary steps towards a political union'.[86]

In fact fifty years of concealment and obfuscation about the ultimate destination of the European voyage had occurred. Different mission statements were unfurled during this ambiguous journey: to accommodate the size and strength of Germany at the heart of the European continent; to ensure secure food supplies; to abolish war on European soil; to promote European growth by building a dynamic trans-national economy; to regulate Europe so that the member states could aspire to enjoy common living standards; to enable Europe to enjoy continued relevance in a multipolar world as new powers jostled with existing ones. But behind these manifestos, all too often different producer groups, nations and assorted lobbies converging on the EU institutions have sought to promote their own particular interests. The EU failed to avoid falling under the sway of an array of forces happy to use the entity as a platform to grow fatter and more influential. Different initiatives from above were launched to try to revive earlier glories in the unification process. But they were often poorly thought-out and contrived, and subject to abrupt modification when reality got in the way of the theoretical blueprint for building Europe. Europe had indeed been built without Europeans but also without sufficient numbers of dedicated leaders, public officials and advocates to ensure that the cause of a united Europe would survive and prosper.

Notes

1 Bruno Waterfield, 'Ordinary people were misled over the impact of the euro', *Daily Telegraph*, 27 May 2010.
2 John Gillingham, *European Integration 1950–2003* (Cambridge: Cambridge University Press, 2003), p. 17.
3 Jean Monnet, letter to Churchill, 2 July 1940, quoted in Frederic J. Fransen, *The Supranational Politics of Jean Monnet: Ideas and Origins of the European Community* (Westport, CT: Greenwood Press, 2001), p. 76
4 Winston Churchill, letter to Monnet, 16 July 1940, quoted in Fransen, *The Supranational Politics*, p. 76.
5 Recollections of Jean-Louis Mandereau in 1981, quoted in Fransen, *The Supranational Politics*, p. 65.
6 Booker and North, *The Great Deception*, p. 29.
7 Booker and North, *The Great Deception*, p. 54.
8 Haller, *European Integration*, p. 21.
9 Haller, *European Integration*, p. 21.
10 Booker and North, *The Great Deception*, p. 83, n. 33.
11 Keith Middlemas, *Orchestrating Europe: The Informal Politics of the European Union* (London: Fontana Press, 1995), p. 10.
12 Middlemas, *Orchestrating Europe*, p. 15.
13 Willis, *France, Germany and the New Europe*, p. 73.
14 Middlemas, *Orchestrating Europe*, p. 17.
15 Ronald Irving, *Adenauer* (London: Pearson, 2002), p. 115.
16 Middlemas, *Orchestrating Europe*, pp. 21–2.
17 Giandomenico Majone, *Europe as the Would-be World Power: The EU at Fifty* (Cambridge: Cambridge University Press, 2009), p. 74.
18 François Duchêne, *Jean Monnet: The First Statesman of Interdependence* (New York: WW Norton, 1994), p. 355.
19 Alan S. Milward, *The European Rescue of the Nation-State* (London: Routledge, 1992), p. 336.
20 See Daniel Hannan, 'The EU is an antidote to democratic governments, argues President Barroso', *Daily Telegraph*, 8 October 2010.
21 Booker and North, *The Great Deception*, p. 79.
22 Booker and North, *The Great Deception*, p. 81.
23 Booker and North, *The Great Deception*, p. 81.
24 Duchêne, *Jean Monnet*, pp. 81–2.
25 Mark Gilbert, *European Integration: A Concise History* (Plymouth, UK: Rowman and Littlefield, 2011), p. 36
26 Haller, *European Integration*, p. 61.
27 Grant, *Delors, Inside the House*, p. 83.
28 Pascaline Winand, *Eisenhower, Kennedy and the United States of Europe* (New

York: St. Martin's Press, 1993), pp. 27–8, 58–9.

29 Gilbert, *European Integration*, p. 50.

30 Booker and North, *The Great Deception*, p. 15.

31 Craig Parsons, *A Certain Idea of Europe* (Ithaca, NY, and London: Cornell University Press, 2003), p. 51.

32 Parsons, *A Certain Idea of Europe*, p. 91.

33 Altiero Spinelli, *The Eurocrats: Conflict and Crisis in the European Community* (Baltimore: Johns Hopkins University Press, 1966), p. 73.

34 John Lloyd, 'The beautiful folly of the European experiment', Reuters, 18 November 2011.

35 Majone, *Europe as the Would-be World Power*, p. 17.

36 Gilbert, *European Integration*, p. 64.

37 Andrew Moravcsik, *Choice for Europe: Social Purpose and State Power from Messina to Maastricht* (Ithaca, NY, and London: Cornell University Press, 1998), p. 180.

38 Booker and North, *The Great Deception*, p. 55.

39 See Zeev Sternhall, 'The "anti-materialist" revision of Marxism', *Journal of Contemporary History*, 22, 1987, pp. 379–400.

40 Dick Pels, 'Hendrik de Man and the ideology of planism', *International Review of Social History*, 32, 3, December 1987, pp. 206–29.

41 Peter Dodge, *Beyond Marxism: The Faith and Works of Hendrik de Man* (The Hague: Martinus Nijhoff, 1966), p. 180.

42 Dodge, *Beyond Marxism*, p. 197.

43 Parsons, *A Certain Idea of Europe*, p. 52.

44 Spinelli, *The Eurocrats*, p. 82.

45 Booker and North, *The Great Deception*, p. 71.

46 Gilbert, *European Integration*, p. 63.

47 See Evelyn Bush and Peter Simi, 'European farmers and their protests', in Doug Imig and Sidney Tarrow (eds), *Contentious Europeans: Protest Politics in an Emerging Polity* (Lanham, MD: Rowman and Littlefield, 2001).

48 Anand Menon, *Europe: The State of the Union* (London: Atlantic Books, 2008), pp. 162–5; also Majone, *Europe as the Would-be World Power*, p. 19.

49 Cris Shore, *Building Politics: The Cultural Politics of European Integration* (London: Routledge, 2000), p. 177.

50 David Brooks, 'The technocratic nightmare', *New York Times*, 17 November 2011.

51 Brigitte Leucht, 'Expertise and the creation of a constitutional order for a core Europe: transatlantic policy networks in the Schuman Plan negotiation', in Wolfram Kaiser et al., *Transatlantic Networks in Regional Integration: Governing Europe 1945–1983* (Basingstoke: Palgrave, 2010).

52 See William Wallace, 'Walter Hallstein: the British perspective', in Wilfried Loth et al., *Walter Hallstein: The Forgotten European* (London: Croom Helm, 1998), p. 190.

53 Roland Vaubel, *The European Institutions as an Interest Group: The Dynamics of Ever-Closer Union* (London: Institute of Economic Affairs, 2009), p. 29.

54 Haller, *European Integration*, p. 155.

55 Duchêne, *Jean Monnet*, p. 315.

56 Booker and North, *The Great Deception*, p. 87.

57 Middlemas, *Orchestrating Europe*, p. 92.

58 Middlemas, *Orchestrating Europe*, p. 92.

59 See Menon, *Europe: The State of the Union*, pp. 44–6.

60 See Wolfram Kaiser, 'Plus ça change? Diachronic change in networks in European governance', in Kaiser et al., *Transatlantic Networks*.

61 Jens-Peter Bonde, quoted by Booker and North, *The Great Deception*, p. 155.

62 Gilbert, *European Integration*, p. 115.

63 Tony Barber, 'A void to fill', *Financial Times*, 27 May 2009.

64 Majone, *Europe as the Would-be World Power*, p. 26.

65 Middlemas, *Orchestrating Europe*, p. 450.

66 Philippe Nemo, 'Europe's endangered soul', *City Journal*, Spring 2010.

67 Friend, *Unequal Partners: French–German Relations*, p. 32.

68 Booker and North, *The Great Deception*, p. 293.

69 Quoted in Booker and North, *The Great Deception*, p. 293.

70 Michael Palliser, DOHB Biographical details and interview, 28 April 1999, Churchill College, Cambridge, Archives, www.chu.cam.ac.uk/archives/collections/ ... Phillips _hayden.pdf, p. 48.

71 Duchêne, *Jean Monnet*, p. 297.

72 Mark Leonard, *Why Europe Will Run the 21st Century* (London: Fourth Estate, 2005), pp. 41–2.

73 Leonard, *Why Europe Will Run*, p. 12.

74 George Ross, 'Policy development and the cabinet system in the Delors Commission', Pittsburg: American Enterprise Institute, no date: http://aei.pitt.edu /7234/1/1002484_1.pdf; Grant, *Delors, Inside the House*, pp. 102–3.

75 Patrick McCarthy, 'Of Richelieu, Adenauer and sundry others', in Patrick McCarthy (ed.), *France-Germany in the Twenty-First Century* (London: Palgrave, 2001), p. 36.

76 Peter Ludlow, 'The European Commission', in Robert Keohane and Stanley Hoffman (eds), *The New European Community: Decision-Making and Institutional Change* (Oxford: Westview Press, 1991), p. 81.

77 Shore, *Building Politics*, p. 196.

78 Shore, *Building Politics*, p. 166.

79 Shore, *Building Politics*, p. 206.

80 Gilbert, *European Integration*, p. 164.

81 Gilbert, *European Integration*, p. 167.

82 Booker and North, *The Great Deception*, p. 379.

83 Haller, *European Integration*, p. 173.

84 Grant, *Delors, Inside the House*, p. 104.

85 Grant, *Delors, Inside the House*, p. 105.

86 Joe Weisenthal, 'Full text of George Soros speech', *Business Insider*, 4 June 2012.

3

France and Germany: the EU's odd couple

The history of the German nation-state has ended. What we can do for the world and for us is the recognition that the nation-state today has been the cause of Europe's catastrophe and the cause of catastrophes in other continents. The nation-state concept is the most destructive force on earth today and we should begin to completely do away with it.

Karl Jaspers (1960)[1]

Dissenters

Proponents of a united Europe have mostly been political winners. Appropriately, some of the key buildings of European government in Brussels are named after its founding apostles.

But there have been prominent dissenters who often counted for much in their own countries and warned that the concentration of power at continental level was no antidote to runaway nationalism. Moreover, they argued, it could provide a backdoor return for narrow and unrepresentative forms of decision-making in which special interests benefited; or else it could expose Europe to new dangers because momentous decisions were taken that were not subject to popular scrutiny.

Germany produced the earliest highly placed sceptic, Ludwig Erhard, the long-running Minister of Economics, the second Chancellor of the Federal Republic, and someone also hailed as the chief architect of its economic recovery. There was also Pierre Mendes-France, the head of arguably the most effective government in the troubled French Fourth Republic (1944–58), who in 1954 refused to throw his weight behind the European Defence Community; later Philippe de Villiers of the Movement for France and the purist Gaullist Philippe Séguin struck blows against the centralisation of the EU which they argued placed French citizens in the worst of all worlds, buried under the crushing weight of both Brussels and Parisian bureaucracy.

But French opposition was bound to be muted. 'The European Union is a

French creation. The major initiatives – from Schuman's plan for a Coal and Steel Community through the Common Agricultural Policy, to the single currency – have been French and have served French interests.' 'The French' Larry Siedentop has argued, had 'an enormous advantage. They know what they want.'[2]

In Britain, implacable opposition from an early stage might have been expected from the Conservative Party to the imposition of a continental order on an island nation which had preferred its own destiny for so long. But until the Premiership of Margaret Thatcher, what was striking was the paucity of that opposition from the party that supposedly articulated British nationalism. Harold Macmillan, the aristocrat who initiated the first overtures to the EU in 1961, managed to conceal the fact that he wished Britain to join an entity committed to disestablishing the nation-state.[3] It was initially intensely pro-European Conservatives like Enoch Powell and Nicholas Ridley who began to spearhead Tory opposition to European entanglements.[4]

The main British opposition to EU membership came from the British Labour Party. Labour figures across the political spectrum expressed their hostility to what was seen as a capitalist club put together in a still volatile and unpredictable continent whose values and aspirations differed from Britain's. Hugh Gaitskell, Douglas Jay, Tony Benn, Peter Shore, Michael Foot and Bryan Gould articulated Labour's apprehensions.[5] Harold Wilson, Labour's leader, was numb to Europe but in search of a political legacy, and his crafty manoeuvring ensured that opponents of entry were neutralised at crucial stages in Britain's turn towards Europe between 1967 and 1975.

Few, if any, notable critics of entry could be found in the other countries which joined the EU, bringing its size up to twelve members by 1985. Ireland, Greece, Spain and Portugal were countries seeking to escape from economic backwardness and (excepting Ireland) authoritarian rule. Opposing the EU seemed absurd (if not perverse) as membership was bound to result in a massive transfer of funds which local Euro-enthusiasts believed would at last unlock the door to modernisation. Denmark was the only dissenter in the early wave of new entrants. It was an old state with strong traditions of civic patriotism which had cause to be wary of large formations meddling in its affairs. This was not such an eccentric attitude as that shown by the decision of countries with not dissimilar profiles, Norway and Switzerland, to reject membership (twice in the case of Norway – in the referenda of 1972 and 1994), Switzerland rejecting external association in a 1992 referendum. There must have been times when top Eurocrats wished Denmark had also stayed out as its voters held up the progress of several key EU treaties and in Jens-Peter Bonde, an MEP for nearly thirty years, had one of the shrewdest critics of EU centralisation.

The inclusion of Sweden, Austria and Finland in 1995 meant that countries which needed to be convinced of the value of further steps on the integration journey (and were strong net contributors to the EU budget) were now also on board. The largest wave of entrants, increasing the EU to 27 members by 2007, mainly comprised former communist countries reliant on EU funding and sponsorship to try and bury the legacy of being trapped in a disastrous political experiment. But they were far from being meek supplicants. Poland negotiated fiercely in a bid to avoid being saddled with entry terms that benefited core EU states looking for captive markets in the East. Vaclav Klaus, the Czech Republic's most prominent politician from 1993 onwards, never hid his view that the cumbersome and centralised EU contained too many similarities to the Soviet model which he had grown up under. He offended believers in the European project, including those like him on the centre-right, by arguing that an entity with utopian goals, but which was wedded to a clumsy and excessive bureaucracy, was too much like history repeating itself for his liking. Other prominent leaders from East-Central Europe could be found who agreed with his outlook.

The convenient assumption that Europeans shared identical values and could thus be subject to uniform regulations was unlikely to find many keen emulators east of the Elbe due to this part of Europe's history of long-distance rule. Searing experiences had convinced many Europeans, captive for over forty years, that democracy could only exist at the level of the nation-state. Horror over the weakening of the original building blocks of European integration – that is, individual countries – grew when, armed with new powers, the EU proved to be such a weak crisis manager in the time of troubles that opened up from 2008 onwards. It also spread to hitherto enthusiastically pro-integration countries such as Finland and the Netherlands. By 2011 they had produced electorally successful parties openly dismissive of the practical value of some of the key EU trans-national controls exercised over their countries. But those temperamentally out-of-tune with the EU style of politics, deal-making done far from the public gaze, or else refusing to believe any longer in a unified political and economic space for Europe, had largely been in the wilderness until 2008.

It was not that they lacked popular support. More crucial was their inability to influence particular institutions which, in member states, EU decision-makers could usually rely on to drive forward the integration project: the civil service, the media and the academic world.

Progress in implementing the supra-national manifesto of Jean Monnet and his followers should have been quicker given the limited strength of their adversaries and the institutional support that these followers came to amass. What held back the integration drive was periodic doubts among policy-makers about the wisdom of the route being taken as well as less edifying bouts of infighting. These were based on the electoral timetables or other political needs of leaders apparently signed up to the European project. Such doubts and recriminations were evident, from the earliest days, in the dual pillars of the new political Europe: France and Germany. From the very heart of the French governing elite, there would be periodic waves of obstructionism, blocking further moves towards integration. Cumulatively, undeclared French Euroscepticism was probably more harmful to the European project than the actions and rhetoric of declared enemies like Margaret Thatcher in Britain.

From the outset, intensive bilateral dealings between leaders of these two states have determined the pace and extent of European integration. Converging Europe has been a story about how these two national giants determined the extent to which their core interests could be reconciled with advancing the European project. In Germany, widespread doubts surfaced only very late with the eruption of the worst crisis in the history of the EU after 2008. In France, uncertainty about how and whether France could preserve its national distinctiveness and broad leverage within the EU has never been far below the surface. Huge doubts had to be swallowed, and bitter grievances emanating from the Second World War set aside, before France could realistically think in terms of partnership with such a recently implacable enemy. Slowly acquired mechanisms of interstate cooperation helped transcend historical grievances, making war less likely as a result; the new atmosphere would also make outright opposition to European integration unfashionable. Intensifying Franco-German cooperation was the motor driving the European project: its architects are in the pantheon of European heroes. Those who feared that a model of centralisation for Europe would throw up new problems were marginalised, although some had distinctive and well-thought-out positions. Their pro-European rivals were not always paragons of democracy or constructive in their dealings with colleagues: they could be short-sighted, their judgement totally shaped by the new ideology meant to stabilise Europe so that memories of the grim warfare among nations were gradually erased from popular consciousness.

From *revanchism* to reconciliation

It is worth recalling that Charles de Gaulle, the official liberator of France in 1944, began his political career in 1944 with radically different ideas of the Franco-German relationship. In a radio broadcast on 5 February 1944 he stated that 'the assurance that French forces will be stationed all along the Rhine, and the separation of the left bank of the river and of the Ruhr basin from the future German state or states ... are conditions France considers essential'.[6]

For three years as de Gaulle's Foreign Minister, Georges Bidault advocated a permanently fragmented Germany with power residing in provinces that eventually would become sovereign entities. In 1946, he stated openly that 'The separation of the Ruhr and Rhineland from Germany is the only way to keep Germany from its national industry – war.'[7] But his successor, Robert

Schuman, succeeded in breaking with *revanchism* and striking out in a new direction. In 1950, he would be able to state what would have been unthinkable just a short time before: 'Five years almost to the day, after the Germans' unconditional surrender, France is carrying out the first decisive act in the construction of Europe, in partnership with Germany. The situation in Europe will be completely transformed as a result.'[8]

Only with great reluctance had France, in 1948, accepted the Anglo-American proposal for the establishment of a West German state with a central government. Its position softened as the confrontation between the Soviet Union and the West, already known as the Cold War, escalated to dangerous levels. In 1952, France gave its backing to the restoration of West German sovereignty to the maximum degree possible without Russian consent.[9] But one territorial issue threatened to undermine the success of a new European understanding.

The Saarland, with one million German inhabitants, located on the west side of the Rhine, had been occupied by France after 1945. It continued to be a symbol of French determination to retain a degree of ascendancy over a defeated Germany. If France controlled its manufacturing industries, then its output of coal and steel would be roughly the same as West Germany's.[10] It has been easily forgotten that Robert Schuman, one of the icons of a common European home, defended French actions to permanently wrest the Saar from Germany and redefine it as an overseas province of France. In March 1950, his Foreign Ministry drew up a Convention which was signed by the puppet government installed by the French High Commission in the Saarland, proclaiming its 'autonomy' and its 'economic union' with France.[11] Chancellor Adenauer's response was low-key and his *rapport* with Schuman contributed to a gradual French climb-down. But it was a protracted affair. The French retreated when it was clear that the overwhelming majority of people in the Saarland had no wish to be separated from Germany. A referendum in 1955 decisively confirmed that and in 1957 the Saarland joined the Federal German Republic as its eleventh *Land*. In between, there had even been a proposal to resolve the problem by making the Saarland the site of a European federal capital (along the lines of the District of Columbia in the USA), but insufficient support was to be found for turning its main city, Saarbrucken, into the future capital of 'Europe'.[12]

Only on 5 May 1955 was the Occupation Statute abrogated and the Allied High Commission wound up. Normalisation of ties was made easier by an acceleration of social and cultural links. The French military government in south-west Germany ironically encouraged this process by bringing large numbers of *lecteurs* to Germany to teach the French language. Social events blossomed into Franco-German societies, work that played an imperative role in hastening *rapprochement*.[13]

Germany's leverage gradually increased due to the advantages it enjoyed over France. It was not preoccupied by costly overseas conflicts or commit-ments and indeed its own defence costs were modest due to the continued presence of Allied forces on its soil. Its politics were also tidy and predictable compared to the fractious kaleidoscope of the French Fourth Republic; and its economy, skilfully shepherded by Ludwig Erhard, showed quick signs of recovery.

The forgotten German Eurosceptic

Erhard, who was Chancellor fairly briefly in the 1960s, is now largely forgotten, at least outside Germany. Bold decisions taken in his war-ravaged country in the late 1940s and careful economic stewardship thereafter provided the crucial groundwork for the German 'economic miracle'. Without the restoration of a prosperous and competitive Germany, little of the funding would have existed that would disarm French resistance to the whole EU concept and subsidise later rounds of expansion.

The only biography to have appeared in English, written by Alfred C. Mierzejewski, perhaps explains why Erhard has become the forgotten man of Europe's post-war recovery. Erhard, it turns out:

> reviled large domestic bureaucracies ... For this reason, Erhard was very suspicious of the drive to create European institutions leading ultimately to a United Europe. He simply could not see the need for such a contrivance. Any such contrivance would inevitably be highly bureaucratic, in his view ... there were so many differences among the various European peoples or among the places where they lived that a single economy or fiscal policy for the entire continent would inevitably fail.[14]

It is not surprising that historians labouring to describe the creation of the European institutions as the logical end-point in the story of Europe have not lingered over the life or public career of Ludwig Erhard. There has been no successful counterpart in the era of stagnation in Europe coinciding with the EU acquiring increasing amounts of powers of decision-making over states. Nor has he been invoked during the current economic emergency as someone whose decisiveness and clear-thinking might provide lessons for climbing out of the economic pit much of Europe has plunged into.

Erhard would surely have been affronted by the *acquis communautaire*. This is the constantly expanding body of rules and regulations, mandated by the Community law, which enables the European Commission to enjoy a monopoly in setting the policy agenda.[15] Seen another way, it is the sum of treaties and negotiated laws which members can only obtain temporary dero-gation from and which, eventually, they will have to comply with in full.[16] In the mid-1990s, countries from former communist Eastern Europe had to comply with over 100,00 pages of laws and directives, making up the 'bible' of EU legislation. Naturally, West Germany's own economic recovery would have been impaired if it had been squeezed into such a bureaucratic strait-jacket in the late 1940s.

Altiero Spinelli, one of the most ardent Euro-federalists, saw Erhard as a maverick, which indeed he was: his 'liberal policy aimed to insert German industry into the world market [and he] did not look with much favour upon the European Community, in which concessions had to be made to French and Italian protectionist tendencies'.[17]

As an alternative to creating an unwieldy supra-national organisation, Erhard placed his faith in the subsidiarity principle in international relations. 'In effect,' according to a biographer, 'he wanted decisions to be made at the lowest possible level, thereby preventing the growth of a large European central bureaucracy.'[18]

A week before the signing of the Rome Treaty in 1957, Erhard said: 'I cannot feign enthusiasm for this treaty ... France has considered the Common Market project solely from the point of view of protection of its economy and cares little for true freedom of trade.'[19] He was the first prominent European to warn that the drive for supra-nationalism was likely to prove a screen behind which national interests would be asserted, sometimes in a crude and uninhibited manner.

He was unlikely to react with equanimity at the unfolding prospect of the French administrative system being imposed on a continental basis. Just fifty years after the formal launch of what became the EU, Charles McCreevy, the outgoing Commissioner for Internal Market Affairs, caused ruffles in a speech on 18 December 2009 responding to President Sarkozy's claim that the appointment of a Frenchman as the new Commissioner for Financial Services was a 'defeat for Anglo-Saxon capitalism':

> President Sarkozy has laid to rest once and for all the myth that EU commissioners are expected to leave aside their home member state national interests ... and act exclusively in the community interest. People forget that the Brussels bureaucracy was designed by the French almost as a copy of how the administration in Paris works.[20]

France in the late 1950s managed, by tough bargaining, to impose many of its own national policy preferences on its new partners at considerable cost, not least to West Germany. For Erhard, France's insistence on a high common external tariff to which Germany would be bound even if it was not in its interest remained a cause of particular unease.[21] He predicted that: 'the result will not be a market for free competition, but an economic burden for Europe'.[22] He thought that the French demand to harmonise social expenditures and labour costs in the new Common Market was a means to increase German production costs: 'Such demands rest on an utterly fallacious interpretation of economic laws and facts, but at one and the same time it characterizes a spiritual attitude which must under no circumstances triumph, unless human initiative and creative forces, yes, even life itself, are to be suffocated in an integrated Europe.'[23] He fought back as best he could despite having a political chief, Adenauer, who was enthusiastic for the nascent project. At Erhard's insistence, the 1955 Spaak Report, planning the shape of the European institutions, had called for regulation of monopolies and trusts whose influence he was seeking to limit in his own country.[24]

Britain, in 1956, had sponsored an Organisation of European Economic Cooperation (OEEC) with the intention of creating a free trade area that could interact with the emerging EEC. This was anathema to the federalist vision of Monnet. But Erhard and the majority of business groups in Germany favoured the creation of a formal link.[25] Besides Erhard's liberal economic views, Germany carried out important trade with the members of the OEEC outside the EEC. But 'at talks in 1957 and 1958, the French delegation made it clear that conditions bolstering French economic interests which had been written into the EEC treaties, should underlie any wider accord'.[26] Walter Hallstein, the German who was the first head of the EU bureaucracy, held views on these matters that were the antithesis of Erhard's and it has been argued that through intransigence and deception, he managed to kill off what was feared to be a rival British 'power-base' that could inconvenience plans for a federal Europe.[27]

Erhard was very much a Cassandra in his doubts about the EU. In the United States, there was cross-party and high-level elite backing for the project. Britain was too absorbed with managing imperial retreat and unfavourable economic trends at home to be able to be a coherent partner and Erhard had a boss who was a strong enthusiast.

Adenauer disarms the French

Konrad Adenauer had never been an enthusiastic German in the political sense even before the disastrous advent of Hitler. He had briefly supported separatism in his native Rhineland at the end of the First World War: he seemed prepared to live with a partitioned Germany since it reduced the influence of the bulwarks of autocratic power in what had previously been the Prussian heartland of Germany. A mystique has grown up about the fourteen-year rule of a ruthless and capable leader avid for power until well into his eighties. Without Adenauer, West Germany might have had a less tidy form of politics. But it is hard to contend that he was the indispensable bulwark of democracy in a country which had suffered different forms of autocratic and dictatorial rule for much of the time since its unification in 1870.

Politically the country was easy to manage; most Germans wished to concentrate on rebuilding the economy so that their own lives, ravaged by inflation, war and unemployment, could finally proceed in a predictable way. For much of the 1950s, Adenauer managed to rule West Germany like a semi-monarch. Remarkably, he spent extended periods on holiday at destinations in the Alps that required ministers to make long trips to see him on state business. He relied on lawyers and civil servants, some of whom had not escaped involvement with unsavoury aspects of the Nazi regime, as his trusted lieutenants.[28] German democracy would have been left by him on a sounder footing if he had instead worked in partnership with his own party colleagues and encouraged people with talent and vision to rise to the top. An Adenauer in charge of a post-national EU state would probably be seen as a provocation as well as confirmation that a united Europe could only work to some degree under a semi-authoritarian direction. His main achievement was in the geo-political realm, smoothing the way for a German return to playing a constructive role in European and international affairs. This was an important turning-point which might not have been accomplished as quickly by a less imperious German ruler; it is worth noting that the Foreign Ministry remained under Adenauer's personal control – he served as his own Foreign Minister until 1955 – and it was staffed with pro-European officials loyal to him.[29]

It hardly counts in Adenauer's favour that he conspired feverishly against Ludwig Erhard becoming Chancellor, proceeding to undermine him as best he could during the three years that he occupied the post. A biographer has compared him with Lyndon Johnson, 'both ... rough and frequently unscrupulous politicians'.[30] He colluded in the state crackdown on the current affairs magazine *Der Spiegel* which had been organised by his Defence Minister Franz-Josef Strauss in 1962.[31] While still revered in his party, the Christian Democratic Union (CDU), he was an official guest of the Spanish dictatorship and 'was much taken' with Generalissimo Franco whom he found 'modest and thoughtful'.[32] But of course his crucial relationship was with France, and after 1958, he became fixated with establishing a partner-ship with the sometimes quixotic and volatile Charles de Gaulle. Between November 1958 and November 1963, the two men met on fifteen occasions, had one hundred hours of talks, and wrote to each other over forty times.[33] Adenauer and de Gaulle met for the first time and 'with some emotion' on 14–15 September 1958. The American academic Julius W. Friend viewed the context of their meeting as being one of 'a semi-sovereign Germany – which the previous war left territorially amputated, historically handicapped, politi-cally divided, militarily occupied, and morally bankrupt'.[34] But West Germany's strengths were becoming harder to conceal. By 1957, it was already the world's third largest exporter, comprising 8.1 per cent of world exports compared to France's 5.1 per cent.[35] In the EU's founding negotia-tions, Adenauer had insisted that German be an official language after it looked as if only French would enjoy such status (the Dutch and Italians in the end also obtaining this level of recognition for their languages).

It would have been hard for bilateral relations to have been normalised if de Gaulle's elemental nationalism had manifested itself in implacable hostility to the European project. Previously, like Mendes-France, he had drawn from the experiences of wartime, and the unity and political and economic health of France, rather than the reconciliation of Europe, was, for him, the chief post-war necessity.[36] But soon after his return to power in 1958, he seems to have reconsidered: the view that 'It was perfectly possible to protect core French interests by playing a full role in the emerging European project' became the new orthodoxy.[37] The readiness of Adenauer to allow France to use the emerging Economic Community for national purposes is likely to have encouraged such a reassessment. Adenauer's primacy at home ensured there was only limited German resistance to EU initiatives, clearly slanted towards France's well-being. Giandomenico Majone has summed up the hard-headed French approach in the following way:

> de Gaulle viewed common European programmes in atomic and space research as convenient ways to tap foreign contributions for the improvement of French national competitiveness rather than as ways for France to contribute to European unity. He also insisted on farm subsidies as a non-negotiable condition for accepting the EEC. Thanks to the CAP, the citizens of other member states help support the income of French farmers by paying higher prices than they would pay otherwise.[38]

An EU emerged where power and advantage was asymmetrically distributed, a clear recipe for dissension in the future. There is no sign that Adenauer, while downplaying German nationalism, saw any contradiction in sponsoring nationalist behaviour by France in what was supposedly a project meant to relegate the national principle to an unimportant role in European affairs. Adenauer remained impassive even when (while he was still Chancellor) signs began to emerge of France using its European platform to revive tensions with the United States. Bernard Connolly has described 'a series of struggles primarily against the United States, over culture, economic philosophy, "spheres of influence" and economic hegemony'.[39]

It was against the lesser Anglo-Saxon rival, however, that de Gaulle launched his first strike. In January 1963, one week before Chancellor Adenauer was to go to Paris to sign a friendship agreement, de Gaulle gave a press conference at which he announced that he would veto the recent British application to join the Community, terming Britain 'an American Trojan Horse'. On his return, Adenauer was attacked by his presumptive successor, Erhard, for not trying hard enough to gain de Gaulle's consent for British entry into the European Economic Community (as it then was). In an interview in the *Suddeutsche Zeitung* in February 1963, Erhard voiced strong doubts on the treaty, arguing that a bilateral treaty with strongly anti-US and anti-British accents was anachronistic and harmful to the West as a whole.[40] In the end, the Bundestag decided to ratify the treaty – with a preamble designed to frustrate de Gaulle's intentions, speaking of 'unification of Europe along the lines of the European Communities, and including Great Britain'.[41] The contents of the preamble were a clear message to France that a German cabinet would not adopt de Gaulle's foreign policy.[42]

France turns on its offspring

In his first Bundestag speech as Chancellor, Erhard spoke of the importance of NATO for German security, proclaiming that his government would continue 'to decide all questions of common interest in close and friendly cooperation with the American government'.[43] He never swerved from this position even in the face of French entreaties. When in 1964 de Gaulle urged Erhard to build a European defence capability independent of the Americans, Erhard asked point blank if the *force de frappe* would be French or European. It would be French, said de Gaulle, but it would be for the protection of Europe.[44] Erhard recalls his reaction: 'I was naturally able to reply, that we have only to choose whether to be dependent on the American nuclear weapon or to be dependent on the French nuclear weapon.'[45]

The most dramatic example of the French obstructionism that impeded the consolidation of the European Community occurred in 1965. On the night of 30 June–1 July, Maurice Couve de Murville, the Foreign Minister, declared that 'a community whose partners do not abide by their agreements has ceased to be a community'.[46] On 1 July, France launched what became known as 'the empty chair crisis' when its permanent representatives to the Community were ordered to return to Paris and it ceased to be represented at meetings of the Council of Ministers.[47] René Mayer, a French Prime Minister during the Fourth Republic, recalls that at an Elysée reception at the height of the crisis, he started telling de Gaulle that as President of the ECSC, he had learnt a lot. De Gaulle interrupted, 'Good! Now forgot everything. I am erasing it all, and we are beginning again.'[48] But in the December 1965 French presidential elections, the percentage of votes that de Gaulle received in the first round fell to only 44 per cent. Monnet was so annoyed with de Gaulle that he endorsed François Mitterrand.[49] De Gaulle was forced into a run-off against his Socialist challenger who made a strong showing (with 45 per cent). This could be seen as a sign that the public wanted an end to the crisis with Brussels.

At the height of the 'empty chair crisis', Erhard pressed de Gaulle hard, eventually threatening to discuss membership with Britain.[50] 'Without Britain,' he had declared in London in January 1964, 'Europe would be only a torso ... Today, when we consider modern technology and all our countless ties, the Channel has ceased to be a dividing line; the expression continental Europe may be a geographical reminiscence, but it is not a political reality.'[51] German political rivals united on Europe and Erhard's victory in the election of September 1965 was widely seen as a vindication of his Atlanticist foreign policy;[52] West German opinion had been appalled by France's decision to quit the military wing of NATO.

Deadlock on foreign policy between Paris and Bonn never let up during Erhard's chancellorship. Even Adenauer was disturbed, appalled by de Gaulle's courtship of the Soviet Union. Speaking to the CDU congress in 1965, he said: 'our destiny is also the destiny of France. If we are devoured by the Russians, the French will be devoured too. It is absurd to think that Communism can become more pliable . . . '[53]

De Gaulle attempted to destabilise Erhard at home but without success. Paris sought to rouse the Adenauer and Strauss factions of the CDU against Erhard by making policy favourable to German agricultural interests conditional on favouring French external goals. When Erhard defeated the CDU's domestic Gaullist faction and held firm, de Gaulle and French officials even resorted to uttering threats about a complete French exit from the EC.[54] Erhard was eventually toppled by his party enemies, in late 1965, but due mainly to domestic economic issues. So the 1963 Franco-German treaty, rather than paving the way for a two-power domination of the EU, remained dormant. Kurt Kiesinger at the head of a 'grand coalition' of CDU and SPD favoured the Franco-German relationship, but little changed in official German policy. Bonn remained opposed to French unilateral goals and was unwilling to make a break with the Atlanticist framework under which it had made a striking recovery.[55]

The European project had become a victim of the political imperatives of the proud and dogmatic leader in charge of the country which had initially been the one to drive the enterprise forward. This would not be an isolated development in the subsequent fifty-year history of the EU. From Valéry Giscard d'Estaing to Nicolas Sarkozy and François Hollande, de Gaulle's successors, anxious for a legacy due to lack of policy success at home, or just in search of any tool that would secure an electoral victory, behaved in an erratic and often parochial way towards wider European questions. Unfortunately, figures like Erhard who had a realistic and pragmatic vision for Europe, acting in concert with the USA, were usually thin on the ground during these periods of opportunistic behaviour. His biographer recalls that 'he was not a statist, a social engineer who sought to create heaven on earth. He was an optimistic but hard-headed thinker who wanted to free people to realise their own potential, while accepting that neither markets nor democracies functioned automatically.'[56]

Erhard might have found de Gaulle's successor, Georges Pompidou, easier to get along with: 'he had little enthusiasm for de Gaulle's quasi-mystical view of the Franco-German bond. The result was a preference for a pragmatic confederal strategy. A British EEC accession was not only acceptable but desirable, both to balance Germany and to bring in another proponent of careful, inter-governmental cooperation.'[57] Pompidou displayed antipathy towards the report of the committee chaired by the Christian Democrat Prime Minister of Luxembourg, Pierre Werner, which in 1970 recommended implementing economic and monetary union by the end of the decade. Indeed, one historian of the EU reckons that Pompidou was 'enraged' by the Werner Report because it so clearly aimed to eclipse the nation-state in such key matters.[58] 'The *Banque de France* must be the bank of France', said the French President. An announcement was made that Bernard Clappier, a faithful protégé of Monnet who had sat on the committee, had acted only as a private expert, without committing France.[59]

After de Gaulle, it became a customary stance of the French political elite to expect the EU to act as a willing instrument for French policy goals. Britain was slow to wake up to this fact. It had joined in 1973 very much swallowing the terms imposed by the founding members, not least France. Sir Con O'Neill, Britain's chief negotiator, believed that the terms for Britain were 'advantageous and not too onerous'. But in his memoir of the negotiations, he expressed his sympathy for the views, expressed below, of an ex-diplomat and senior civil servant, both now sitting in the British parliament:

> In a debate in the House of Commons on 20 January 1971, Sir Anthony Meyer said: 'It has been said by many honourable Members in the debate that everything depends on the terms. Frankly, I do not think that it depends on the terms at all. I believe that it would be in the interests of the country to join the EEC whatever the terms.'
>
> In a debate in the House of Lords on 27 July 1971, the late Lord Crowther Hunt said: 'It has always been clear, ever since we committed our biggest mistake for 200 years by refusing to be one of the founder-members of the Common Market, that we should have to pay a price to get in, and the price is very much lower than I expected it to be. But, in any case, you do not haggle over the subscription when you are invited to climb into a lifeboat. You scramble aboard while there is still a seat for you.'[60]

The Labour government of Harold Wilson sought to re-negotiate terms 'without conviction'. The Foreign Secretary, James Callaghan, found himself confronted by an evasive and opaque French negotiating approach which the other national members seemed prepared to accept. According to John Cole, the chief BBC political correspondent, Callaghan complained that 'when you believed you had agreed on something during the lunch-break, you got back into the meeting to find the French had changed their minds, and though the Germans, Italians and Dutch might talk behind their hands, they would all go along with the French in the end'.[61]

Europe: an extension of French power

France's proprietorial role towards the EU rankled with the British Labour figure Roy Jenkins. By contrast with Wilson and Callaghan, he was an ardent pro-European who was the first Briton to hold a major European office, as President of the European Commission from 1977 to 1981. On 19 December 1978, he recorded in his diary a meeting with the French Foreign Minister, Jean François-Poncet:

> The French do get into an enormously over-excited state and find it difficult to believe there can be different interpretations of things and that people who don't agree with them are not necessarily knaves or fools. They treat people as craven, threaten them too much, and believe that they will succumb to 'a thunderbolts of Zeus' treatment. I think it stems from the fact that the French government is too hierarchical and authoritarian, and that they are all terrified if they cannot bring home to Giscard exactly what he wants. This corrupts people like François-Poncet, who is in general a decent, sensible, intelligent man. The whole interview left a disagreeable taste in my mouth.[62]

François-Poncet had issued a threat that unless a French demand was satisfactorily addressed: 'We could call off direct elections, it could affect the whole direction of the community.'[63] Erhard had been one of only a few other European figures prepared to openly criticise French methods of negotiation, complaining about Paris's failure to honour previous agreements with West Germany.[64]

Valéry Giscard d'Estaing was perhaps the most unambiguously pro-European figure to have served as French President in the last sixty years. Since 1969, he 'had pushed for broad policy coordination, an exchange rate mechanism, a stabilisation fund, pooled reserves, and even a single EEC representative at the IMF'.[65] But he also at times seemed to embody the French desire for a 'strong Europe with weak institutions' that could easily be managed by a lead EU player like France.[66] Frustrating negotiations that Roy Jenkins had with Giscard in the late 1970s left him convinced that it was Giscard's hope that he could turn the Commission into a strengthened secretariat of a European Council to be presided over by a permanent president.[67] In West Germany's Chancellor, Helmut Schmidt, he had an interlocutor who shared his enthusiasm for accelerated European integration. With both of them starts a long phase in which France sought to tie Germany into common financial and economic arrangements even though their respective economies were arguably ill-matched for such coordination. The new monetary coordination was agreed by the two leaders in meetings, heavy with symbolism, that were held in the autumn of 1978 in Aachen, former capital of Charlemagne's empire.[68] It was, as one observer noted, 'an initiative … in the Monnet style with Mr. Schmidt and M. Giscard d'Estaing operating outside the normal channels, through trusted agents'.[69] Both men communicated easily in English, seeing and telephoning each other frequently.[70] In the history of the EU, there has been no equivalent bilateral relationship among pro-integration leaders unless one ranks Jacques Delors as a powerful leader rather than a super-bureaucrat (someone who established a deep rapport with Helmut Kohl). Both Giscard (aged 88 in 2013, while Schmidt was aged 96) have lived long enough to see the European integration project plunge into a major crisis, perhaps not least due to the rush to implement hastily devised plans for pooling sovereignty.

From 1981 to 1995, François Mitterrand dominated French politics during an era when the EU's power and influence considerably expanded. Initially, he was a devotee of de Gaulle's concept of *L'Europe des patries*. He 'did not want political union unless it was firmly inter-governmental'.[71] However, a bold re-evaluation took place in 1983 as it became clear that the left-wing economic strategy of pursuing economic growth and expanding the economic role of the state even further was leading to a balance-of-payments crisis and big falls in the value of the franc.[72] Mitterrand, whose commitment to socialism had always been equivocal, executed a radical policy U-turn. Cuts in public spending and a reduction of taxes on business were signals that he wished to join up his economic policies with those of his partners. During the French EEC presidency, Mitterrand 'surprised everyone by calling for supranational-style EEC reforms, even endorsing (if somewhat ambiguously) the European parliament's recent utopian Draft Treaty on European Union (the work of Altiero Spinelli)'.[73]

The establishment of Economic and Monetary Union started to become a top French priority in the economic realm. Kohl had accepted Mitterrand's proposal that Jacques Delors become President of the European Commission in 1984. Even though it was seen as Germany's turn to fill the top bureaucratic office, Kohl did not object about renewing his term in 1988. The enthusiasm of much of the German elite for a single currency excited Mitterrand and his advisers and revived an underlying French approach to the EU: 'The French wanted to gain politically what their weakness made impossible economically: part of the control over European monetary and economic policy from the Germans'.[74] From the end of 1987, Delors and Kohl had private meetings, sometimes as often as once a month. They usually met in Kohl's home and talked via interpreters.[75] It was their belief in the federal destiny of Europe that forged these close bonds (actually closer than the ones between Delors and Mitterrand, who was suspicious about surrendering the limelight to someone whom he viewed as an agent of France).

Delors himself never completely lost sight of this role of defending French interests at the supra-national level. To Bernard Connolly, a Commission official who came to view the most ambitious convergence plans as outright folly, he was a faithful exponent of the view that: 'Only by extending the borders of the state from the French nation to "Europe" can that state hope to retain its domestic power.'[76] Supporting evidence for such a claim can certainly be found in his reluctance to forego protectionism. In 1992, Ray MacSharry, the Competition Commissioner, was actually involved in a confrontation over tariffs on US farm produce. He was at the time engaged in important talks designed to promote trade with the USA. Delors's biographer Charles Grant relates that the Commissioner 'accused Delors of interfering and spoiling a deal', claiming that his 'main concern was the timing of a deal rather than the substance'. MacSharry, who briefly resigned, claimed: 'Delors told me he did not want a deal before the French elections [due in March 1993] because of the upheaval it would cause in France. Delors denies ever saying that.'[77] In his industrial strategy, Delors also showed concern to channel benefits to the car, textile, defence and electronics industries 'which happened to be France's problem sectors at the time'. But Grant relates that the Edinburgh summit in 1992 squashed the proposal to spend more money on 'industrial competitiveness'.[78]

The monetary sacrifice for Europe

In 1988, at the start of his second presidential term, Mitterrand had announced that it would be consecrated to 'Europe. He was largely true to his word so that, by the end of March 1993, he announced that he would not appoint as Prime Minister anyone not committed to the *franc fort* and the Franco-German "couple".'[79] Dramatic events had required attention to be focused on the geopolitical architecture of Europe. The sudden retreat of Soviet power in Eastern Europe placed the German question firmly back on the agenda. Regarding the fate of East Germany, Kohl felt that a swift unification with its western neighbour was the best of all the options available. In December 1989, just after the collapse of the Berlin Wall, Mitterrand had expressed concern to the German Foreign Minister, Hans-Dietrich Genscher, about the likelihood that absorption with German unification tasks would mean Germany would turn its back on the integration process. In such an eventuality, Mitterrand thought that the risk existed of a return to traditional balance-of-power politics in Europe.[80]

Chancellor Kohl decided to publicly back the French initiative for monetary union in order to overcome these anxieties and stabilise the Franco-German relationship in the new and challenging times opening up.[81] He signed up to the project just before the Strasbourg European Council meeting in December 1989. The dismantling of the Deutschmark occasioned very little debate despite the currency having been one of the great success stories of the Federal Republic. It was a symbol of the practical, achievement-orientated Germany, contributing by its economic success to normalising conditions in Europe. Politicians were then in charge of France and Germany who, arguably, lacked qualifications to make careful economic judgements on issues of such magnitude. They were taking a leap into the unknown: there was no guarantee that a European single currency would maintain its value as well as the Deutschmark had done. But there were only occasional fears expressed, such as the one emanating from Edmund Stoiber, Prime Minister of Bavaria, that the Deutschmark could be replaced by a 'confetti currency'.[82]

Perhaps the decision to abolish the national currency appeared to be a small one in light of the momentous challenges that Germany was suddenly facing. In February 1990, Kohl surprised the Bundesbank with a plan for rapid monetary union between the eastern and western halves of Germany. This did produce domestic ructions: Karl Otto Pohl, the President of the Bundesbank, described the idea as very premature and considered resignation.[83] The 1949 constitution had given the Bundesbank the authority to check the central government in key financial issues. But its autonomy was put aside because of the unprecedented challenges the forty-year-old German state suddenly faced. Warnings about the impact of financial parity proved to be only too prescient as much of the East German economy was rendered uncompetitive by this monetary move.[84]

Without joint Franco-German sponsorship, the single currency would have been unlikely to see the light of day. But it was very much an elite undertaking with only the faintest resonance in society. One analyst made this observation about the French mood at the end of the 1980s:

> French public opinion ... exhibited shallow support for monetary integration in principle. Polls showed 60–70 per cent in favour of unspecified monetary cooperation in 1989. But on neither right nor left did politicians see the technical and liberal EMU project as an electoral winner. In the campaign for EP elections in June 1989, the left ignored EMU, the right avoided it, and the strong pro-EMU centrist list of Simone Veil was shocked to receive fewer votes (8.4%) than the ... National Front, the Communists, or the Ecologists.[85]

In France, the Maastricht Treaty (of which the proposal for a single currency was the most important element) was put to the voters in a referendum. Thanks to a strong campaign to preserve the franc from orthodox Gaullists led by Philippe Séguin, voters in 1992 endorsed the proposals by only a slim margin. To stave off defeat, in a pre-vote television address President François Mitterrand had assured the French public that, contrary to the explicit language of the treaty, European monetary policy would not be left to European central bankers but would be subject to important political oversight.[86] Such would be the case in practice. In a few years, deficit ceilings would be breached by France and Germany. Their respective political weight ensured that the sanctions included in the Maastricht treaty for a large budgetary imbalance were simply waived. If a member got into severe difficulties because of over-spending, in theory it could not be rescued by the ECB and, thanks to inter-bank arrangements, it would be hard to limit any such crisis to a single distressed member.

But no hard thinking was done about throwing together frugal and profligate countries in a currency zone where central control was limited but states were still unable to use traditional tools, such as devaluation or adjusting interest rates, to extricate themselves from difficulty.

Euro enthusiasts assumed that the single currency could acquire the status of the Deutschmark and financially underpin a united continent. Since referenda are not part of German constitutional practice, it was impossible to debate the pros and cons of this argument. In the German party system, fidelity to 'more Europe' was almost a default position. But Hans-Otto Pohl had said in an interview that: 'if the idea spread and the German population understood what it [European Monetary Union] is about – namely, that it centres on their money, and that decisions on it would be taken not by the Bundesbank, but by a new institution then I would imagine that considerable resistance might arise'.[87] But it would only be after the imbalances between members led to a steep crisis that a powerful critique of the decision to repudiate the Deutschmark would occur (perhaps the best-selling 2012 book by Thilo Sarrazin, *Europa braucht den Europa nicht* (Europe doesn't need the Euro) marks the start of the new phase). By this point, it was clear that the eurozone members still continued to pursue their own economic interests and had yet to switch to adopting a pan-European economic outlook.

The limits of Franco-German solidarity

In between, there were sporadic attempts to construct a Franco-German axis in order to consolidate the cause of European integration. Following German unification, the overtures mainly came from Germany and it was the French partner which chose to draw back.

In 1994, two prominent Christian Democrats, Wolfgang Schäuble and Karl Lamers, argued for a 'hard-core' of members to step forward in order to accelerate or deepen the integration process. The Schäuble-Lamers Paper recommended the establishment of a core group of five countries with a Franco-German partnership at its centre. This vanguard would move towards economic and monetary union and defence and security policy at a faster pace than set out in the Maastricht Treaty.[88]

Jacques Delors's views on Europe's future were very close to those expressed in this document. But despite enjoying very high popularity ratings in France, he declined to run for the French presidency in 1995. Strong elements of the French left remained hostile to supra-nationalism. The influential left-nationalist Jean-Pierre Chevenement warned that '[this] modification of the state system ... [would] mean the end of the French Republic, and thus of France'.[89] The prospect of a 'strategic bargain' between France and Germany on political union which was up for discussion in a forthcoming inter-governmental conference was thus diminished.[90]

It was Jacques Chirac who in 1995 became France's President, someone who in the late 1970s had exclaimed against a 'Europe which is dominated by Germano-American interests'.[91] Later, he was willing to pay lip-service to pro-EU orthodoxy – but only up to a point. Prospects for a new Europe shaped by Franco-German statecraft were impaired by Chirac's requirement to cohabit politically with the French Socialists in the late 1990s.

Nevertheless, in a speech meant to commemorate the 50th anniversary of Robert Schuman's declaration, Joschka Fischer, the German Foreign Minister, called in May 2000, for the creation of a 'European Federation' with both a European Parliament and a European government. He proposed a bicameral European Parliament, comprising a directly elected chamber and one chosen along the lines of the US Senate or German Bundestag on a regional basis.[92] He advocated a 'federation of nations' in a bid to reach out to EU 'inter-govern-mentalists'.[93] What became known as the Humboldt declaration attracted cross-party backing in Germany itself. But the official French response was a frosty one. Within two weeks, the French Foreign Minister, Hubert Vedrine, had published an open letter criticising Fischer's plans as unrealistic. Referring to France's upcoming EU presidency, he pointed out that there was a difference between launching proposals for Europe's long-term future and making a good job of being the Council President.[94] He feared that an 'accumulation of struc-tures and interlocking competences', such as Fischer's proposals were likely to create, 'would rapidly become unbearable and the national level would have to be done away with ... For most nation-states and their peoples, this would cause immense problems of identity and democracy.'[95]

'France,' in the words of Julius Friend, 'wanted the EU to be the real power France could no longer be – but declined to surrender to the EU portions of sovereignty necessary to give the EU powers of swift decision necessary to implement a real foreign policy.'[96] It failed to supply pro-integration champions ready to work effectively with German decision-makers to build a sound and well-managed structure for EMU, one that would be a platform for European unity. Even if there had been figures in government on either side of the Rhine with the knowledge of economics and the political will to try, creating such an optimal currency union would have been a difficult feat given the contrasting economic performances and prospects of both countries.

Instead, there was a rather low-grade and complacent approach to launching the euro. Problems that would come back to haunt the EU after 2008 were simply swept aside. It was political criteria that determined the structure and implementation of the new stage in European integration. Perhaps this ought not to be any surprise. France and Germany, in the preparatory stages and in the first decade of the euro, both lacked the govern-mental continuity that had marked previous times. Domestic political rivals were almost evenly matched and there was a reluctance to devote close attention to big challenges outside the national policy arena.

On the surface, after 1989 France had appeared keen to lock Germany into common European structures as its eastern neighbour grappled with immense nation-building challenges. Much of the German political world proved amenable but Mitterrand's successors turned out to be parochial or irresolute in nurturing the relationship. Instead, Germany's economic exceptionalism was simply further underlined by the way the currency union operated. The low interest rates that the European Central Bank set in order to help Germany cope with the challenges of re-unification would decouple Germany from much of the rest of Europe. The resulting weakness of the euro assisted German exports in non-EMU countries, but the rates were too low for a number of other countries in EMU. This led to accelerating inflation, which benefited Germany's price competitiveness, setting off a credit boom, which increased demand for German goods elsewhere in EMU.

Two centre-right governments were in office in Paris and Berlin when the eurozone eventually entered a full-scale crisis in 2009–10. The approach of Angela Merkel and Nicolas Sarkozy to an emergency which, by 2011, could no longer be dismissed as a crisis of liquidity in some unimportant participating states often appeared to be shaped around domestic political concerns. France and Germany maintained an uneasy common front opposed to debt restructuring which it was feared would turn the eurozone into a debt transfer union in which German trade surpluses were used to resuscitate crisis-ridden members. In public Sarkozy insisted that France and Germany made up a 'privileged' economic partnership. But a 2011 opinion poll whose findings were first published in *Le Monde* found that only 18 per cent of Germans believed that their country should consider France its 'privileged partner'.[97]

Sarkozy had declared early in 2011: 'Chancellor Merkel and myself will never – do you hear me, never – let the euro fall ... The euro is Europe. And Europe spells 60 years of peace.'[98] But there was a reluctance to admit that there were striking deficiencies in the construction and implementation of monetary union in Europe. Instead the emphasis was placed on austerity measures in countries with unsustainable debts, or else plans for new forms of economic centralisation without any concern about their accountability. Such a stance caused the *Economist* to remark in March 2011: 'Sarkozy does not care for Merkel's economic medicine, but wants a euro-zone "economic government" to restore lost French influence (one senior eurocrat remarks that France needs Germany to disguise its weakness and Germany needs France to disguise its strength).'[99] An informal Franco-German leadership body even made its appearance the following autumn, at a period when the crisis sharply intensified. The *Grupe de Francfort* was depicted by the British financial journalist Ambrose Evans-Pritchard as 'something that would have been familiar in the old Soviet Union – a self-appointed body of powerful individuals prepared to topple national governments if they failed to toe the line. The GdF met four times on the sidelines of the Cannes summit, issuing ultimatums to Greece and Italy that have destabilised the administrations in both countries.'[100] Lorenzo Bini Smaghi, a member of the executive council of the European Central Bank until 2012, argued later that it was no coincidence that Silvio Berlusconi was rapidly ousted as Italy's Prime Minister after he proposed pulling Italy out of the single currency in talks with other governments. But this coercive version of earlier Franco-German alignments, involving Giscard and Schmidt and Delors and Kohl, quickly ran out of steam and was unable to produce any effective response to a spreading crisis.[101]

Sarkozy himself would soon suffer defeat in the French presidential election of May 2012. Merkel made half-hearted attempts to sustain him, even intervening on his side early in the campaign until it became clear that a lot of French voters were unimpressed. Figures released during his re-election bid showed that France's trade deficit had reached an all-time high in the previous year, raising serious questions about French competitiveness. According to the French treasury, France's share of global trade fell from 7.8 per cent in 2003 to 6.2 per cent in the final quarter of 2011. The Irish economic expert David McWilliams commented that 'France is gradually losing its vitality and presence in global export markets. French imports climbed 11.7 per cent last year while exports slumped.'[102]

France's new Socialist President, François Hollande, briefly exhibited a few signs of wishing to lead a Latin bloc in the eurozone and challenge the austerity agenda which his predecessor and Merkel both saw as the only acceptable crisis remedy. For a time Merkel found herself isolated at the almost constant EU summitry from which opaque plans and initiatives emanated for resolving the crisis. But Hollande failed to devise an alternative strategy to the one centred on austerity and played a role of diminishing importance in the crises that buffeted the eurozone during a troubled first year as France's President. In June 2012, Merkel broke a longstanding taboo and spelled out the contrasts between the two economies: 'If you look for instance at the development of unit labour costs between Germany and France in the past 10 years, then you see that at the start of the millennium Germany looked rather worse or at best as good as our neighbour in a lot of factors, while the differences have now been growing a lot more strongly, also a topic that must be discussed in Europe, naturally.' She also described her own country as Europe's 'stabilising anchor and growth engine' and told German business leaders that Europe should actually talk about what had hitherto been a taboo subject – the growing gap between the bloc's two biggest economies and traditional allies.[103]

In the autumn of 2013, François Heisbourg, a senior French foreign policy insider, published a book in which he depicted the euro as 'a cancer' which needed to be removed to preserve the rest of the European project. He wrote with realism about the EU's accelerating loss of legitimacy and believed that Germany's refusal to aid France in the 2012 Libya crisis exposed the limits of the Franco-German partnership at the top of the EU.[104] It would be very much in character if the momentum to dissolve the euro originated from the very elite that had been one of its mightiest champions a few decades ago.

Conclusion

Much of the architecture of a common Europe had been the fruit of French and German efforts. But the relationship had grown lopsided and dysfunctional as crisis stalked the EU's most ambitious exercise in integration. Germany had shed its introspection and timidity and from 1989 much of its elite was prepared to embark on a journey towards European statehood. France by contrast appeared to have lost its nerve and a cool response to overtures for radical integration was offered at the end of Mitterrand's presidency and under his successor Chirac. From de Gaulle to Chirac and Sarkozy, French strategy towards the European Union was too often based exclusively on ways of extracting national advantage from Europe or else promoting the personal agenda of a head of state enjoying semi-regal powers. It is no exaggeration to say that an offspring conceived by France suffered unnecessary neglect thereafter due to a wayward and selfish mother. A well-run European entity in which there was genuine national parity and efforts made to bridge the democratic deficit was all too often frustrated by French capriciousness. Indeed, the blows directed against the cause of building an EU with strong economic and political authority by France were harder ones than those mounted by any Eurosceptics.

Notes

1 Friedrich Hackmann and Dominique Schnapper, *The Integration of Immigrants in European Societies* (Stuttgart: Lucius & Lucius, 2003), p. 55.
2 Larry Siedentop, *Democracy in Europe* (London: Penguin 2001), p. 114.
3 Booker and North, *The Great Deception*, p. 126.
4 See Anthony Forster, *Euroscepticism in Contemporary British Politics: Opposition to Europe in the Conservative and Labour Parties Since 1945* (London: Routledge, 2002); and Nicholas True, 'European Union', in Lord Howard of Rising (ed.), *Enoch at 100* (London: Biteback, 2012), pp. 5, 16, 20.
5 Coherent critiques of EU membership from Labour Party figures include Douglas Jay, *Chance and Fortune* (London: Hutchinson, 1980) and Peter Shore, *Separate Ways: Britain and Europe* (London: Duckworth, 2000).
6 Willis, *France, Germany and the New Europe*, p. 16; Irving, *Adenauer*, pp. 108–9.
7 Willis, *France, Germany and the New Europe*, p. 80.
8 Willis, *France, Germany and the New Europe*, p. 80.
9 Willis, *France, Germany and the New Europe*, p. 137.
10 Irving, *Adenauer*, p. 116.
11 Willis, *France, Germany and the New Europe*, p. 73; Irving, *Adenauer*, p. 118.
12 Irving, *Adenauer*, p. 120.

13 Willis, *France, Germany and the New Europe*, pp. 196–7.
14 Alfred C. Mierzejewski, *Ludwig Erhard: A Biography* (Chapel Hill and London: University of North Carolina Press), p. 38.
15 Majone, *Europe as the Would-be World Power*, p. 32.
16 Booker and North, *The Great Deception*, p. 129.
17 Spinelli, *The Eurocrats*, p. 89.
18 Mierzejewski, *Ludwig Erhard: A Biography*, pp. 40–1.
19 Willis, *France, Germany and the New Europe*, p. 265.
20 *Daily Telegraph*, 21 December 2009.
21 Irving, *Adenauer*, p. 127.
22 Irving, *Adenauer*, p. 127.
23 Ludwig Erhard, *Prosperity Through Competition* (London: Thames and Hudson, 1958), p. 214.
24 Moravcsik, *Choice for Europe*, p. 149.
25 Willis, *France, Germany and the New Europe*, p. 278.
26 Willis, *France, Germany and the New Europe*, p. 278.
27 Booker and North, *The Great Deception*, pp. 113–15.
28 Charles Williams, *Adenauer: The Father of the New Germany* (London: Little Brown & Company, 2000), pp. 386–9.
29 Moravcsik, *Choice for Europe*, p. 100.
30 Williams, *Adenauer*, p. 490.
31 Williams, *Adenauer*, pp. 507–11.
32 Williams, *Adenauer*, p. 535.
33 Gilbert, *European Integration*, p. 76.
34 Friend, *Unequal Partners: French–German Relations*, p. viii.
35 Willis, *France, Germany and the New Europe*, p. 265.
36 Willis, *France, Germany and the New Europe*, p. 179.
37 Willis, *France, Germany and the New Europe*, p. 278.
38 Majone, *Europe as the Would-be World Power*, p. 17.
39 Connolly, *The Rotten Heart of Europe*, p. 383.
40 Julius W. Friend, *The Linchpin: French–German Relations, 1950–1990* (Washington, DC: Praeger, 1991), pp. 39–40.
41 Willis, *France, Germany and the New Europe*, pp.315–17.
42 Willis, *France, Germany and the New Europe*, p. 316.
43 Friend, *The Linchpin*, p. 43.
44 Friend, *The Linchpin*, p. 44.
45 Friend, *The Linchpin*, p. 44.
46 Willis, *France, Germany and the New Europe*, p. 345.
47 Willis, *France, Germany and the New Europe*, p. 345.
48 Willis, *France, Germany and the New Europe*, p. 407, n. 99.
49 Booker and North, *The Great Deception*, p. 157.
50 Moravcsik, *Choice for Europe*, p. 203.
51 Willis, *France, Germany and the New Europe*, p. 328.
52 Willis, *France, Germany and the New Europe*, p. 348.
53 Willis, *France, Germany and the New Europe*, pp. 335–6.
54 Duchêne, *Jean Monnet*, p. 213.
55 Duchêne, *Jean Monnet*, p. 203.
56 Mierzejewski, *Ludwig Erhard: A Biography*, p. 41.
57 Parsons, *A Certain Idea of Europe*, p. 91.

58 Parsons, *A Certain Idea of Europe*, p. 161.
59 Parsons, *A Certain Idea of Europe*, p. 161.
60 Sir Con O'Neill, *Britain's Entry into the European Community: Report on the Negotiations of 1970–1972* (London: Frank Cass Publishers, 2000), pp. 357–8.
61 John Cole, *As It Seemed To Me – Political Memoirs* (London: Weidenfeld and Nicolson, 1995), p. 96.
62 Roy Jenkins, *European Diary, 1977–1981* (London: Collins, 1989), pp. 364–5.
63 Jenkins, *European Diary*, p. 364.
64 Williams, *Adenauer*, p. 516.
65 Parsons, *A Certain Idea of Europe*, p. 162.
66 Anand Menon, 'France and the ICG of 1996', *Journal of European Public Policy*, 3, 2, June 1996, pp. 239, 249.
67 Jenkins, *European Diary*, p. 372.
68 Parsons, *A Certain Idea of Europe*, p. 168.
69 Parsons, *A Certain Idea of Europe*, p. 187, quoting Piers Ludlow.
70 Friend, *The Linchpin*, p. 87.
71 Friend, *Unequal Partners: French–German Relations*, p. 33.
72 Gilbert, *European Integration*, p. 119.
73 Parsons, *A Certain Idea of Europe*, p. 180.
74 Friend, *Unequal Partners: French–German Relations*, p. 36.
75 Grant, *Delors, Inside the House*, p. 41.
76 Connolly, *The Rotten Heart of Europe*, p. 379.
77 Grant, *Delors, Inside the House*, p. 174.
78 Grant, *Delors, Inside the House*, p. 156.
79 Parsons, *A Certain Idea of Europe*, p. 291.
80 Webber, 'Successful and genuine failures', pp. 7–8.
81 See Heinrich August Winkler, *Germany: The Long Road West, Volume 2, 1933–1990* (Oxford: Oxford University Press, 2007), p. 474.
82 Martin Holmes, *Franco-German Friendship and the Destination of Federalism* (London: Bruges Group, 1999).
83 Connolly, *The Rotten Heart of Europe*, p. 93.
84 Connolly, *The Rotten Heart of Europe*, p. 92.
85 Parsons, *A Certain Idea of Europe*, p. 214.
86 See Martin Feldstein, 'EMU and international conflict', *Foreign Affairs*, 76, 6, November–December 1987, p. 63.
87 Connolly, *The Rotten Heart of Europe*, p. 117.
88 Friend, *Unequal Partners: French–German Relations*, p. 63.
89 Friend, *Unequal Partners: French–German Relations*, p. 64.
90 David Buchan, 'Tilt in the balance of power', *Financial Times*, 13 December 1994.
91 Gilbert, *European Integration*, p. 115.
92 Joschka Fischer, *From Confederation to Federation: Thoughts on the Finality of European Integration* (London: The Federal Trust, 2000), p. 17.
93 Fischer, *From Confederation*, pp. 22–3; Webber, 'Successful and genuine failures', p. 20.
94 Webber, 'Successful and genuine failures', p. 20.
95 Hubert Vedrine, 'Points de vue – réponse à Joschka Fischer', *Le Monde*, 12 June 2000, quoted by Webber, 'Successful and genuine failures', p. 20.
96 Friend, *Unequal Partners: French–German Relations*, p. 93.
97 Open Europe, 'Je t'aime … moi non plus', 21 January 2011.

98 'Failure of the Euro would be cataclysmic', *EUObserver*, 27 January 2011.
99 Charlemagne, 'The divisiveness pact', *Economist*, 10 March 2011.
100 Editorial, *Daily Telegraph*, 'Europe's politburo', 8 November 2011.
101 See Lorenzo Bini Smaghi, *Morire di Austerita* (Milan: Il Mulino, 2013).
102 David McWilliams 'Germany is too strong – a Yes vote just solidifies this', *Sunday Independent*, 8 March 2012.
103 'Merkel takes dig at French economy', *The Irish Times*, 15 June 2012.
104 See François Heisbourg, *La fin du rêve européen* (Paris: Stock, 2013).

4

The flight from nationalism towards the elusive European identity

I thought the Euro would be so successful that it would lead to political union and that it would be attractive for other states to join. This was a mistake.[1]
Ruud Lubbers (Prime Minister of the Netherlands 1982–94), 2011

Manufacturing a common identity

A primary goal of the EU has been to promote a popular sense of European consciousness so as to enable allegiances to shift from individual nation-states to a European centre.[2] But despite the progress in moving towards economic and legal standardisation, there has been an acute shortage of basic ingredients for this feat to be easily accomplished. The ideal of a common country called *Europa* is still only embraced by a minority.

Active sponsorship emanates from the EU for works of history exploring how the term 'Europe' entered common currency and became a political concept in its own right. Cosmopolitan intellectuals like Count Coudenhove-Kalargi and Denis de Rougemont promoted the concept in the age of turbulent nationalisms before 1945. Today, the salesmen for supra-nationalism often hail from similar cosmopolitan backgrounds. There are not enough such evangelicals for Europe to form a critical mass and they are different in their tastes and associations from citizens whose lives, in most respects, remain fixed within national parameters. The decades since the ending of the Cold War have also revealed that there are insufficient common interests to drive forward plans for a European state. During the high noon of European integration, subterfuge had been required to create a confederation of states. Today, most of the resulting institutions are unloved, with a lugubrious bureaucracy known as the European Commission substituting for a venerable monarchy or a heroic republic.

A lengthy financial crisis – which initially was dismissed as a temporary crisis of liquidity affecting several unimportant eurozone countries, only to turn into a systemic emergency exposing the disfunctionality of the currency union in fundamental respects – has undermined faith in the EU's more vaulting goals. Effective common responses to the crisis have eluded EU decision-makers. As capital has fled homewards from stricken countries like Spain, Greece and Ireland in a desperate search for security, the pan-European character of the financial system has unravelled even as the euro continues as a seventeen-nation currency. The crisis has cruelly exposed how distant the EU is from having a balanced continental economy where slump in one of its parts can be contained by progress elsewhere. Indeed, there is free movement of labour for most of the twenty-eight EU members, but emigration continues to be not intra-European but predominantly extra-European. The vast pool of young unemployed in Spain and Portugal are not migrating to Northern Europe, with its incipient labour shortages due to an ageing population, but prefer, instead, to cross the oceans to former colonies in Latin America and Africa, places which retain the coloniser's language.[3]

Language remains a great divider, thwarting the emergence of a genuine European conversation. After 1973 Denmark insisted on Danish interpreters at all open meetings of the European Parliament, even though nearly all Danes present would be able to use English, and today very expensive provision is made for twenty-one official languages at the EP.[4] Just 18 per cent of people aged 18–34 perceive themselves to be proficient in another language (usually English) according to EUROSTAT, the European Union's statistical agency.[5] Linguistic barriers not only obstruct continental political debate and impede the creation of a truly European identity, but they have acute practical short-comings. The severity of the euro crisis has even been ascribed to mono-lingualism. In 2011, the German financial journalist, Olaf Gersemann asked:

> Why were institutions such as Germany's central bank, or the EU Commission not made aware during the last decade of the extent of the problems in Greece and Portugal? Because experts depended on the Greek and Portuguese governments for whatever information they were getting. Not knowing the languages meant they couldn't independently read Greek and other newspapers, which would have made the situation abundantly clear. This is an ongoing problem.[6]

No EU decision-maker has spoken up in favour of the adoption of an efficient and neutral 'bridge language'. Advocates continue to be found for Esperanto; Edoardo Campanella reckons that 'the most painless and effective solution for Europe would be to teach Esperanto to all children in primary school. About 100 hours of instruction will suffice for most Europeans.'[7]

Turkey witnessed a semi-successful ideological makeover in the 1930s that focused on reform of the language and the alphabet. It was designed to rid everyday culture of its rural idioms and turn it into a supporting prop for nationalism; it was also carried out with fewer resources than the EU could muster. But the circumstances were exceptional, following a successful bid to repel an attempt by several of the European powers to partition the country.

There is also at least one successful example of nationhood thriving within the context of linguistic pluralism: in centuries of unbroken independence, Switzerland never succeeded in adopting one common language, hardly to its detriment. A widely shared commitment to preserving the freedom of a small country located in the very heart of a turbulent continent made up for the lack of a common tongue. In compensation, there was a set of strongly decentralised state institutions, shaped around popular sovereignty, which commanded support transcending ethnic and religious cleavages. The political system of the EU will be truly fortunate if it is able to devise institutions which possess a fraction of the legitimacy enjoyed by the various pillars of Swiss group identity.

It was during the third decade of its existence that the EU decided to throw its energy behind promoting a European consciousness. In 1984 the European Council set up a 'Committee for a People's Europe' whose task was to promote a collective identity which would support the deepening of European integration. From the outset, it was decided that a set of symbols was needed for communicating the principles and values upon which the Community was based.[8] The hope was that it would dislodge the cultural supremacy of nationalism, without which the task of acquiring political legitimacy for a common European state appeared unattainable.

Jacques Delors's Commission proposed Community-wide public holidays marking key moments in the history of European integration, such as Jean Monnet's birthday and the date of the signing of the treaty launching the ECSC. Thus 9 May, the anniversary of the Schuman Plan, was officially designated Europe Day.[9] Massive high-rise buildings in the 'European' quarter of Brussels have been erected in the last forty-five years as the EU's responsibilities have widened. These glass and concrete edifices have been named after the statesmen who were the pioneers of the European cause. The latest edifice was unfurled in June 2011 at a dinner for the leaders of EU member states, devoted to a discussion about the threat of Greek bankruptcy and new austerity cuts. Herman Van Rompuy, the head of the European Council, handed round a glossy brochure to EU leaders regarding a €240 million headquarters. It is to be called 'Europa' and will look like a giant glass egg when it is finished.[10]

Transparency surrenders to deal-making

When the biggest European story in many years burst forth in 2009, most Europeans were still wedded to a print and broadcasting media that was largely national in character. The saga of the single currency was unable to confirm the hopes that one of its architects, Jacques Santer, had invested in it. On the eve of its appearance, he had written:

Countries which share a common currency are countries ready to unite their destinies as part of an integrated community. The Euro will bring citizens closer together, and will provide a physical manifestation of the growing rapprochement between European citizens which has been taking place for the past forty years or more.[11]

The real face of European integration has been the civil service, which occupies much of the space in the European quarter of Brussels. Turning it into an inspiring symbol has been an unavailing task. The mission of building a common European entity is sometimes lost sight of in national rivalries, as when the top commission posts are allocated every five years. In the year 2000, three countries comprised almost 40 per cent of senior, Grade A, officials: France (15 per cent); Italy (12.3 per cent); Spain (10.5 per cent); in addition, Italy had a striking 29.7 per cent of D grade staff, mainly comprised of service workers.[12] Nepotism of quite striking kinds was evident in the staffing of the European Parliament. Jens-Peter Bonde, a tenacious fighter for transparency during his twenty-nine years as an MEP, recalls that in 1979 'Parliament was fairly Mafia-like. A general director recruited 18 young Italians from his home village and installed them in an office where they received wages for the whole village.'[13]

The European Commission is notable for being an *independent* civil service, one that is not habitually taking orders from governments or parliaments.[14] But this independence may well contribute to its poor image: the absence of strong oversight by a legislature or executive may make it prone to financial inefficiency and even corruption. The European Court of Auditors refused to clear the Commission's accounts for many years, starting in 1994.[15] In 2002, when the Commission's new chief accountant, Marta Andreasen, raised shortcomings in accounting methods, such as the absence of double-entry book-keeping to forestall irregularities, her superiors reacted with hostility.[16] She was suspended from her post where she oversaw 130 people in the accounts department of the Commission after she raised the matter with the European Parliament. She was kept on at full pay but not allowed to enter the Commission buildings, before eventually being dismissed.[17] This well-publicised episode was bound to be a disincentive for any official, perhaps inspired by a sense of European patriotism, who wished to draw attention to state or private financial practices in Greece or Spain that contributed to the severity of the eurozone crisis. Whistleblowers were frowned upon in an organisation whose historical destiny it apparently was to prepare the way for a new stage in European history. When the script proved defective, not a single head rolled at the European level after years of often striking incompetence. Instead, the key decision-makers expected to be treated with seriousness even when their rule-breaking and improvisations became ever more apparent.

The amateurism which held sway at the top of European institutions meant that it was unavoidable that they would become a hub for pressure groups as soon as they accumulated more power and wealth. The desire to gain material rewards through obtaining contracts or turning their proposals into EU law mounted in the Delors era and after. Some lobbying and professional campaigning groups are actually funded by European taxpayers through subsidies from the European Commission. The Taxpayers Alliance in the UK claims that between 1997 and 2012, nearly €100 million was allocated to environmental groups by the Commission's 'Life +' programme. Often their publicly funded campaigns resulted in sharply rising energy costs for citizens thanks to their growing influence in EU policy-making.

Two analysts, after comparing the influence of pressure groups at the European level and in the member states, reached the conclusion that 'the EC system is now more lobby orientated than in any national European state'.[18] According to Roland Vaubel, many EU bureaucrats share a common vision with lobbyists. Both favour political centralisation, they are often impatient with transparency, and they have no desire for voters to intrude into their affairs. They 'form an alliance against the median voter – against democratic control'.[19]

Since 1995, citizens can direct complaints about their treatment at the hands of European institutions to an Ombudsman. The holder of the position is elected by Parliament and Nikiforos Diamandouros, in place since 2005, has reinforced its credibility as a vigilant body keen to narrow the gulf between citizens and the entities of the EU. Upon taking up his post, he stated that:

> As the institution that gives rise to around 70% of the Ombudsman's inquiries, it is vital that the Commission take a leading role in dealing with maladministration and in promoting a service culture with respect to citizens.[20]

In 2012, he felt the need to issue a reminder that 'European Union officials should be conscious that the Union's institutions exist in order to serve its citizens. They should also always act as if under the closest public scrutiny and be willing to explain their activities.'[21]

It is hard to soften the image of the confederation of functionaries and technocrats at the top of the EU power structures. But occasional attempts are made. After the European Constitution was derailed by referendum defeats in two founder states in 2005, a concerted effort was made to ensure that Commission staff were patient and approachable with members of the European public. By 2007, the Commission had launched a new 'EU agencies campaign' telling citizens, 'Whatever you do – we work for you'.[22]

A shortage of European role models

Investing the EU with glamour and appeal would be much easier if, among the twenty-eight members, there were successful role models which encapsulated some of the achievements and aspirations of the EU.

Germany is virtually alone in the EU in enjoying untrammelled economic success, but the conditions which enabled it to thrive during the era of the single currency have helped keep many other states in deep recession. Chancellor Merkel has regularly insisted that in countries seen to be living beyond their means, living standards would have to be drastically adjusted through austerity in order to eradicate debts and accomplish the recovery of the eurozone. Addressing a rally of supporters in May 2011, she asserted that Southern Europeans were not working enough, while it was Germans who were expected to bail them out: 'It is also about not being able to retire earlier in countries such as Greece, Spain, Portugal than in Germany, instead everyone should try a little bit to make the same efforts.' She declared that 'We can't have a common currency where some get lots of vacation time and others very little. That won't work in the long term.'[23] Greeks riposted by pointing out that the OECD had shown that they toiled 2,017 hours each year, which is more than any other European country. Germany, by contrast, according to OECD figures, was second from bottom, the average worker toiling 1,408 hours a year.[24] It is hard for the EU to insist that it is an antidote against intolerant nationalism when huge fall-outs occur in which millions of Greeks and Germans acquire mutually antagonistic views of each other because of its failed policies.

Before the post-2009 crisis placed EU states into the separate camps of being creditor or debtor nations, Ireland had been the lead model for how a once poor country could flourish under EU tutelage. In 1998, when Jacques Santer, then President of the European Commission, addressed Irish parliamentarians, he noted how 'it is rare to find any period of such profound transformation which has been as successfully managed as here in Ireland'.[25]

The economic breakthrough which began around 1988 was admiringly dubbed the Celtic Tiger for emulating Asian countries in attracting prestigious companies through which rapid export-led growth boomed. It was North American firms which dominated the new investors and the Irish economy would do far more business with Britain and the USA than with its continental EU partners for many years to come. A major advantage for most of the 1990s was the independent exchange rate policy that Ireland enjoyed from 1993 to 1999. Turbulence on the money markets led Ireland to float its currency. It obtained a highly competitive exchange rate, boosting Irish exports and inhibiting competing imports. It was no small achievement for Ireland to build a pharmaceutical, medical and software industry far from Europe's geographic core.[26]

But Ireland was far from being a glowing example of the 'smart economy' in action, 'the best place in Europe to turn research and knowledge into products and services', as its Prime Minister Brian Cowen put it in 2010.[27] The OECD reported in 2008 that Ireland, before the crash, was one of the lowest spenders per capita on research and development, and on education in general, with very large teacher/student ratios and weak support infrastructure.[28]

Unwise decisions in the previous decade had seen the Irish state channel hundreds of millions of euro in subsidies or tax incentives into the property sector.[29] It was assumed that Ireland could continue to boom thanks to a property-driven bubble based on the low interest rates of the eurozone. Even if politicians, state officials and regulators had identified the acute dangers Ireland was exposed to by 2007, it would have been hard to cool down the economy. Membership of the eurozone meant that raising interest rates or devaluing the currency were no longer powers belonging to the government in Dublin.

The EU showed no sign of alarm even as economists started to speak out about the peril the nation was in thanks to the banking sector having lent three times the country's income in often reckless transactions. At the end of 2008, the total stock of foreign borrowing by Irish banks was around €110 billion. Four years earlier, in 2004, Ireland's banks had only borrowed just over €15 billion from abroad.[30] Low interest rates fuelled the reckless acquisition of foreign debt, culminating in a run on Irish deposits and a collapse of Irish bank shares in 2008. In a colossal misjudgement, the Irish government then decided to guarantee the assets and liabilities of a massively overextended banking sector.

Speaking in Dublin on 27 April 2011, Klaus Regling admitted that the frenetic policies of economic expansion being pursued In Ireland 'were not criticised really by outside bodies, who were in charge of doing this, of supervising the economy – the IMF, the OECD, the European Union, including me, myself in my job'.[31] He had been head of the Commission's Directorate General for Economic Affairs (2001 to 2008) and now was in charge of the European Financial Stability Facility (the bail-out fund for insolvent members of the eurozone).

The Irish state continued to buy toxic bank assets while making plans to sell off the state's own physical assets, destroying the balance sheet in the eyes of one observer.[32] Another was certain that by embracing such a strategy, soon Ireland would 'no longer [be] a nation but merely a bankrupt branch of the ECB'.[33]

By 2012, Ireland was well on the way to losing the equivalent of €41 billion, the amount of receipts it had received from the EU budget over the entire period from 1973 to 2009. Much of this money would be routed from Irish taxpayers to European private creditors of Irish private banks. Indeed, by the start of 2011, a substantial portion had already been paid over, to be replaced with sovereign debt.[34] Massive spending cuts were imposed to service the debt. Meanwhile, Irish gross domestic product figures continued to be buoyant in 2011–12 thanks to the orders flowing into the branch plants of multinational companies (ones which were lightly taxed). But gross national product figures, reflecting the economy owned and run by Irish people, were increasingly dire. A collapse in the purchasing power of the Irish consumer threatened the viability of much of the small and medium business sector and confronted Ireland with the spectre of a long-term slump.[35] Given the prestige that the EU derived from the Irish 'economic miracle', its collapse gravely undermined the EU's image as a successful agent of development and modernisation among its weaker members.

Minstrels for Europe

The most active proponents of European integration laid emphasis on the EU's economic prowess. But the worth of the social experiment was usually summed up in non-economic terms. Thus Mark Leonard, the advocate of supra-nationalism with, arguably, the strongest profile after 2005, believed the case for European unity sprang from the way that it identified Europe as a progressive social model fit for emulation by the rest of the world. In his book, *Why Europe Will Run the 21st Century*, he wrote:

> By creating the largest single internal market in the world, Europe has become an economic giant that, according to some calculations, is already the biggest in the world. But it is the quality of Europe's economy that makes it a model: its low level of inequality allows countries to save on crime and prisons ... its social model gives people leisure and time with their families ... As the world becomes richer ... the European way of life will become irresistible.'[36]

He is a self-confident example (unruffled even by recent setbacks) of what the German social scientist Max Haller called '"Strong" or privileged social groups (in terms of education and knowledge, occupational positions, financial resources) [who] will favour integration much more than the population at large or "socially weak" groups in particular.'[37]

By 2008, more than €2.4 billion was being extracted from the EU budget annually to back a wide variety of efforts designed to promote European integration.[38] Much of it was concentrated on cultural, educational and citizenship initiatives designed to convince people of the merits of 'ever closer union'. Universities were a particular target. They were institutions, the most illustrious of which had since medieval times been based around transnational bodies of academics and students. Without the intervention of the EU being needed, many academics (particularly in the social sciences and humanities) were already distrustful of the claims of nationalism and receptive to alternative ways for organising humanity.

From the era of Delors onwards, the EU devoted considerable time and resources to building a powerful constituency of support across the academic world. The key instrument was the Jean Monnet project. This makes available money for the establishment of academic chairs which 'must deal specifically and entirely with the issue of European integration'. By May 1998 there were 409 Jean Monnet chairs distributed across the EU. These were split between 40 per cent in Community Law, 23 per cent in European Political Science, 28 per cent in European Economics, and 9 per cent in the History of the European Construction Process.[39] By 2001, 491 European universities hosted 'European Centres of Excellence', more than a quarter of them in Britain. The Commission's own grants lasted only three years, but to win them the universities had to guarantee that the projects would remain in place for at least four more years.[40] It would have been understandable if Britain had been singled out as a target, given the persistence of Eurosceptic views across much of society. The importance of altering 'hearts and minds' in its universities was shown in 2009 when a memo from Dominic Brett, Head of Public Diplomacy at the European Commission Representation in the UK, was leaked to the think tank Open Europe. Using the huge mailing list of the University Association for Contemporary European Studies (UACES), he offered Commission staff to speak to students, either by visiting their universities or by hosting meetings in London, about topics central to the activity of the EU such as climate change and the Lisbon Treaty. The communications strategy of the EU is clear about the Commission having the role of 'build[ing] up support for the European Union's policies and its objectives'. But Open Europe saw this as 'a completely unacceptable use of public money', especially since 'the EU has no mandate for education policy'.[41]

Much scholarship has been devoted to elaborating the view that the European Union is the culmination of a process building up over three thousand years of European history in which the continent, often in the face of great adversity, has struggled to acquire a common voice. In 2011, it was decided to erect a 'House of European History' in Brussels to chronicle the voyage towards unity. Much attention focused on the soaring costs, up from £58 million at the outset to an estimated £136.5 million by the end of 2015. But a scheme meant to promote an awareness of European identity was also dogged by conflicts about how to interpret a stormy past. Due to an inability to agree about events such as those from 1939 to 1945, the European Parliament decided that the exhibits in the museum would only cover the period starting from 1946.[42]

The EU's choice of ERASMUS, SOCRATES and LEONARDO as acronyms for its major educational exchange programmes also shows a conscious desire to be associated with great names in European thought and art.[43] But it is unclear how lofty ambitions designed to emphasise a contemporary Europe built around a 'shared heritage, moral ascendancy and cultural continuity' have been fulfilled in practice.[44] More enthusiasm for academic exchange schemes has been shown in some countries than in others and little evidence has been presented to suggest that they are the foundations for a new European consciousness among highly educated younger citizens. The social sciences and humanities are broad fields of study which have entered into crisis as a result of the financial downturn after 2009. For over forty years, graduation in their disciplines and subject areas led to a career, very often in a low-level bureaucratic occupation, for millions of Europeans. But such careers are fast receding for many young Europeans. Nevertheless, the European dream still burns bright for academics able to play a direct role in shaping EU policy. By 2006, academics were involved in a huge number of committees, perhaps as many as 3,999, drawing up legislation on behalf of the Commission alongside lobbyists.[45] Their involvement was very effective for the EU as it reduced its operating costs and enabled its own size to be concealed. Booker and North have written:

> contracts [to academics] were often issued under the 'research' budget [of the EU], which automatically compelled member states to contribute to 'co-funding'. By this means, not only was the Commission able to increase its spending at the expense of member state taxpayers, but it was able to call on the services of a much larger workforce than represented by its own employees.[46]

A surprising feature of the EU's efforts to champion a European consciousness is the extent to which it remains a bureaucratic process without active involvement from the private sector. Few wealthy capitalists with intellectual pretensions and a political vision have shown any desire to pledge part of their fortune towards the dream of a single unified Europe. Far more independent-minded industrialists, from Robert Owen and Friedrich Engels onwards, have championed socialism than seem willing to identify with the cause of a united Europe. Just one highly idiosyncratic figure, George Soros, the hedge fund speculator and economic philosopher, occupies an eminent but solitary position as a capitalist crusader for Europe (see Chapter 2, p. 60).

Perhaps the key medium for socialising citizens in a European direction is the electronic media. Following referendum defeats for the Maastricht process in the early 1990s, Delors set up a 'Comité des Sages' assisted by advertising executives to strengthen the EU's media profile. Since 1998 a multi-lingual television channel, accessible to every EU household possessing cable television, has existed. *Euronews* claims 2.6 million viewers weekly; in 2011, the EU tripled its financial contribution to *Euronews* to €15 million, providing one-quarter of its budget and enabling it to open eleven new journalistic bureaux worldwide.[47] What resulted too often seemed like propaganda for the EU rather than dispassionate coverage of its activities; Jan A. Johansson, writing on a website championing Eurosceptic voices, suggested that 'television programmes that critically evaluate the activities and money spent by the EU institutions will never be seen on *Euronews* [which has] a political line in favour of increased supra-national governance'.[48]

Double-speak on nationalism

The continued presence of nationalism of course generated solidarity behind the cause of European unity. The doctrine's supposedly antiquated character encouraged the view that it was more practical and visionary to organise economic affairs on a trans-national basis: the single currency was justified because, with the abolition of exchange rates, both travel and business could become cheaper and less cumbersome. Turning the EU into a fully integrated 'United States of Europe' with a central European treasury able to enforce common rules on government spending for individual countries appeared a logical next step for many. Such a financial union appeared to be a recipe for enduring peace, a clear improvement on nation-states whose competition had spilled over into outright belligerence at certain disastrous moments in modern European history. Doubters like the philosopher Roger Scruton believed it was unreasonable to identify 'the normality of the nation-state through its pathological examples'. He drew on the writer G.K. Chesterton who had argued that to condemn patriotism because people go to war for patriotic reasons is like condemning love because some loves lead to murder.[49]

The automatic credibility enjoyed by trans-national initiatives in the face of nationalist excesses led to one unfortunate side-effect: they were not checked in advance to make sure that they could work in the real world. It was only when the euro crisis was far advanced that the view that there had never been 'an example of a successful and durable currency union that was not backed up by a political union – otherwise known as a nation', began to be tolerated in the *Financial Times*. It had evolved from being the voice of Britain's financial centre, the City of London, to being a newspaper which sought to reflect official EU opinion, a journey which has seen it move to being 'a corporatist paper of the Centre-Left'.[50] The appearance of euro notes and coins in January 2002 caused it to hail the new currency as 'a triumph of political will ... Its physical launch is a testament to a generation of visionary leaders who pursued a dream.'[51] In May 2008, with the storm clouds gathering over the single currency, a *Financial Times* leader exclaimed: 'However improbable the celestial design, it has succeeded in real life'.[52] In the subsequent four years, the newspaper had to report worsening tensions between core and periphery eurozone members and between EU states inside and outside the eurozone of a sharpness not recalled in the era before the arrival of the currency union.

In December 2011, when a leading ratings agency deprived France of its triple A status, Christian Noyer, head of the French Central Bank, argued that ratings agencies should downgrade Britain before France; and it was not long until the Prime Minister, François Fillon, publicly noted that Britain had a higher debt and larger deficits than France. There may well have been understandable frustrations, in a country with a political culture more nationalist in character than most others in the EU, that it lacked the freedom of action still possessed by Britain in the economic sphere. Professor Martin Feldstein, a leading critic of the euro since its planning stages, argued that Britain was unlikely to default on its debt ahead of France because it retained its own currency:

> When interest and principal on British government debt come due, the British Government can always create additional pounds to meet those obligations. By contrast, the French government and the French central bank cannot create Euros. If investors are unwilling to finance the French budget deficit – that is, if France cannot borrow to finance that deficit – France will be forced to default.[53]

After 2008 the sense of expectation about a European political take-off largely vanished. Sovereign debt and competitiveness crises inside the eurozone, stemming in large measure from internal imbalances and irresponsible lending to peripheral countries, and combining with a larger global financial crisis, managed to silence many, though not all, evangelists for a common European economy.[54]

Even during the pre-crisis phase of the currency union, nationalism had continued to shape economic policy within the EU irrespective of the rhetoric. France was the exemplar in this regard due to the active role that a cohesive state played in economic affairs, and a protectionist attitude towards French jobs was usually displayed irrespective of the colour of the government. This was shown in 2011 when the ailing private carmaker PSA Peugeot Citroën announced job losses; the Industry Minister Éric Besson also immediately promised that all jobs in French plants would be spared. The state was already using its holdings in companies to block the transfer of production facilities to lower-cost countries, although it was noted that protectionism of this kind only brought limited relief due to production costs rising and goods manufactured at home becoming too expensive.[55] At other times, French policy-makers retreated from nationalism if it became impractical for France to realise economic objectives on its own. An article in the German press noted that 'French politicians become convinced Europeans' in order to accomplish 'the creation of EADS, Europe's largest aerospace and defence group' giving it a continuing ascendancy in this important economic sector. But Chancellor Merkel blocked a merger with the British defence giant BAE in 2012 because, despite calls from senior German Europhiles for a pan-European defence industry, she did not believe it was in Germany's best interests at that time.[56]

In 2004, Nicolas Sarkozy brokered the merger of the Franco-German pharmaceutical group Aventis with the French company Sanofi, so creating the third largest pharmaceutical company in the world. Yet when Siemens wished to take over a troubled French rival, he blocked its designs. He also ensured that the proposal to include a commitment to a single market with 'free and undistorted competition' failed to become a part of the EU treaties.[57]

Economic convergence is often a cover for power-plays which retain a national dimension. French and German managers in EADS are bound to eye each other suspiciously, especially since it will be hard to ensure that any plant closures are managed in a way that respects national balance. Attempts to regulate the financial sector are capable of stoking cross-national rivalries that were supposed to have been buried with the dawn of European integration. Inexperienced European parliamentarians are capable of being manipulated by large, state-orientated financial sectors in countries like France which aim to crush competitors in Britain with regulations that target smaller firms.[58]

Germany, even before the eruption of the currency crisis, was also emphasising its own national economic interests, sometimes in controversial ways. Thus from 2005, it spurned the common energy policy sought by its central and East European neighbours in favour of a strictly bilateral arrangement with Russia.[59]

In the 1990s, Germany's business and financial establishment were the monetary union's strongest advocates. But by 2012, there was mounting evidence that keeping the eurozone together was no longer such a major priority. The preoccupation in political and economic circles was how to shield Germany from the worst effects of a Europe-wide economic crash. Some of the solutions proposed, such as linking up with the developing 'BRIC' countries, or forming a core eurozone of North European creditor nations, clearly were shaped around specific German rather than wider European concerns.[60]

Unheeded warnings

Leading politicians in Finland, an ally of Germany in the eurozone's so-called creditor bloc, spoke candidly in 2012 about their suspicions about momentous decisions being taken over the heads of Europe's citizens. Timo Soini, leader of the True Finns party, was already a well-known critic of the exclusive and ineffective way the crisis was being handled. But in August 2012, Erkki Tuomioja, the country's veteran Foreign Minister and a member of the Social Democratic Party, voiced deep suspicions of plans by what he described as 'a gang of four' EU insiders to corral member states into some form of fiscal union. 'I don't trust these people,' he said, among whom he included the European Central Bank chief Mario Draghi.[61] Such palpable distrust is corrosive for European elite solidarity, especially in a time of crisis, and disheartens a proponent of 'more Europe' like Jürgen Habermas who, instead, sees this as a time to take risks for Europe.[62]

In Germany by March 2012 only 35 per cent of voters desired 'turning the EU into a fully integrated "United States of Europe"' according to a You-Gov-

Cambridge poll.[63] Leading Germans had warned in 2010 about support for the EU falling away due to over-regulation and an obsession with imposing common standards in areas far from crucial for the cause of European integration. Former German President Roman Herzog, along with the Director of the German-based Centre of European Policy think tank Luder Gerken, argued that the EU needed to change course or risk 'complete collapse'. Joined by the Dutch Liberal politician and former EU Commissioner Frits Bolkenstein, they complained that 'Brussels legislates regardless of the people's wishes and of long established traditions and cultures'. They warned that the EU must win back support for its existence, which it had lost from many citizens and even from many parts of the economy. Without this endorsement there was 'a risk of permanent damage to the people's acceptance of the fundamental principle of European integration with immeasurable consequences for the EU, including the possibility of it completely breaking down'.[64]

The Working Time Directive, which banned state or private firms from allowing employees to work more than 48 hours a week, was an EU ordinance that caused particular indignation in Britain. Originally, thanks to Britain having opted out of the Maastricht Treaty's Social Chapter, it appeared that it was unaffected by it. But in December 2008, British Labour MEPs in the European Parliament were instrumental in ending the British waiver.[65] Three million people who worked more than 48 hours a week were affected. According to Charlotte Leslie MP, who organised a British parliamentary debate on the issue in April 2012, limiting 'medics to working a 48–hour week is having a devastating effect on patients' treatment, doctors' training and the expertise of future consultants'.[66] Vince Cable, the Business Secretary who belonged to the pro-EU Liberal Democrats, soon after complained of the 'dreadful economics' and 'illiberal' nature of this Brussels directive.[67] The British Steelworkers Association found that 90 per cent of employees polled were hostile to the directive, fearing that it would result in job losses as competitors overseas took advantage of the resulting decline in industrial productivity.[68] The campaigner against EU red tape, Open Europe, placed the Working Time Directive at the top of the list of the ten most costly EU regulations. In 2009, it claimed that unless it was scrapped or overhauled, it was likely to cost the UK economy £32.8 billion by 2020.[69]

The EU's mania for policies of standardisation has definite limits when it comes to sensitive subjects such as those in the realm of immigration. This was clearly shown in the spring of 2011 when a meeting of interior ministers of the EU refused to support the call from Italy and Malta for a policy of 'burden-sharing' towards the growing volume of asylum seekers from North Africa. 20,000 North African migrants were already languishing on the tiny Italian island of Lampedusa, with more on the way due to civil war in Libya. After the meeting, Roberto Maroni, the Interior Minister, complained about 'an institution which takes action quickly only to bail-out banks ... I wonder if it really makes sense [for Italy] to remain part of the EU'.[70] The EU's Home Affairs Commissioner, Cecilia Malmström, had recently argued that: 'The need for a common EU policy on asylum and immigration is urgent ... I hope that the current situation also contributes to the EU taking several steps forward towards a common asylum and immigration policy.' Sweden, her home country, had taken close to 30,000 refugees in 2010 as opposed to neighbouring Finland grudgingly accepting only 700.[71] But a policy based on distributing the intake of refugees fairly is likely to be stillborn. This is just the most graphic issue indicating the daunting obstacles in the way of an authentically European political system emerging, shaped around the pursuit of common policies.

Ossified politics at a European level

The party blocs in the European Parliament have proven too heterogeneous to be the basis for stable competing formations. Sometimes, sharper differences exist within a particular political family than between ostensibly rival ones. This was shown when the Dutch Liberal Frits Bolkenstein clashed in 2010 with Guy Verhofstadt, the Belgian leader of ALDE, the Liberal group in the European Parliament. He openly called Verhofstadt's proposals to launch EU taxes and EU bonds 'ridiculous', saying 'if they do that, then we don't know where it will end'.[72] Verhofstadt's predecessor as ALDE's head, Graham Watson MEP, was known to be to the left of some of the Socialist MEPs, according to Julian Priestley, a former secretary-general of the Parliament.[73]

Absence of solidarity in the left-wing grouping now known as the Party for European Socialists has been visible for many years. In 1982, when Spain elected a Socialist government that had made membership of the Community its top priority, the new Prime Minister, Felipe González, hoped that 'Socialist solidarity' would erode France's tenacious defence of her producer interests.[74] He was swiftly disillusioned. Under Mitterrand negotiations moved no more quickly than they had under Giscard. French worries about agricultural competition and the likelihood that Spanish entry would lead to a reduction in the size of the subsidies allocated to French farmers held matters up. It was only when Mitterrand converted to a pro-European stance in order to divert attention from domestic policy failings that the impediments blocking both Spanish and Portuguese entry were suddenly lifted, enabling both to join in 1985.[75] For its part, Greece, which had only joined in 1981, made its backing for the latest enlargement round conditional (in 1984) upon the creation of 'integrated Mediterranean programmes', from which it could benefit.[76] (By now Greece was led by the radical left party, Pasok.) Much later, in the spring of 2012, François Hollande failed to get the support of partners on the European left to renegotiate the fiscal treaty. It complicated his bid to replace

Sarkozy as President, which was accomplished only after a narrow electoral victory in May 2012.[77]

Besides the predominance of sensitive national concerns, the absence of high-calibre political actors has impeded a post-national form of politics in Europe. In too many cases, the national contingents of MEPs sitting in the European Parliament are dominated by figures who have been passed over for elective office in their domestic politics. Not a few regard the European assembly as a sinecure, as shown by the opposition of many to moves to curtail opportunities for supplementing generous salaries by exploiting loopholes in the expenses system.[78]

The impetus for a common European politics might be expected to come from the left owing to its internationalist rhetoric. But its politicians, at European level, are increasingly absorbed with issues that detach them from mainstream society. They devote far less energy to traditional Social Democratic issues like social insurance and the minimum wage than to non-economic and niche causes like renewable energy, liberal lifestyle issues like gay marriage, various forms of identity politics and promotion of amnesty for illegal immigrants. The left, in a number of countries, has come to embrace the worldview of *bobos* (bourgeois bohemians) which has made it a champion of liberal middle-class perspectives. This has enabled conservatives and populists to make inroads into working-class electorates in a number of countries.[79]

It was the early twentieth-century sociologist Robert Michels who first noticed the trend towards careerism leading the leaderships of left-wing parties to begin to 'despise, and then actively conspire, against the lower income groups that they purported to champion'.[80] Left-wing parties (and indeed numerous trade unions) have been reluctant to back immigration controls even though a rapidly increasing labour force depresses wage levels for settled workers (irrespective of their ethnicity). Such factors have impeded the emergence of a new European politics but such a new departure might still be attempted if common ground is found on the political left for a joint approach to tackling the financial crisis.

The German Social Democratic party (SPD) under the influence of Sigmar Gabriel, had by the late summer of 2012 moved towards accepting the pooling of European debt and mutual budgetary oversight. It remains to be seen how much consensus on the European left exists for a programme emphasising democratic oversight of major economic concerns, and perhaps even policies of redistribution and growth designed to replace the austerity regime in place from 2008 onwards.

European universalism collides with national interests

It is clear that any European-style New Deal would have to dispense with plenty of elitism and indeed a record of collaboration with dominant economic interests by governments like those of Tony Blair and Gerhard Schröder. Attention would need to be devoted to re-imaging political identity and allegiance. Intellectuals on the left, such as Jürgen Habermas, have toiled to promote an inclusive citizenship: one that extends not just beyond national but also European categories in order to encompass global concerns. The EU has given backing to becoming a normative power enabling it to evolve into a world community hopefully deserving of emulation. In 2007, a communiqué from the European Commission showed that there was backing for evolution down such an idealistic path:

> The EU is, and must aspire to become even more, an example of a 'soft power' founded on norms and values such as human dignity, solidarity, tolerance, freedom of expression, respect for diversity and intercultural dialogue, values which, provided they are upheld and promoted, can be of inspiration for the world of tomorrow.[81]

In 2008, Jose Luis Zapatero, the Spanish Prime Minister, said that the EU should aim to be 'the most important world power in 10 years'.[82] But as long as the EU held back from embracing pacifism, it would have to spend money on defence and security and, even before the arrival of a full-scale recession, there was 'no sign of EU willingness to spend the money required to play the leading role'.[83] NATO figures showed that the US spent 4 per cent of its GDP on defence in 2007, compared to an EU average of 1.6 per cent. The US spent $545 billion in 2007 while the UK spent $63 billion, France $60 billion and Germany $41 billion.[84] In 2011, the US Defence Secretary Robert Gates questioned whether NATO could survive in the light of such spending disparities.[85] He spoke out in the middle of a Franco-British decision to throw active support behind rebels in Libya who would later succeed in toppling the forty-two-year regime of Colonel Muammar Gaddafi. But coordination with the rest of NATO had been difficult to secure. Germany's unhappiness prevented a common position emerging and showed the difficulties in coordinating a common EU foreign policy. In March 2011, Guido Westerwelle, the German Foreign Minister, pointedly observed that President Sarkozy of France had been pursuing a bold unilateral policy and that even his own Foreign Minister, Alain Juppe, was kept in the dark about his decisions.[86]

The EU often prefers to emphasise not its defence role but its contribution to reducing global poverty and promoting sustainable economic development. It had a very large external aid budget of €12 billion by 2010. But its aid role was shrouded in ambiguity. By 2011 only 46 per cent of EU aid was reaching lower income countries, compared with 74 per cent of UK aid and 58 per cent of EU member state governments' aid. Instead of poverty, according to a 2011 report, 'it appears that geographical proximity and ties with former colonies continue to determine the destination of much of the EU's aid budget'. Thus, the wealthy tropical islands of New Caledonia received on average €16 per person from EU aid in 2010, despite being basically just as rich as the average EU country.[87]

From the inception of the EU, France in particular has sought to project its influence in former colonies and wider regional spheres of influence by utilising EU resources. The Union of the Mediterranean, created in 2008 at the instigation of Nicolas Sarkozy, is a case in point. It was intended to strengthen ties between the EU and North Africa and the Middle East. But controversy ensued when France and Spain reached essentially a private deal to share its presidency on a two-yearly basis. Holding the rotating EU presidency in the second half of 2010, Belgium thought the role would devolve to it after the French presidency was over. Karel de Gucht, the Belgian Foreign Minister, wrote an indignant letter to his Spanish counterpart, expressing his 'amazement' about how the rules determining the way in which the EU should be represented on the world stage had been violated in this instance.[88]

Fishing wars and the mirage of post-national governance

If outwardly altruistic initiatives are undermined by turf wars between the European participants, then policy areas where there is competition between members over finite resources often reveal a glaring absence of European consensus. Fishing is perhaps the primary example.

The size of the Spanish fishing fleet and the long-term success of Spanish governments in giving it a privileged place in European fishing policy has created recurring tensions with other maritime states and indeed with the Commission itself. In 2002, Spain was partly excluded from access to Community waters; when this ban expired, the Commission used an obscure clause in the Amsterdam Treaty to prevent fishing stocks being endangered through over-exploitation by Spanish vessels.[89] Spain tried to override the Commission by enlisting the support of its Commission member, Loyola de Palacio, who the rules state must not act in the national interest.[90] She broke these rules by writing to Franz Fischler, the Fisheries Commissioner, to 'express my concerns about the thrust and impact of your proposal to reform the Common Fisheries Policy'.[91] But Spain was in a strong position due not least to being the holder of the rotating EU presidency in the midst of this upset. Instead of de Palacio being reprimanded, instead it was the Commission functionary in charge of fishing, Steffen Smidt, a Dane, who was removed. His salary continued to be paid by EU taxpayers but he was deprived of a job.[92] It was claimed that a phone call from the Spanish Prime Minister, José Manuel

Aznar, to the Commission President Romano Prodi, led to the official's removal.[93] Jens-Peter Bonde, the Eurosceptic Danish MEP, demanded an inquiry but the affair was successfully hushed up. The fullest account in English is to be found in his memoir of his twenty-nine years as an MEP.

Spanish fishing activities in the waters of Northern Europe, and the inability of the EU to impose an effective check because of the leverage enjoyed by Spain in its affairs, has had a rancorous impact. Bilateral relations with Britain and Ireland have been affected. The collapse of fish stocks and the decline of communities which for centuries derived an existence from fishing has deepened national antagonisms. As EU decision-makers struggle to deepen the integration process, they can ill-afford the collapse in European solidarity that such episodes ultimately bring in their wake. But key EU decision-makers, whose continuing power derives from winning occasional elections, often seem reluctant to learn such lessons.

In 2012, France's Nicolas Sarkozy was at the centre of Franco-German efforts to obtain a common EU response to handling the post-2009 financial crisis. At the start of his re-election bid in March 2012, without any warning to his colleagues, he threatened to pull France out of the EU's borderless Schengen Agreement unless action was taken to reduce the number of illegal immigrants. 'We can't leave the management of migration flows to technocrats and tribunals,' he declared, warning that 'the Schengen Agreement can no longer respond to the seriousness of the situation. It must be revised. There is a need to implement a structural reform that we have implemented for the euro.'[94] Arguably, Chancellor Merkel had behaved in a similarly uncollegiate manner when, in the aftermath of the Fukushima nuclear emergency in Japan, she announced that Germany was pulling out of nuclear energy projects without bothering to tell her lead ally France, which had collaborated with Germany for decades on joint civil nuclear projects.[95]

The improvised nature of Sarkozy's attack over Schengen was hard to conceal. As with much else in the EU, it was a bureaucracy based on French norms that shaped the working of the Schengen machinery. Pointing to action on the euro crisis as a model for dealing with high levels of immigration was unlikely to rescue Sarkozy's lacklustre presidency and he duly lost. But other cornered leaders are likely to use low politics as a survival strategy even if it clashes with core EU values. This ensures that the manifestos of visionaries who dream of a citizens' project for Europe which becomes a laboratory for transforming the world on a just and equal basis, remain stillborn. Mark Leonard's *Why Europe Will Run the 21st Century* is perhaps the boldest in the claims that it makes for 'Europe'. Leonard and other intellectuals with a pan-European profile, such as Jürgen Habermas, enjoy occasional cameo roles as legitimisers of a project with progressive overtones. But in their lucid moments, they surely are aware that when countries like France and sometimes Spain are able to avoid adhering to the key rules of membership but expect lesser members to fully abide by them, it sabotages the EU as a viable model for post-national governance.

The desire of particular nations to turn the EU into an arena for advancing what is seen as their core interests revives wariness and suspicions about leaving one's fate in the hands of others. It destroys the hope expressed by the historian of European integration Alan Milward in 1995 that a powerful but understated sense of 'allegiance' to the EU would develop in time across most of Europe.[96]

Eurocrats struggle to find a model

There are insufficient common interests to drive European integration forward and the original ones – preserving Franco-German peace and containing Russia – have diminished in relevance. An untidy and sprawling bureaucracy is in charge. It assumes that because Europe is a continent, it is therefore also a natural political unit. The absence of powerful common bonds and elected institutions with power over the executive do not instil a sense of caution or humility as the architects of integration hurry to build a European political edifice.

Regions were promoted by Jacques Delors to enable Brussels to bypass nation-states and legitimise a new tier of authority. Over a longer period, immigrants were invested with group consciousness rather than the emphasis being placed on encouraging them to integrate with their host countries. Encouraging the retention of rural cultures in a heavily urbanised space like Western Europe is an unwanted consequence of promoting radical forms of multiculturalism. Arguably, it blocks the upward mobility that enabled the USA to absorb successive waves of immigrant groups. The USA has managed to acquire the features of a unitary community which elude the EU even though the USA remains strikingly decentralised in the way that it functions politically.

By contrast, José Manuel Barroso, President of the European Commission, appears to be inspired by older models of governance indigenous to Europe. Speaking in 2007, he declared: 'We are a very special construction unique in the history of mankind, Sometimes I like to compare the EU as a creation to the organisation of empire. We have the dimension of empire.'[97] When, during his tenure as the head of the IMF, the prominent pro-European politician Dominique Strauss-Kahn proclaimed that the EU also needed to become an 'empire', Dan O'Brien, the economics editor of the *Irish Times*, pointed out to him that many smaller European countries had cause to be wary of such an arrangement.[98] But the expression of such desires by top Eurocrats may be impossible to suppress given the quasi-imperial role that politicians and bureaucrats are able to enjoy in the career structure of the EU. They receive only a fraction of the parliamentary oversight that they could expect when operating in their domestic political arenas and media scrutiny is often unexacting as well. The Lisbon Treaty, promulgated in 2009, boosted the power of these functionaries. It gave the EU the hallmarks of a state but not one that could be described as at all democratic in character.

Heinrich August Winkler, a German critic of the enlargement which saw the EU almost doubled in size between 1995 and 2007, also sees imperial aggrandisement as a motivating factor. He complained of 'European Bonapartism' and argued in 2005 that

> What Europe does not need are ahistorical utopias, such as the end of the nation-state, the existence of a European nation, and the wish of geo-strategists like Joschka Fischer, Volker Rühe and Günther Verheugen, to push the domains of the EU to the borders of Syria, Iran and Iraq, so that Europe may finally become a world power.[99]

America: an endless preoccupation

The need to keep up with, or even surpass, the United States in economic weight and geo-political leverage became a scarcely concealed EU objective as integration was gathering pace. The importance that transatlantic rivalry acquired is ironic given the extremely active role that successive US Presidents, the State Department and even the CIA played in seeking to advance the cause of a United Europe from the 1950s onwards.[100] But there is no building – or even room – in the European quarter of Brussels commemorating the important American contribution to this cause. In 1990, when Jacques Delors criticised the United States for allegedly undermining the CAP, a casual observer might easily have assumed that Washington had been a long-term adversary of the cause given the sharpness of the language:

> The Americans should stop insulting us. I am not going to be an accomplice to the depopulation of the land. It's not up to the Americans to tell us how to organize our farm policy and the balance of our society. Their attitude is to treat the EU as if it had the plague and then encourage the rest of the world to join in.[101]

In 2008, when Irish voters rejected the Lisbon Treaty and its formula for greater EU centralisation, Jean-Pierre Jouyet, the French Europe Minister, detected American machinations behind the setback: 'Europe has powerful enemies on the other side of the Atlantic, gifted with considerable financial means. The role of American neo-conservatives was very important in the victory of the No.' *The Economist* commented: 'Mr Jouyet's outburst is frankly embarrassing, and only makes sense if you live in a world of Lilliputian Euro-narcissism, imagining that each raincloud that opens over Brussels was sent by dark forces from far away, intent on stopping the EU from becoming a mighty superpower ... Europe is quite capable of preventing its own rise, without help from any hidden hands.'[102]

Mounting US preoccupations with the European financial crisis were viewed as an unnecessary intrusion even after several years of instability. When the US Treasury Secretary arrived for a regular summit of EU finance ministers in September 2011, the Swedish and Austrian foreign ministers (both from non-NATO states) issued disparaging statements. Timothy Geithner was there to boost policies of fiscal stimulus but the most influential European participant, Germany's Wolfgang Schäuble, was emphatically opposed: 'That has never been the European model and it won't be.'[103] Several months later, Valéry Giscard d'Estaing issued a statement clearly blaming ill-intentioned American interests for the crisis:

> It is a crisis manufactured from without. We find ourselves in a destabilised monetary configuration, where the European currency is the subject of a deliberate and organised attack by the financial markets, particularly the Anglo-Saxon ones.[104]

Inhibitions about American participation in crisis measures would abate as EU decision-makers failed to agree on concerted action but, at the G20 summit in Mexico in June 2012, when José Manuel Barroso was asked by a Canadian journalist to explain why North Americans should 'risk their assets to help Europe' he replied:

> Frankly, we are not here to receive lessons in terms of democracy or in terms of how to handle the economy. This crisis was not originated in Europe ... this crisis originated in North America and much of our financial sector was contaminated by, how can I put it, unorthodox practices, from some sectors of the financial market.[105]

One abiding memory that David Brooks, a leading columnist on the *New York Times*, recalls from his time as a correspondent in Brussels in the 1980s was the scorn that the functionaries had for the type of multi-level representative politics that were commonplace in the USA: 'Off the record, Europe's technocrats would say the most blatantly condescending things: History had taught them that Europe's peoples were not to be trusted and government should be run from the top by people like themselves.'[106]

How to convince the sceptical masses?

A transatlantic breach in political culture was clearly exposed in the aftermath of one of the greatest body-blows to the pro-integration cause, the 2005 referendum defeats for the European Constitution in France and the Netherlands. Rather than admit that the builders of one Europe had completely lost touch with most voters who were unimpressed by plans to greatly increase the bureaucratic dimension of the EU, leading figures argued the very opposite.

At a Brussels press conference, Jean-Claude Juncker told journalists: 'many of those who voted "no" were voting for more Europe. If some of their votes were added to the "yes" vote, we have won.'[107] Guy Verhofstadt, then the best-known Belgian on the European stage, 'claimed that the French and Dutch voters had rejected the Treaty, not because it was too ambitious, but rather because it was not sufficiently ambitious: it did not go far enough in the direction of a supranational welfare state'.[108] Academic backers of this perspective were to be found who argued that putting high levels of state resources into European citizenship, by making social assistance a right for everyone, would help the concept become a reality.[109]

The EU was already becoming less reticent about pouring considerable funding into citizens' initiatives which were seen by critics as propaganda efforts meant to champion more integration or else defend specific ideological agendas. In the 2007–13 financial cycle, €215 million was due to be spent on a 'Europe for Citizens' project. In 2010 part of it was set aside 'to foster action, debate and reflection related to European citizenship and democracy, shared values, common history and culture through the activities and cooperation of think tanks and within civil society organisations at European level'. According to the Open Europe think tank, 'these kinds of funding streams are shamelessly biased towards groups which more or less share the Commission's political agenda of further integration and/or defending the EU status quo'.[110] Being often surrounded by true believers meant there was a growing temptation to exaggerate the degree of support for integration. In 2010, Eurobarometer published the findings of a poll in which it was claimed 75 per cent of Europeans were in favour of giving the EU a stronger role in the coordination of member states' economic and budgetary policies.[111] Respondents had only been asked about inter-governmental cooperation and there was no mention of the role of the EU or the term 'European economic governance'. The result might have been rather different if this question had been asked instead: 'Do you think that the EU should be given more powers to monitor your country's economy, including decisions on public spending and taxation?'

In 2007, the EU was already spending €15.7 million on Eurobarometer opinion surveys. According to *The Economist*, 'the Frenchman who invented them called the polls a means of promoting integration, by showing Europeans in different nations where they agreed and disagreed'.[112] Max Haller, a German critic of EU centralisation, believes that the themes and questions are often lopsided. 'Questions on critical issues such as waste, bureaucratism, corruption and the like are not included at all,' he argues. 'The Common Agricultural Policy is one of those controversial issues' but bland questions are asked which avoid 'the many fundamental problems and contradictions of this policy'.[113] Haller has compared Eurobarometer with 'commissioners (*maîtres de requêtes*) of the French *Ancien Régime* who had to visit and inspect the provinces and collect all kinds of data which could be relevant for the preservation of central power'.[114]

Using another French political example, Pascal Lamy, Jacques Delors's *chef de cabinet*, seemed to confirm the impulse a̶ ̶ ̶g top functionaries about acting as benevolent but controlling guardians for the people. He once observed that: 'Europe was built in a St-Simonian way from the beginning, this was Monnet's approach ... The people weren't ready for integration. So you had to go on without telling them too much about what was happening.'[115] Citizens were treated not as partners but often as obstacles to be circumvented. Commission President Barroso displayed this reflex to perfection in 2008 when he insisted that overwhelming voter hostility in Britain to joining the single currency should be no cause for despondency:

> We are now closer [to Britain joining the euro] than ever before. I'm not going to break the confidentiality of certain conversations, but some British politi- cians have already told me, 'If we had the euro, we would have been better off'. I know that the majority in Britain are still opposed, but there is a period of consideration under way and the people who matter in Britain are currently thinking about it.[116]

Unsurprisingly, exposure to such patronising attitudes did not swing many British citizens towards the European cause. But the integration process had a real impact on many working in the British civil service who were exposed to the historically far more elitist and secretive practices to be found in Brussels. The transformative effect of Europe on the British bureaucracy may only have deepened the cleavage between it and citizens in whose name officials were supposed to act, not least due to the role of civil servants in implementing EU law.

European justice: a citadel of true believers

A leading specialist on the evolution of European law, Joseph Weiler, has noted the scarcity of academic critiques of the elite-driven process of European integration, especially as it affected the fields of justice and law. One explanation offered was the theoretically based neglect of the legal aspect of integration among political scientists and economists.[117] But another was more unsettling. There exists an 'almost unanimous non-critical approach ... towards the Court of Justice' owing to the fact that 'Community law and the European Court were everything an international lawyer could dream about: the Court was creating a new order of international law ...'[118] His concerns were taken much further by Max Haller who, in 2008, claimed that the lure of status and practical rewards among academics in the burgeoning field of European Union law had obliterated any critical perspective:

> From the sociological, elite-theoretical viewpoint, we may only add that this wonderful new world of law was not only a huge intellectual challenge but provided also ample new opportunities for new jobs and careers. These jobs

are highly rewarding not only in terms of incomes (the incomes of the ECJ judges are among the highest in the EU system) but also in terms of a challenging and powerful new professional role. Membership in the ECJ or expert work carried out for it makes it possible for lawyers to take over a quasi-political role. Court decisions, as any legal act, everywhere have some political sides to them. In the EU and the ECJ, this aspect of the legal role has become essential. The European legal expert is a paradigmatic example for the thesis well-known in the sociology of professions that new institutions and organisations often also create new professions.[119]

Members of the ECJ are cocooned from European public opinion, so it is perhaps not surprising that their institution has endorsed 'legislative over-enthusiasm at EU level'.[120]

In successive judgments by the ECJ, the reach of EU law has been extended into politically sensitive areas such as welfare and pension rights, gender, disability, health and safety and workplace rights.[121] Haller believes that the ability of the ECJ and the European Court of Justice to overrule democratically elected governments comprises a major part of the EU's democratic deficit.[122] Lord Patrick Neill, a senior British legal expert, warned in 2000 about the dangers of 'judicial activism' from an over-zealous European Court. In his view, 'the ECJ has indulged in "creative jurisprudence" on many occasions'. It has also 'frequently adopted strained interpretations of the texts actually agreed by member states' and introduced 'doctrines and rights of action which cannot be found in those texts'.[123]

A backward step arguably occurred when, after 2004, national governments ceased to be able to advance policy proposals for areas of law which the EU enjoyed responsibility over. Competition of policy ideas from both national and supra-national sources was replaced by a Commission monopoly. Weiler was unable to find scholars prepared to criticise the exclusion of the democratically legitimated national governments from policy initiation in such a politically sensitive area.[124]

Much sympathy exists among scholars of the EU towards the exercise of what the political scientist Robert Dahl called guardianship. This is 'deliberation among experts … [with] claims to be more "truth-orientated" due to being better designed to weigh all aspects of a problem impartially than [a] majoritarian democracy' could do.[125] The idea that in important policy areas something like a science of the public good exists and that only specialists will possess such knowledge is widely assumed.[126] This perspective is used to defend the process of *comitology*, whereby officials and experts from the member states close ranks with Commission bureaucrats to devise new laws and regulation. It is thought to result in 'a more deliberative and "truth orientated" discursive process than, say, legislatures'.[127] But sceptics have warned that woolly and idealistic thinking is at work here:

Experts can be particularly susceptible to 'group think', which may be reinforced rather than challenged by such processes. Insider, expert norms can be
self-serving products of an entrenched paradigm, within a given professional
community that may have become immunised from critical scrutiny and/or the
legitimate concerns of citizens.'[128]

No other international organisation enjoys such clear supremacy of its laws
over the laws of member governments as does the EU, and it has the backing
of the European Court of Justice to adjudicate disputes.[129] Human rights has
become an increasingly central issue for the EU, since it helps define its
progressive role. The Strasbourg-based European Court of Human Rights
(ECHR), although emerging from the Council of Europe, has been assigned by
the EU to play a decisive role in this regard. It enforces the European Charter
of Human Rights which, under the Lisbon Treaty, the EU had become a full
institutional signatory of. Britain endorsed the treaty in 1998, meaning its
parliament was obliged to enforce its ruling that prisoners must be given the
vote. The ECHR's forty-seven judges, many from countries such as those in
the former Soviet Union where human rights are fragile or harshly restricted,
found in 2006 in favour of British prisoners being entitled to vote. No
political party, or recognisable segment of the electorate, supported such a
move but Britain's parliament in 2011 was powerless to stand in its way.
Twenty-two MPs voted in favour but ten times that number opposed the
proposal which proceeded to become law.[130]

ECHR judgments are often seen to privilege groups on the margins of
society whose behaviour sometimes conflicts with the norms of the rest of
society. Thus, since 1998, lawyers representing 'travellers' who practise a
nomadic lifestyle have been able to argue that, as an ethnic minority, they have
the right to pursue this traditional way of life. To deny this right would result
in discrimination as the 1998 Act allows them to move around the country
settling on property which is not theirs.[131] Roger Scruton has written that:
'Increasingly, in Europe, the idea of human rights is being used in this way to
cancel national traditions and undermine managed environments in the
interest of international ideals that are imposed without counting the cost to
those who must conform with them.'[132] Group rights have been championed
by the ECHR which, according to the British journalist Charles Moore, is
largely under the sway of liberal jurists who regard 'democracy as little more
than a series of unenlightened opinion polls in which majorities vote to
oppress minorities'.[133]

A range of NGOs have made common cause with different arms of the EU
thanks to sharing a political vision shaped around the promotion of universal
values. Laws and regulations which endorse a trans-national perspective are
seen as advancing the views of an enlightened single world perspective against
narrow local chauvinism.[134] Focus groups and committees have been recruited
to draw up laws and regulations that, when imposed, often curtail some of the

previously recognised rights of European citizens. The EU's legitimacy has been eroded by failing to proceed cautiously and see that the rights of one group of people to pursue their particular lifestyle can sometimes only be guaranteed at the expense of the rights of another to enjoy privacy or access to public or private space. Funding streams have been directed towards groups which promote an idealistic or highly intrusive 'Europe' at the expense of citizens' rights as expressed through the working of national parliaments.

The widening of the scope of human rights has taken the 1950 Charter on Human Rights far beyond what was intended by many of its architects, according to the former British Law Lord Leonard Hoffmann. He stated in 2011 that the Strasbourg court had grabbed such power to 'micro-manage the legal systems of the member states' that British judges have ended up following the court with decisions 'which would have astonished those who agreed to our accession to the convention in 1950'.[135] Professor Michael Pinto-Duschinksy, a political scientist who in 2012 resigned from a commission reviewing the impact of the ECHR on Britain due to the absence of progress in addressing some of the key problems, has argued that Britain should retain the 1950 Convention but place its jurisdiction in the hands of the highest British court.[136] He and others believe that enabling a court in which the membership is comprised not just of judges but unqualified political appointees risks creating strife and bitterness. It is another indication of how the EU has shown active partiality towards lobby groups that are vocal and sometimes militant in their behaviour, and is quite ready to assume that they represent the popular will. There is little evidence from opinion polls that its cultivation of such forces has narrowed the gulf between the centralised entity and the citizenry of Europe.

The EU expands; so does Euroscepticism

If the peoples of the twenty-eight EU states are viewed as clay in the hands of empire builders, then it may be no surprise that they remain stubbornly national in many of their attachments. The Italian EU specialist Giandomenico Majone believes that 'no "Europeanization" of the masses has taken place even remotely comparable to the "Nationalization of the masses" perceptively analysed by George Mosse in the case of Germany' in the nineteenth century (or indeed in France during the same period).[137]

Enthusiasts for union cling to a different perspective. Paschal Fontaine, former assistant to Jean Monnet (1973–77) and *chef de cabinet* to the President of the European Parliament (1983–87), has invoked Monnet in saying that 'we are not forming coalitions among states but unions among peoples'; it is primarily a 'humanistic' enterprise involving a 'coming together' among peoples of different national cultures.[138] He claimed that the creation of 'a people's Europe' was already 'the Commission's avowed political objective in the 1970s'.[139] But this 'European people' arguably only took powerful shape in the writings of academics and advocates for a total break with existing loyalties. It is a concept with certain similarities to the 'revolutionary working-class', proclaimed by its sponsors as a dynamic force destined to transform the entire economic order.

Confusion and sometimes acrimony often reigned at the top of the EU concerning how best to complete the journey towards European post-nationalism. Sharp differences existed between Jacques Delors and his successor as Commission President, Romano Prodi, over strategy. In an interview for *Le Monde* in 2000, Delors launched 'an unprecedented attack on Prodi's plans for enlargement, warning that they threatened to "dilute" economic integration and would undermine the ambitions harboured by the existing member states' for faster integration.[140]

After the end of the Cold War, Mitterrand displayed the customary French caution towards the arrival of new members with a large agricultural sector. He was opposed to any speedy admission of the former Warsaw Pact states in 1991 and he dangled a pretentiously titled 'assizes of confederation' in front of them. It was a new confederation, which would have included the Soviet Union and would have been limited to 'soft' issues like the environment, economic cooperation and culture. There was forthright opposition to any scheme that would park countries like Poland and Hungary in a grouping with the Soviet Union. Mitterrand also blundered in an address given in Prague by saying that it would be 'decades and decades' before they could come into the EU.[141] He found himself isolated and at the 1994 European Council meeting in Essen a comprehensive strategy to prepare these countries for accession was agreed. But the entry terms were not generous ones. The powerful French agricultural lobby ensured that changes made to the CAP in June 1999 at the Berlin summit would benefit existing members far more than applicants.[142] This was a bitter pill for Poland to swallow: it had roughly 40 per cent of the total population of all candidate states and also the largest agricultural sector – a nominal 25 per cent of the population on the land.[143] In 1999, the GDP per capita of the accession states ranged from Slovenia's €14,492 down to Bulgaria's €4,871. The corresponding EU average was €20,650.[144] A dramatic exodus of migrants began from poor parts of rural Poland and from other accession states which had a perceptible impact on labour market conditions across Western Europe. According to a French critic of the premises underlying EU expansion, industrial interests intent on gaining access to cheap labour and keeping wages low lobbied for a swift removal of restrictions on the movement of people.[145] What was surprising was the absence of concern in the European trade union movement about the impact of open borders on the collective bargaining power of workers. Except in a few countries like Germany, trade unions increasingly represented white-collar workers in bureaucratic occupations. The retreat of manufacturing and extractive industries had led to a decline in union membership: by 2007, the percentage of trade union membership in the labour force had fallen to 28 per cent in Britain, 20 per cent in Germany, 10 per cent in Spain and 8 per cent in France.[146]

Enlargement also benefited the EU's most centrally located member, Germany. It had access to a future market of roughly 100 million consumers and the EU's insistence on rapid economic liberalisation proved a huge boon for German firms. They were able to acquire market domination over a range of sectors in countries further east where local industry was too weak to effectively challenge well-produced and competitively priced German goods.

Whatever challenges arose from constantly expanding borders and continued heavy emigration from non-European countries to different parts of the EU, its functionaries generally welcomed the rapid pace of change. Philippe Nemo has written: 'the bigger Europe gets, the more power, resources, and jobs flow to the bureaucracy in Brussels, and the more geopolitical prestige the Eurocrats gain. Thus the European machine has become self-propelled.' However, he went on to warn that the EU has committed itself to a project that the peoples of Europe no longer understand. He complained of the 'blindness' of the functionaries to the impact of their decisions and believed it was aggravated by their tendency to 'live and socialise only among themselves, influencing and reassuring one another in the politically correct ideology that they absorb from the equally superficial media'.[147] It is therefore perhaps not surprising that when, in 2009, fifty top Commission officials and 203 members of the European Parliament in nine EU member states were asked about their attitudes to Turkish membership of the EU, 44 per cent said it was 'a good thing' compared to 21 per cent of the general public.[148]

Interests prevail over ideals

Concentration on the financial dimension of European integration from the early 1990s onwards enabled segments of the EU's wealthy and mobile sectors to close ranks, opening up a division with much of the rest of society. In the EU system, trade unions have been unable to fulfil the role of defenders of ordinary citizens' economic and social interests; it is clear from the meagre presence that they have in EU consultative bodies that they have shrunk to a minor ranking (certainly compared to bodies representing agricultural or employers' interests).

Once they were plunged into the post-2009 financial crisis, EU leaders struggled to show that they were acting on behalf of the broader concerns of European citizens rather than defending vested interests, particularly in the over-extended financial sector. Their statements failed to carry conviction. When Barroso said in October 2010, 'I am pleased to stand before you this morning and confirm that Europe is closer to resolving its financial and economic crisis ... We are showing that we can unite in the most difficult of times', it was a statement of hollow reassurance, of which there would be plenty of others to come.[149] Not surprisingly, polling data, coinciding with Barroso's declaration, showed that a plurality of EU respondents (46 per cent) believed that each of the EU's national governments should have primary responsibility for dealing with the economic crisis. With a few exceptions, majorities in the eurozone countries said the euro had been a bad thing for their economy, including France (60 per cent) and Germany (53 per cent), but also Spain (53 per cent) and Portugal (52 per cent).[150] By mid-2012, with the crisis revealed to be systemic and not confined to a handful of imprudent eurozone members, trust in the EU had reached an all-time low according to the latest Eurobarometer survey. It stood at 31 per cent, a 3 per cent decrease since autumn 2011. At the same time, the average level of trust in national governments and parliaments had increased, reaching 28 per cent for both. Especially in countries with searing memories of authoritarian rule, the EU had benefited from being viewed as a bulwark of freedom, a counter-balance to unpredictable and sometimes high-handed national politics at home.

The institutional crisis in the eurozone exposed as feeble the far-fetched claim made by two leading academic proponents of advanced integration in 2005 that it was the existence of the EU and its supra-national agenda which had preserved the relevance of nation-states. Ulrich Beck and Anthony Giddens had argued that:

> The EU is an arena where formal sovereignty can be exchanged for real power, national cultures can be nurtured and economic success improved. The EU is better placed to advance national interests than nations could possibly do acting alone: in commerce, immigration, law and order, the environment, defence and many other areas.[151]

The EU's role as a collective sustainer of constructive nationalism appeared very threadbare as the post-2009 crisis gathered pace. The European cause found it hard to draw on the resources of allegiance and identity commonly available to many nations during periods of difficulty.

Although mass European society had moved in a secular direction, religion still retained different levels of influence in many important EU states, but there were few EU notables who un-selfconsciously espoused religious values, acting as points of contact between the major churches and EU institutions. Relations between the EU and the Vatican had never been the same since, in 2004, the Italian Christian Democrat Rocco Buttiglione was forced to withdraw his candidacy for the post of Justice Commissioner after he admitted that as a loyal Catholic, he believed homosexuality to be a sin.[152] Tellingly perhaps, it was a dispute over a contentious *cultural* issue that threatened to spark off a huge conflict between Parliament and the Commission rather than anything concerning the conduct and quality of democracy or pressing economic issues. In 2003, France had objected to a reference to

Europe's 'Christian heritage' in the preamble to the proposed Constitution.[153] The resulting draft had little to say about the role of faith in shaping contemporary Europe. It was hardly surprising that the EU Commission's group on Ethics in Science and New Technologies had not a single church person on it, despite the issues with important moral dimensions that were under consideration.[154]

In tranquil as well as stormy times, leaders struggled to offer inspiring European metaphors capable of leading people in a pro-integration direction. The absence of symbols and values shaping a European narrative made it hard for them to offer counterweights to signs of fragmentation on an ethnic or religious basis. On 16 October 2010, as the economic storm intensified, Angela Merkel delivered a sharp condemnation of the German record on building multiculturalism. She declared it to have been an abject failure:

> Immigrants should learn to speak German ... We kidded ourselves a while, we said: 'They won't stay, some time they will be gone,' but this isn't reality. And of course, the approach [to build] a multicultural [society] and to live side-by-side and to enjoy each other ... has failed, utterly failed.[155]

Britain's David Cameron made similar remarks about multiculturalism also when speaking in Germany in February 2011; Merkel had sought to rehabilitate the idea of a 'lead culture' able to integrate newcomers as successfully as appeared to happen in the United States. But it was hard to see how this could easily be accomplished if many Germans, as well as state institutions, remained diffident about their own culture.[156] At least the problem of a growing underclass segregated from mainstream society and shut out of the productive economy was starting to be recognised, one that put unwanted strain on European cohesion. But positive answers towards building social cohesion and integrating immigrants and their descendants through education and fulfilling work were unlikely to come easily in the midst of a recession.

Neither would it be easy to enable citizens to feel that they had any kind of political ownership of the new European institutions if their further centralisation was required in order to vanquish the financial emergency. The use of EU power is supposed to be governed by the principle of subsidiarity.[157] It is laid down that the central organs of the EU would only take charge of those areas of decision-making that were beyond the capacity of individual state members to handle effectively. But in 2010, a former German President, Roman Herzog, and a former EU Commissioner, Frits Bolkenstein, openly warned that the EU institutions cannot be relied upon to enforce the subsidiarity principle because they are only interested in extending their powers. They went on to complain that the European Court of Justice would do nothing to enforce the principle. Its rules are legally binding on member-states and take precedence over domestic law.[158] 'The Court has an interest in a constant expansion of its areas of competence. The same is true for the European

Parliament.'[159] They argued that the EU's future was in jeopardy unless national governments learnt to categorically say no to the horse trading and alliance brokering in the Council of Ministers, when the suggested legislation contravenes the principle of subsidiarity or goes beyond the EU's areas of competence.

For such historically minded politicians as Herzog and Bolkenstein, who had lived through wars and privations, Mark Leonard's claims that the EU represents 'the most exciting experiment in democracy in the world' and that a major problem for 'Europe's democratic revolution' was that it 'has gone largely unnoticed by its citizens' are likely to be seen as deeply misplaced.[160] As head of a major think tank that regularly hosts meetings with top national and EU decision-makers, Leonard displays a naivety which suggests that the EU is ill-equipped to pass through its time of troubles. The post-2009 crisis is a test of the EU's vigour and statesmanship and it shows little sign of rising to the challenge. It is too theoretical in its approach, too wedded to special interests, and quite unprepared to take a completely fresh look at its institutions and their methods and be prepared to radically redesign them.

From Yugoslavia in the early 1990s to Iraq after 2003 and Libya in 2011, it has been unable to devise a common foreign and security policy due to clashing national interests. It has sought to accomplish change on too wide a range of policy fronts. This has involved it moving on from regulating markets and ensuring self-sufficiency in food, to trying to arrange currency stability, fend off climate change, and impose a suffocating and very costly regulatory regime of 'health and safety'. Britain's David Cameron complained in 2009 that the UK had spent more than £35 billion complying with EU employment and health and safety law in the previous decade.[161]

Goodwill is frittered away by pursuing unpopular policies for ideological reasons or to justify the existence of a vast system of bureaucracy. EU spending has gone up just as nearly all governments have been trimming or slashing budgets to cope with the economic crisis; the single currency debacle is not the only major policy failure that has beset the EU. From 2008 the Emissions Trading System was the EU's flagship policy designed to make it the global leader in renewable energy. It was supposed to give companies incentives to switch to green energy sources, but by 2013, the EU was forced to concede that the policy was not working. There was a failure to reduce carbon emissions and polluters had even been rewarded with large subsidies.[162] Following the explosion at Japan's Fukushima nuclear reactor in March 2011, Germany's Angela Merkel had been the principal champion of green energy, ditching nuclear power overnight. But two years later, the members of her centre-right coalition at the European Parliament were voting to retreat from costly investments in renewable energy. In Germany itself, where energy bills were 40–50 per cent above the European average, the strains being placed on its energy mix proved unsupportable by 2013 and flagship climate programmes were scaled back.[163] This was an example of the EU retreating from a favoured policy that had become a huge liability, threatening to alienate business interests and consumers alike from governing parties. But so far, it has been the exception to the rule. When complex policies create clear winners and losers (such as the notorious CAP), 'the EU reflex is never to question or scrap the policy, since political dogma, vested interests and institutional inertia rule [this] out'. According to Helen Wallace, normally a keen advocate of the expansion of EU influence, 'In political science, it's called "past dependence". You are so locked in by what you have done before that you end up doing a version of it again and again.'[164]

Conclusion

The EU shows no sign of being capable of renewing itself in the current crisis. Nations big and small which have experienced setbacks of different kinds in the last two hundred years have sought with varying degrees of success to restore their vigour. But all the indications are that the key EU decision-makers prefer to reinforce those centralising features which have robbed the EU of real legitimacy. Too many ongoing suspicions and rivalries have prevented it from accomplishing Monnet's hope of 'fulfilling unions among peoples'. It is an alliance of interests rather than ideals. It remains obsessed with diminishing the strength of its national members through various restrictions and power-grabs. These stratagems merely weaken Europe since the centre has shown itself incapable of adequately exercising national responsibilities on numerous policy fronts. The bureaucrats, intellectuals, lawyers and post-national politicians who continue to work for the kind of centralised Europe that has not been seen since the age of absolutist empires are incapable of inspiring an attractive and enduring European identity. Their distrust of conventional democracy and inability to supplant it with political arrangements that enjoy widespread interest or participation combine an economic crisis with a political crisis. The commitment to equality, one of the few substantial themes in the European narrative, has already been discarded in an intensifying crisis. The EU had sought legitimacy across Europe by guaranteeing the human necessities that ensured a tolerable life for most of the continent's inhabitants. But confronted by an elemental crisis, its leaders showed that social justice was not a fundamental concern. A generation of young people has been sacrificed in one country after another in order to enforce the deflationary strategy seen as necessary to allow a dysfunctional currency union to stagger on and its chorus of supporters to salvage their credibility. The EU has been revealed as an entity not so different in its essential drives and worldview from other past European systems of authority. They were forms of authority designed to prolong the ascendancy of privileged forces. Such a narrow perspective failed to shield them from storms that ultimately toppled them as shown by the collapse of royal absolutism in Europe between 1789 and 1918. But at least in striving to defend narrow elite privileges, old European hierarchies could appeal to traditional symbols and values which enjoyed genuine appeal. By contrast, the symbolic authority of the twenty-first-century European order is threadbare. It has enforced punishing austerity on millions to safeguard the interests of a narrow set of financial and bureaucratic players. It is likely to receive an unprecedented rejection in the elections for the European Parliament in May 2014 in a contrasting set of countries. But it will be hard for democracy to play any central role in rescuing the European project from its gravest errors. Financial decisions have been taken in order prop up the currency union, most notably the socialisation of vast amounts of private debt, which cannot easily be undone. A polarised European Parliament and the prospects of fresh financial shocks due to the way the European elite has destabilised large parts of the global economy seem hard to avoid.

It is hard to see how *Europe* can be invoked as an effective rallying-cry in order to initiate a retreat from disastrous policy-making. Efficient and innovative decision-making has been almost completely absent from the EU's corridors of power for a long time. Unelected elites have taken decisions which appear prejudicial to their own interests and not just the welfare of Europeans in general. The induction of China into the World Trade Organization in 2001 appears increasingly senseless given the way that a centrally planned political system and economy is able to massively undercut European production costs and prices.

With a dazzling lack of foresight, the EU assumed it could remain a pivotal economic player by fully embracing globalisation, internationalising production and even labour forces, and pressing ahead in a reckless manner with liberalisation of the financial arena. The euro was envisaged as guaranteeing a front row place for the EU in the globalised economic world. Instead, burdened by an unworkable monetary system which has led to an accumulation of vast amounts of public and private debt, Europe faces the likelihood of future economic shocks that it is now ill-equipped to absorb. The current crisis of representation could easily turn into a full-blown political one in which desperate rulers try to abandon remaining democratic niceties just as they have discarded the EU's own rule-book for handling eurozone difficulties with overwhelmingly ruinous results.

Notes

1 Marsh, 'Faltering ambitions and unrequited hopes', p. 46.
2 Shore, *Building Politics*, p. 222.
3 Edoardo Campanella, 'Europe's crisis of tongues', Project Syndicate, 10 August, 2012.

4 Simon Clark and Julian Priestley, *Europe's Parliament* (London: John Harper Publications, 2012), pp. 162, 172.

5 Campanella, 'Europe's crisis of tongues'.

6 Olaf Gersemann, 'Top ten reasons why the euro was a dumb idea', *Die Welt*, 29 November 2011.

7 Campanella, 'Europe's crisis of tongues'.

8 Shore, *Building Politics*, p. 46.

9 Shore, *Building Politics*, p. 49.

10 Andrew Rettman, 'Van Rompuy's "egg" goes down badly at EU summit', *EU Observer*, 24 June 2011.

11 Jacques Santer, 'The euro, instrumental in forging a European identity', *Info Europe*, No. 8, May 1998.

12 Shore, *Building Politics*, pp. 184–5.

13 Jens-Peter Bonde, *Mamma Mia: On 25 Years of Fighting for Openness in the EU* (Copenhagen: Forlaget Vindrose/Nota, n.d.), p. 58.

14 Vaubel, *The European Institutions*, p. 29.

15 Vaubel, *The European Institutions*, p. 36.

16 Marta Andreasen, *Brussels Laid Bare* (Devon: St Edwards Press, 2009), p. 48.

17 Bonde, *Mamma Mia*, pp. 31–5.

18 S.S. Andersen and K.A. Eliassen, 'European Community lobbying', *European Journal of Political Research*, 20, 2, p. 178.

19 Vaubel, *The European Institutions*, p. 39.

20 European Ombudsman speech by P. Nikiforos Diamandouros, on the occasion of the formal dinner with the EU institutions, bodies and agencies to mark the 10th anniversary of the European Ombudsman Institution, Brussels, 17 November 2005: www.ombudsman.europa.eu.

21 Toby Vogel, 'Principles for EU officials', *European Voice*, 21 June 2012.

22 Open Europe, 'How many people work for the EU?', 29 January 2007.

23 Valentina Pop, 'Merkel under fire for "lazy Greeks" remark', *EUObserver*, 19 May 2011.

24 Charlotte McDonald, 'Are Greeks the hardest workers in Europe?', BBC News, 26 February 2012.

25 Ray MacSharry and Padraic White, *The Making of the Celtic Tiger: The Inside Story of Ireland's Boom Economy* (Cork: Mercier Press, 2000), p. 154.

26 See Tom Gallagher, *Journey Without Maps: Ireland and the EU during the European Financial Crisis* (Brussels and London: New Directions, 2012), pp. 12–13.

27 'Disinvestment in education is the path to an "innovation island"?', *Ireland after NAMA*, 15 March 2010: http://irelandafternama.wordpress.com.

28 'Disinvestment in education', quoting Irish radio (RTE), 9 September 2008.

29 Shane Ross, *The Bankers: How the Bankers Brought Ireland to its Knees* (Dublin: Penguin Ireland, 2009), pp. 123, 129.

30 Stephen Kinsella, 'Five years after crash, what have we learned?', *Irish Independent*, 20 August 2012.

31 *Sunday Independent*, 1 May 2011.

32 David McWilliams, 'We're being played for fools', *Sunday Business Post*, 24 April 2011.

33 Tom McGurk, 'Who will hoist the Jolly Roger?', *Sunday Business Post*, 17 April 2011.

34 Colm McCarthy, 'Sarkozy's grandstanding on our corporation tax misses the point', *Sunday Independent*, 16 January 2011.
35 Thomas Molloy, 'Half of Irish businesses on verge of collapse, new survey shows', *Irish Independent*, 31 July 2012.
36 Leonard, *Why Europe Will Run,* p. 7.
37 Haller, *European Integration*, p. 21.
38 Lorraine Mullally, 'Bad news for democracy', *EUObserver*, 30 July 2008.
39 Martin Ball et al., *Propaganda: How the EU Uses Education and Academia to Sell Integration* (London: Bruges Group, 2004).
40 Booker and North, *The Great Deception*, p. 477.
41 Open Europe, 'EU Commission officials – coming to a uni near you', 13 August 2009.
42 Bruno Waterfield, 'House of History cost estimates double to £137 million', *Daily Telegraph*, 3 April 2011.
43 Shore, *Building Politics,* p. 57.
44 Shore, *Building Politics,* p. 57.
45 Booker and North, *The Great Deception*, p. 359.
46 Booker and North, *The Great Deception*, p. 359, n. 7.
47 Martin Banks, 'EU triples its financial contribution to Euronews', *The Parliament*, 13 January 2011: www.theparliament.com.
48 Jan A. Johansson, 'Euronews: channel of propaganda', *EUD, Alliance for a Europe of Democracies*, 18 January 2011: www.eudemocrats.org/eud/news.php?uid=296.
49 Roger Scruton, 'The nation-state and democracy', *The American Spectator*, 14 February 2007.
50 Daniel Hannan, 'If Nicolas Sarkozy thinks the FT is a free market newspaper, God help France', *Daily Telegraph*, 16 April 2012.
51 *Financial Times*, 2 January 2002.
52 *Financial Times*, 26 May 2008.
53 Jonathan Russell, 'Martin Feldstein: French "don't get" problems at euro's heart', *Daily Telegraph*, 29 December 2011.
54 Martin Wolf, 'The "grand bargain" is just a start', *Financial Times*, 29 March 2011.
55 Jochen Bittner et al., 'Europe's seven deadly sins: 2', *Presseurop*, 15 December 2011.
56 Open Europe, 'BAE/EADS deal collapse shows national interests still rule when it comes to defence', 11 October 2012.
57 Bittner et al., 'Europe's seven deadly sins: 2'.
58 See Daniel Hannan, 'EU regulation is making the next crash inevitable', *Daily Telegraph* (Daniel Hannan's blog), 14 September 2012.
59 Philip Stephens, 'Europe's German question', *Financial Times*, 26 March 2010.
60 Wolfgang Münchau, 'Germany is stuck between a brick and a volte-face', *Financial Times*, 6 February 2012.
61 Ambrose Evans-Pritchard, 'Finland prepares for break-up of eurozone', *Daily Telegraph*, 16 August 2012.
62 Jürgen Habermas, *The Crisis of the European Union: A Response* (Cambridge: Polity, 2012), pp. 123–4.
63 *Daily Telegraph*, 17 March 2012.
64 Open Europe, 'It concerns the EU's very existence', 21 January 2010.
65 Open Europe, 'Time's up?', 16 March 2009.
66 Open Europe, 'The EU and the NHS', 27 April 2012.

67 Open Europe, 'Cable gets it 100% right on EU regulation (almost)', 8 May 2012.
68 Open Europe, 'Time's up?'.
69 Open Europe, 'The top 100 most costly EU regulations', 21 December 2009.
70 Open Europe, 'Italy is testing the limits of EU integration', 12 April 2011.
71 Open Europe, 'Italy is testing'.
72 Open Europe, 'Bolkestein vs. Verhofstadt', 3 August 2010.
73 Clark and Priestley, *Europe's Parliament*, p. 206.
74 Gilbert, *European Integration*, p. 128.
75 Gilbert, *European Integration*, p. 128.
76 Gilbert, *European Integration*, p. 129.
77 *Eurointelligence Daily Briefing*, 18 March 2012: www.eurointelligence.com.
78 Honor Mahony, 'Call for EU anti-fraud office to investigate MEPs' expenses', *EUObserver*, 21 February 2008.
79 See Cas Mudde and Cristobal Rovira Kaltwasser, *Populism in Europe and the Americas: Threat or Corrective for Democracy?* (Cambridge: Cambridge University Press, 2012).
80 See Juan J. Linz, *Robert Michels, Political Sociology, and the Future of Democracy* (New Brunswick: Transaction Publishers, 2006), pp. 5, 33–46.
81 Open Europe, 'Compare and contrast', 1 August 2008.
82 Open Europe, 'Worlds apart', 14 August 2008.
83 Open Europe, 'Worlds apart'.
84 Open Europe, 'Worlds apart'.
85 *New York Times*, 10 June 2011.
86 Open Europe, 'EU common position on Libya blown apart', 11 March 2011.
87 Open Europe, 'EU external aid: who is it for?', 18 April 2011.
88 'EU's Union for the Mediterranean drifts into irrelevance', Brussels Blog, *Financial Times*, 1 June 2010.
89 Booker and North, *The Great Deception*, p. 489.
90 *European Voice*, 8 May 2002.
91 Gareth Harding, 'Fish tale at European Commission', United Press International, 2 May 2002.
92 *European Voice*, 30 May 2002.
93 Daniela Spinant, 'Ombudsman urges committees to look at fish scandal', *EU Observer*, 28 May 2002.
94 Nikolaj Nielsen, 'Sarkozy threatens to end EU passport-free travel', *EUObserver*, 13 March 2012.
95 For energy collaboration, see Artur Ciechanowicz and Rafal Sadowski, 'The future of the Franco-German tandem', Warsaw: Centre for Eastern Studies, 11 July 2012: www.osw.waw.pl.
96 See A.S. Milward, 'Allegiance: the past in the future', *Journal of European Integration History*, 1, 1995, p. 12.
97 Bruno Waterfield, 'José Manuel Barroso: "What we have is the first non-imperial empire"', *Daily Telegraph*, 11 July 2007.
98 Dan O'Brien, 'Interplay of biggest powers pits self-interest against bailout rate', *Irish Times*, 28 May 2011.
99 Quoted in Majone, *Europe as the Would-be World Power*, p. 56.
100 Booker and North, *The Great Deception*, p. 55. See also a series of articles in the issue of the *Journal of European Integration History*, 6, 2, 2000 devoted to American relations with Western Europe and the EU between 1950 and 1974.

101 Booker and North, *The Great Deception*, p. 321.
102 Charlemagne, 'France's minister sees a neocon plot', *Economist*, 26 June 2008.
103 Leigh Phillips, 'EU finance chiefs cool on German plans for Europe', *EUObserver*, 19 September 2011.
104 *Presse Ocean*, 16 January 2012, interview with V. Giscard d'Estaing.
105 *Daily Telegraph*, 20 June 2012.
106 Brooks, 'The technocratic nightmare'.
107 Booker and North, *The Great Deception*, p. 568.
108 Majone, *Europe as the Would-be World Power*, p. 128.
109 See Philippe Schmitter and Michael Bauer, 'A (modest) proposal for expanding social citizenship in the European Union', *Journal of European Social Policy*, 11, 1, 2001, pp. 55–66.
110 Open Europe, 'Questionable EU priorities', 23 August 2010.
111 Open Europe, 'A classic example of EU spin', 26 August 2010.
112 Charlemagne, 'Ask a silly question', *Economist*, 21 February 2008.
113 Haller, *European Integration*, p. 260.
114 Haller, *European Integration*, p. 259.
115 Michael O'Neill, *The Struggle for the European Constitution: A Past and Future History* (London: Routledge, 2009), p. 10.
116 Taxpayers Alliance, 'Every one of the people matters, Mr Barroso', 1 December 2008.
117 J.H.H. Weiler, *The Constitution of Europe* (Cambridge: Cambridge University Press, 1999), p. 205.
118 Weiler, *The Constitution*, p. 205.
119 Haller, *European Integration*, p. 106.
120 Stephen Weatherill, 'The constitutional context of (ever-wider) policy-making', in Erik Jones, Anand Menon and Stephen Weatheril, *The Oxford Handbook of the European Union* (Oxford: Oxford University Press, 2012), p. 578.
121 O'Neill, *The Struggle*, p. 272.
122 Haller, *European Integration*, p. 335.
123 Shore, *Building Politics*, p. 138.
124 Weiler, *The Constitution*, p. 165.
125 Richard Bellamy, 'Democracy without democracy? Can the EU's democratic "outputs" be separated from the democratic "inputs" provided by competitive parties and majority rule?', in Peter Mair and Jacques Thomassen (eds), *Political Representation and European Union Governance* (London: Routledge, 2011), p. 8.
126 Bellamy, 'Democracy without democracy?', p. 8.
127 Bellamy, 'Democracy without democracy?', p. 9.
128 Bellamy, 'Democracy without democracy?', p. 9.
129 Robert Keohane and Stanley Hoffman, 'Institutional change in Europe in the 1980s', in Robert Keohane and Stanley Hoffman, *The New European Community: Decision-Making and Institutional Change* (Oxford: Westview Press, 1991), p. 11.
130 Charles Moore, 'If Strasbourg has its way, we will all end up as prisoners', *Daily Telegraph*, 12 February 2011.
131 Roger Scruton, *Green Philosophy* (London: Atlantic Books, 2012), p. 371.
132 Scruton, *Green Philosophy*, p. 374
133 Charles Moore, 'The civil servants are the masters now', *Daily Telegraph*, 16 March 2012.

134 Scruton, *Green Philosophy*, p. 249

135 Moore, 'If Strasbourg has its way'.

136 See Michael Pinto-Duschinksy, *Bringing Rights Home* (London: Policy Exchange, 2011), p. 1.

137 Majone, *Europe as the Would-be World Power*, p. 23, referring to George L. Mosse, *The Culture of Western Europe in the 19th and 20th Centuries* (London: John Murray, 1963); see also Eugen Weber, *Peasants into Frenchmen: The Modernization of Rural France, 1870–1914* (Stanford, CA: Stanford University Press, 1986).

138 Quoted in Shore, *Building Politics*, p. 16.

139 Paschal Fontaine, *A Citizen's Europe* (Luxemburg: OOPEC, 1993), p. 7.

140 *Scotsman*, 19 January 2000.

141 Friend, *Unequal Partners: French–German Relations*, p. 58.

142 Friend, *Unequal Partners: French–German Relations*, p. 95.

143 Friend, *Unequal Partners: French–German Relations*, pp. 94–5.

144 Friend, *Unequal Partners: French–German Relations*, p. 93.

145 Philippe Nemo, 'Europe's endangered soul', *City Journal*, Spring 2010.

146 See 'Trade union', Wikipedia.org/wiki/trade_union.

147 Nemo, 'Europe's endangered soul'.

148 Vaubel, *The European Institutions*, p. 33, quoting European Elite Survey, Center for the Study of Political Change, University of Siena, May–July 2006 (as published by Roper Center for Public Opinion research MCMISC 2006–Elite) and Transatlantic Trends 2006, Topline Data, June 2006.

149 *Daily Telegraph*, 30 October 2011.

150 Open Europe, 'Economic governance: a tale of two polls', 16 September 2010.

151 Ulrich Beck and Anthony Giddens, 'If the EU were abolished, we would have less control over our affairs', *Guardian*, 4 October 2005.

152 Booker and North, *The Great Deception*, p. 547.

153 Booker and North, *The Great Deception*, p. 523.

154 TaxPayers Alliance, 'Your techno-moral guardians', 29 October 2009.

155 'Angela Merkel says the un-sayable', *Globe and Mail*, 19 October 2010.

156 Oliver Marc Hartwich, 'Germany proves clumsy with foreign matter', *Australian*, 21 October 2010.

157 Gilbert, *European Integration*, p. 164.

158 Roland Flamini, 'Judicial reach: the ever-expanding European Court of Justice', *World Affairs Journal*, November/December 2012.

159 Open Europe, 'It concerns the EU's very existence'.

160 Leonard, *Why Europe Will Run*, p. 95.

161 Open Europe , 'It's going to get a whole lot worse', 2 December 2012.

162 Oscar Reyes, 'EU's flagship climate policy is sinking fast', *EUObserver*, 16 April 2013.

163 'Funding shortfall: Germany forced to cancel climate change programmes', *Der Spiegel*, 18 March 2013; 'Tilting at windmills', *Economist*, 18 March 2013.

164 Paul Taylor, 'Over-complex Europe keeps making same mistakes', Reuters, 14 May 2012.

5

The steady retreat of democracy in the EU

Integration via absolutism

One of the chief casualties of the extended economic crisis in the EU has been democratic politics. The EU's own mechanisms for decision-making have been set aside at particular moments; a core group of countries has assumed responsibility for crisis management. Indeed, between 2010 and 2012 it often seemed as if Germany's Angela Merkel and France's Nicolas Sarkozy were acting as dual monarchs, acquiring exceptional powers to handle a deepening emergency. Usually, there was not even the pretence of seeking the views of smaller partners, or pretending that their concerns weighed heavily on the minds of the 'Merkozy' duo as they had came to be known by 2010. The European Parliament was never invoked in order to obtain legitimacy for decisions that would make national taxpayers liable for huge amounts of debt.

In fact, the EP has continued its practice of being absorbed with non-economic issues. It has remained largely impassive even when the response of the European crisis managers has been to prop up the financial sector and postpone any idea of restructuring it so that it might better serve the EU's strategic goals. Largely with taxpayers' money, banks have been re-financed in order to buy government bonds and preserve the illusion of underlying financial stability. Along the way, certain policies have been jettisoned after their soundness was previously proclaimed by leading European officials, usually without much explanation or even attempts to obtain the confidence of the wider public. By the autumn of 2011, the core EU states were prepared to intervene in the internal governance of some of the most troubled eurozone members in order to assert technocratic rule over parliamentary government. Plans for a fiscal union were floated from the end of 2011 that would erode national controls over tax-raising and spending. In September 2012, the ECB's head, Mario Draghi, marked a new departure by announcing that the ECB would intervene financially so as to lower the high interest rates (yields) that were impeding countries on the peripheral zones from selling their bonds and thus raising revenue.

He offered a third way of combined fiscal and economic oversight but stopping short of political union. How the new central oversight of finances could be reconciled with minimum democratic requirements was not made clear, but one thing was confirmed: financial decisions would be located more firmly than ever before in the hands of technocrats and functionaries in the EU institutions and increasingly subordinate national bureaucracies.[1]

Since the start of the crisis, there had been continuing reliance on the expertise of the bureaucratic elites which in no small measure had been responsible for the EU's descent into crisis. Failure had long paid off at the heart of the EU, or else had attracted few of the penalties which normally face decision-makers in the national context. There was no sign that the proponents of a state, already dubbed in some quarters as 'Euroland', were capable of obtaining the legitimacy for the sizeable transfers from rich to poorer areas of the currency union without which its continuation is hard to envisage.

Support from intellectual elites on the left and business lobbies on the centre-right was not lacking for centralised economic governance. The motives of particular interest groups and lobbies for wishing to transfer powers from the national to the supra-national level varied of course, but even in the midst of a structural economic crisis, there was striking common ground for proceeding towards more ambitious forms of integration. Neither left- nor right-wing advocates of 'more Europe' appeared to be deterred by the numbness or hostility of the general populace even in previously pro-integration states. It was only in countries where a sense of alienation had given rise to populist challenges to the European order (Finland, the Netherlands and Italy) that elites had become more circumspect.

Arguably, the attempt to keep the European project afloat, even in crisis conditions, by operating above the heads of the people was a continuation of a practice which had been noticeable since the foundation of the European institutions. Little effort was invested in creating a popular base from which the architects of a new Europe could obtain support in challenging times and broad legitimacy overall. Craig Murray, a former British diplomat, recalls how, when serving in Poland in the mid-1990s, he was struck by the elitist assumptions behind the EU project. At one conference in Warsaw, organised by the Konrad Adenauer Foundation, he recalled how:

> speaker after speaker outlined what they called 'the role of elites' in promoting EU integration. That was the title of one of the sessions. The thesis was put forward, quite openly, that European Union was a great and noble idea which had always been moved forward by great visionaries among the elite, and that popular opinion may be relied on to catch up eventually, but should not be allowed to stop the project.[2]

Such an outlook, conveyed by the official foundation of the German Christian Democratic Party, was regularly expressed by politicians across the spectrum, especially at moments of tension in EU affairs. Following French and Dutch rejection of the European Constitution in 2005, the Spanish Foreign Minister, Miguel Moratinos, together with ministers from Belgium and the Czech Republic, made the claim that these 'No' votes were 'much less an outright rejection of the Constitution than untimely protest by a disgruntled but above all misinformed public'.[3] The Dutch Prime Minister, Jan Peter Balkenende, was a relatively isolated voice when he called on his fellow national leaders to reflect and display some humility, and accept that the challenge at that point was 'not always more and always further' integration, but instead 'how can we bring Europe closer to the people'.[4]

In Britain, against the background of undiminished public scepticism about the benefits of EU integration, top political figures periodically displayed the patronising attitudes ingrained in continental EU states about integration's inherent worth. In 1998, the leaders of the Labour and Liberal Democrat parties, along with the senior Conservatives Michael Heseltine and Kenneth Clarke, felt it necessary to drop normal hostilities and meet in central London to launch a new campaign, sponsored by the 'Britain in Europe' group, to educate the British people on 'the benefits of being in Europe'.[5] Britain's beef had, until recently, been subject to an EU ban owing to an outbreak of 'mad cow' disease in 1996. Yet Germany and France continued to refuse to allow British exports to resume, resulting in both Britain and the European Commission taking legal action. Germany lifted its ban in 2000 but France only did so in September 2002, nearly a year after the ECJ had said it was acting illegally.[6] Yet in 1994, Douglas Hurd, the British Foreign Secretary, had cited as one of the benefits of EU membership the fact that 'the French cannot block our lamb or the Germans our beef'.[7]

The EU's failure to regulate conflicts between members is testimony to its lack of authority, especially over those who see it as a platform for advancing national interests. But the entity has picked itself up from successive setbacks perhaps for one overriding reason. It offers politicians, and especially bureaucrats, the right to rule without democratic interference. This is something which the American commentator, David Brooks, has described as 'the holy grail'. It gives tremendous scope and power to 'the arrogant gray men who believe they can engineer society, oblivious to history, language, culture, values and place'.[8]

Rule of the functionaries

The essentially bureaucratic nature of the EU, allowing all crucial decisions to be made by elites, has been defended by many social scientists. Ernst Haas, the American author of the first social scientific study of the integration process, believed this to be the acceptable norm.[9] He spawned a school of thought which argued that the basic problem was not how to 'Europeanise the masses'; rather the problem was how to make 'Europe without Europeans'.[10] The aim was to build permanence without the people. It places the EU at variance with other historical attempts to establish the dominance of new public values and institutions, ranging from religious evangelicalism, Marxist state proselytism and of course the efforts of national elites to spread their authority over the masses from around 1800 onwards.

Supra-nationalism, Jean Monnet's term for the new European concert, lacks any specific meaning other than experimenting with forms of governance that keep democracy at arm's length. It is only at rare moments that the undemocratic character of the EU is singled out as a virtue rather than an uncomfortable reality. One such moment occurred in 2010 when the President of the European Commission, José Manuel Barroso, openly described the EU as an antidote to democratic government. In justifying the EU's handling of the economic crisis, he declared: 'Governments are not always right. If governments were always right we would not have the situation that we have today. Decisions taken by the most democratic institutions in the world are very often wrong.'[11] Barroso, especially at such a difficult moment, was unlikely to direct attention to the EU's long list of policy failures. But to Daniel Hannan MEP, a publicly funded body which rejects any public oversight of its affairs is ill-equipped to surpass democratic states in effective governance. After Barroso's speech, he wrote:

A random cross-section of the population will almost always have more collective wisdom than a group of self-selected and necessarily self-interested experts. It cannot be repeated too often: the oxen are wiser than the grasshoppers.[12]

In the absence of the sanctions faced periodically by national politicians at the ballot-box, EU decision-makers have far more incentives to retain defective policies. Their chances of dismissal or disgrace are not high. This context perhaps helps to explain why the audacious and high-risk policy of creating a currency union in the absence of key stabilising elements was pursued with such uncritical acceptance at the top of the EU from the 1990s onwards.

Senior bureaucrats have become the chief defenders of a financial experiment whose political advocates, Kohl, Delors and Mitterrand, are dead or else in retirement. It does not bode well for democracy that they are often more inflexible in their attachments to particular policies than perhaps most politicians. The veteran Danish Euro MEP Jens-Peter Bonde recalls an experience from the 1980s when he held the rotating post of spokesman for the parliament's own budget. One day he arrived to find that his civil servant, Julian Priestley, had already written his report: 'not bad but not critical enough',

Bonde concluded before deciding that the European taxpayer would be better served if he wrote it himself.[13] But perhaps most of Bonde's counterparts would have been content to deliver unaltered the speech that had been crafted by a dedicated and artful functionary. Reflecting in his memoirs, Bonde believed that when abuses or mistakes occurred, hard-pressed politicians at the top of the Commission were often the ones *less* likely to blame than the top layers of the Commission bureaucracy.[14] One telling example of the whip-hand that bureaucrats can try to exercise over Commissioners dates from 2006. In the autumn of that year, Günther Verheugen, the Industry Commissioner, told the *Süddeutsche Zeitung* that there was a 'permanent power struggle' going on between EU Commissioners and their top civil servants. He said that the civil servants had 'too much power' and that he had 'strongly criticised' some of them for thwarting his deregulation drive. He then told the *Financial Times* that this failure to deregulate was costing the EU economy €600 billion a year.[15]

That weekend pictures of Verheugen and his chief of staff Petra Erler holding hands on a trip to Lithuania were published in the German press. The following week *FT Deutschland* reported that EU officials were openly calling for Verheugen to resign over his attack on Commission staff.[16]

Self-confident functionaries prepared to subvert the authority of their superiors, especially if their own status or performance is questioned, are wedded to their own procedures. Change is unwelcome to bureaucratic routines even if others see it as unavoidable because of poor results in terms of policy delivery. The bureaucratic mindset usually has little patience with the realities of a Europe that remains stubbornly diverse in many of its characteristics. There is rarely any desire to build a multi-faceted Europe that reflects the organic realities of the diverse societies that Europe continues to have.

This is reflected in the opaque language contained in EU reports and statements. A lack of concern with communicating clearly to the inhabitants of the EU is encapsulated in the draft of the Lisbon Treaty agreed by the twenty-seven members in October 2007: it 'consists of some 65,000 words of detailed inserts written in the usually dense and utterly impenetrable legalese of treaty-lingo, and to be appended to the extant treaties'.[17] The EU is a factory for laws and regulations which has created a growing ascendancy for lawyers. All too often they use a nomenclature or jargon that widens the gulf between the EU and the citizen.

A Czech journalist observed in 2012 that 'EU texts and speeches are frequently filled with dogmas and propositions delivered in a moralising and solicitous tone ... It is an illustration of just how much the Union's elites lack self-reflection upon their failure to grasp that it is oversized ambitions that have plunged the Union into the crisis we have today, and of their inability to extricate themselves from the dead end of programmed centralisation.'[18]

Subtle and byzantine legal minds have been used to frame legislative proposals that advance a supra-nationalist agenda far more boldly than appears to be the case at first sight. Europhile politicians skilled in procedural arts have been able to bounce these proposals past unprepared advocates of an inter-governmental EU. This was the case at the Inter-Governmental Conference that met in Milan in 1985 to prepare for the Single European Act. Bettino Craxi, the Italian Prime Minister, caught Margaret Thatcher unawares by calling for a single majority vote on a draft law which was largely the work of trusted lieutenants of Jacques Delors, the Commission President. Christopher Booker and Richard North have written:

> In principle, it [the Commission] should have had no formal part, but Delors, Emile Noel, and Francois Lamoureux, his institutional expert, attended the working meetings of foreign ministers and officials. These meetings were used to define the agenda and impede governments from advancing ideas of their own. The Commission used its familiarity with the integration agenda to freeze out or discredit proposals meant to uphold inter-governmentalism. All proposals were drafted by these three, without reference to other Commissioners.[19]

Most of the five-yearly Commission terms have seen the feudalisation of power within specific bureaucratic fiefdoms and networks. But the Delors cabinet was a dramatic break with the norm. It was a hierarchical one shaped around an ethos of explicit commitment to building a trans-national Europe.[20] Jacques Delors's outsized ambitions obtained a fruitful outlet thanks to the longstanding dominance of the French administrative model in EU affairs. It was a mixture of the formal and informal. There was 'a formal system with rigid bureaucratic structures and rather inflexible legal rules with informal approaches based around personal networks grafted on to it'.[21] Roy Denman, an EU official fully committed to the integration ideal, nevertheless found the methods of Delors and his henchmen hard to reconcile with his hopes for Europe:

> When he [Delors] arrived [in 1984] the French had a major influence in the Commission. By the time he left, in 1994, they had a stranglehold. During his time more than half the twenty Director generals were sacked ... In almost all cases their fault had been to voice reservations about Delors policies or French interests. Where in a key *Directorate generale* the French did not have a senior figure, '*Hommes de confiance*' were placed ... All this meant changing the Commission into a Tammany Hall with a French accent.[22]

French bureaucratic norms were adapted to an often unstable or fluctuating political situation in which administration was supposed to be based around supposedly immoveable procedures. The reality was often a fluid situation in which a strong-willed and self-confident operator could show a surprising degree of improvisation. John Mole has written about the French approach to governance that was transported to Brussels half a century ago:

Rules and procedures are rarely broken but they are constantly distorted, manipulated and ignored if they do not serve the purpose to which they were intended ... Beneath the apparent structure of the organisation, there is usually an invigorating sub-culture based on informal networking and characterised by flexibility, scepticism and energy.[23]

Peter Mandelson, the EU Commissioner for Trade between 2005 and 2008, was one of the few British politicians to take easily to this opaque bureaucratic world. But other British officials floundered or surrendered to the norms of the Brussels system, as David (now Lord) Williamson seems to have done. He was the Secretary-General (or chief civil servant) to the Commission President from 1987 to 1997. According to a biographer of Delors, he 'has become more enmeshed in the Delors network than [Emile] Noel ever was ... Williamson has not stood up to Delors or Lamy. Those close to Leon Brittan are particularly critical of Williamson for having allowed Lamy to rewrite the minutes of commission meetings.'[24] (Perhaps unsurprisingly, Williamson was made a Commander of the *Légion d'honneur* by France.)

Many British recruits had a more uncomfortable experience, however. They 'were uncertain how to lobby or network' in a bewildering administrative arena 'where the political, bureaucratic and financial worlds intersected'.[25] This was confirmed by an official seconded from Whitehall to try and improve UK recruitment to the Commission during the 1990s. One Commission official was quoted as saying 'there is a different ethos and employment culture in the UK and Nordic countries'.[26]

A bureaucratic labyrinth with more than its fair share of plots and manoeuvres was not necessarily more efficient in terms of delivering results. The French bureaucracy remained wedded to old methods after 1945: unlike the civil services of Germany, the Netherlands and Denmark, which were all radically reorganised after the war and kept files in a centralised filing system in each ministry, France and Italy did not undergo this process and there was an acute dependency on duplicating files.[27] The Delors era was concerned with centralising power without simultaneously modernising the bureaucratic agencies which he hoped would wield it. Indeed, Charles Grant has written: 'Some of the Commission's worst features have survived the Delors decade ... decisions on jobs are seldom made without months of struggle between rival networks of influence.'[28]

Unfortunately, the European Parliament acquired much of the institutionalised culture of the Commission as its size and powers gradually expanded over a thirty-year period. This would place on hold hopes that it could be a real democratic forum able to check the hierarchical and sometimes arbitrary features of the existing pillars of EU authority.

In 1976, the foreign ministers of the then nine-member EU approved the European Elections Act. The European Parliament was almost doubled in size, and a five-year term between elections was agreed, the first direct elections occurring in 1979. But there were obstacles in the way of it becoming a respected political forum in which citizens of EU nations felt well represented at Community level. The EP has no permanent home: it sits in both Brussels and Strasbourg, an odd arrangement which is fixed by a protocol in the Treaty of Amsterdam. France is attached to the Strasbourg seat and, since it is written into a treaty, unanimity from the Council would be required for a change to occur that would save money and CO_2 emissions and arguably make the EP a more efficient parliamentary organ.[29]

The EP's legitimacy was further corroded because it lacked the usual powers of a parliament. It may well be the only one in the world that does not have the right to propose legislation, and the setting of tax rates is also beyond its control. Three large party groupings have emerged: the European Socialists on the left, the Association of Liberal Democrats on the centre-left, and the Popular Party on the centre-right. But for many years, they voted in common much more often than the parties in many national parliaments would ever do. Assessing a thirty-year record, Roland Vaubel concluded in 2009 that they form one large party: 'the party of EU centralisation. The European parliament represents itself.'[30]

Stillborn change: the Santer affair

A show of independence was evident in 1995 when the EP proved reluctant to approve the appointment of Jacques Santer as President of the European Commission. His nomination passed by only 260 votes to 238 with 23 abstentions. The second holder of the post from Luxembourg, Santer had been a compromise candidate after Britain had vetoed the Belgian Christian Democrat Jean-Luc Dehaene who was widely seen as the continuity candidate likely to try and consolidate Delors's supra-national agenda. A period of drift ensued in a Commission with high-ranking former national politicians who were unlikely to fall in behind the leadership of a former Luxembourg Minister of Finance. Civil servants in the Commission even refused to comply with Santer's decision that they hand over their office phone numbers so that they could be lodged in an official directory.[31]

It is no secret that the Commission and Parliament often view each other with suspicion despite their supposed commitment to a common future for Europe. In January 1999, when the Court of Auditors uncovered evidence of abuse of office in the Commission, Santer was confronted by a threat from the EP to pass a motion of censure against the Commission. Under the Maastricht Treaty, it now had the power to dismiss a Commission by a two-thirds majority. In light of the parliament's own 'luxurious allowances and expenses', the political scientist Mark Gilbert called it 'one of the most egregious examples of the pot calling the kettle black in modern political history'.[32] Santer played for time by agreeing to allow a commission of independent experts to look into the accusations.

The investigating committee had few of the independent voices that Jens-Peter Bonde, a tireless campaigner as an MEP against abuses of power, thought were needed. The larger political groups on the left and right preferred to nominate 'their own loyal party henchmen' who it was expected would 'quieten the uproar'.[33] However, when the Commission sought to obstruct the committee in its work, any readiness to perform a whitewash faded. From a Dutch EU official, Paul van Buitenen, the committee was able to receive 5,000 pages of documentation containing evidence of irregularities, much of which the Commission had refused to release to them.[34] Santer tried to hang on even when the report of 'the wise men' concluded that 'it is difficult to find anyone who has even the slightest sense of responsibility' for the abuses that had been uncovered. Technically, the Commission could only be brought down if two-thirds or more of MEPs voted against it. The two commissioners who bore the heaviest criticism in the report were both Socialists, but the Socialist parliamentary group, led by Britain's Pauline Green, declined to close ranks on a tribal basis and allow Santer to survive on a minority vote. She called on the college of commissioners to resign *en masse*. This led to furious manoeuvring among the office holders and their national backers. President Chirac refused to permit Edith Cresson, the most heavily criticised commissioner, to be made a scapegoat by resigning alone. The Spanish Commissioner Manuel Marin received similar support from his Prime Minister. Santer himself refused to go alone. One of the least-criticised commissioners, Austria's Franz Fischler, broke the impasse when he announced his intention to resign. The Commission finally resigned in its entirety when the Belgian member Karel van Miert pointed out that the pension rights of colleagues who were thrown out in a vote of no confidence were less secure than of those who resigned voluntarily.[35] They all finally resigned on 15 March 1999.

Many years later, Santer would be plucked from retirement, aged 75, in 2012 to head the board of the Special Purpose Investment Vehicle (SPIV) which was designed to raise enough funding to ensure the viability of the eurozone rescue fund for insolvent member states.[36] Meanwhile, in 2006 the ECJ found that Edith Cresson had acted in breach of her obligations as a commissioner. But the court decided not to impose any further penalty such as depriving her of her pension rights.[37]

The crisis had erupted against a background of corruption scandals in France which indicated shortcomings in public ethics as the Mitterrand era was replaced by that of Jacques Chirac, President of France from 1995 to 2007. In the 'wise men' report, most attention had focused on Edith Cresson, the Commissioner for Research, Science and Technology. An unpopular figure at home in France, she left office after less than one year as Prime Minister in

1991–92 and was packed off to Brussels. She had appointed her dentist as a personal scientific adviser and when asked to explain such 'cronyism', she replied that it was 'good for people, even if they were friends, to experience life in EU institutions'. She went on to blame the charges against her on an 'Anglo-German conspiracy' and a 'German-inspired bid to damage France', remarkably claiming that she was 'guilty of no behaviour that is not standard in the French administrative culture'.[38] This resort to nationalist posturing when irregularities or failures are exposed is a trait that clashes with the EU's self-image as a mature pan-European entity. It would be revived when the post-2009 financial crisis revealed serious geographical fissures in the by now twenty-seven-member EU.

The sense of entitlement artlessly displayed by Cresson was also a particular feature of the French governing classes which had exercised such a long-term hold over EU affairs. The extent to which such an elite was hated by many ordinary French citizens struck Daniel Hannan, the Conservative MEP, when he campaigned in the 2005 French referendum on the proposed European constitution and found that many people viewed their politicians as a kind of occupying force because of their proprietorial attitude towards the state.[39]

The North–South cultural fault-line

The crisis which rocked the EU at the end of the 1990s briefly brought to the surface the view that the then thirteen-member EU was divided on a North–South basis in its attitude to public morality. The argument was expressed in a few quarters that the attitudes of political elites to using state resources for private or political gain was less censorious in Southern Europe than further north. A German MEP, Ingo Friedrich, stated in 1998 that 'a completely different attitude towards patronage prevailed' in the Mediterranean countries.[40] This remark was prompted by the decision of MEPs from Southern Europe to close ranks in January 1998 when there was a first attempt to dump the Commission. Surveys into high-level corruption in Europe and the desire of political forces to stamp it out showed that the issue was taken more seriously in most North European EU states than in the South and that citizens in Scandinavian countries, the Netherlands, Germany and some others tended to be far less alienated from the political class on account of the better behavioural standards to be found in its ranks.[41]

By 2010 reticence had faded about discussing flagrant uses of state patronage for vote-winning purposes. The American commentator Walter Russell Mead was in no doubt that Greek politics is straight out of 'the school of Huey Long [a still-celebrated populist politician from Louisiana who was assassinated in 1935 just as he was mounting a bid for the US presidency] ... who famously told supporters that "If you're not getting something for nothing, you're not getting your fair share"'.[42]

'I cannot downplay the shock that the Greek debt-crisis has caused with my Finnish electorate that believes in fair play and following the rules,' declared Finland's Europe Minister, Alexander Stubb, in 2011.[43] Greek analysts were by now providing copious evidence of how deep-seated a culture of graft, runaway patronage and stifling red tape was in politics, often buttressed by corruption in state institutions as well as in private business and trade union circles. Nikos Tsafos, an economist responsible for the informative 'Greek Default Blog', was in no doubt that Emmanouil Roidis, a Greek humorist writing in 1875, summed up the elemental force driving Greek politics in an accurate manner and that the so-called Europeanisation of Greece had made no dent on underlying realities:

> Elsewhere parties come into existence because people disagree with each other, each wanting different things. In Greece, the exact opposite occurs: what causes parties to come into existence and compete with each other is the admirable accord with which they all want the same thing: to be fed at the public expense.[44]

Entry into the EU in 1981 seems to have only exacerbated a tendency for the party in power to spend resources rather than concentrate on raising them. A left populist party was elected to office shortly after Greece obtained EU membership, dominated by a scion of one of Greece's most influential political dynasties. Andreas Papandreou proclaimed his Panhellenic Socialist Movement (Pasok) to be a liberation movement rather than a conventional party. Its discourse championed the dispossessed and legitimised an 'underdog mentality' but the beneficiaries of his rule which lasted (with some breaks) until 1995 were mobilised groups such as trade unions, bureaucrats and favoured business groups.[45]

In Greece, the share of state spending went from 24 per cent of GDP in 1980 to 43 per cent in 1988, a 19-point rise. Revenues, by contrast, rose less than 7 points from 20.4 per cent to 27 per cent. Crucially, transfers such as subsidies, grants and social assistance rose from an average 25 per cent of the budget in 1980–82 to 32 per cent in 1986–88 (reaching an astounding 37 per cent in 1998).

In 1980, Greece had a debt-over-GDP ratio of 22 per cent which in 1988 rose to 61 per cent and then in 1993 reached 98 per cent of GDP. Without the soft budget conditions provided by the EU, it is quite possible that state profligacy on such a scale would have led Greece to default in the mid-1980s.[46] Instead of an early default, the incongruous existence of a semi-developed clientelistic state within a successful regional bloc like the EU enabled the structural failures of Greece to be masked for many years to come.[47]

In senior EU ranks, there was no effort to become familiar with underlying Greek political conditions or reflect on whether Greece could enjoy successful development within the EU. Instead, membership, forced along by Valéry

Giscard d'Estaing when French President in the late 1970s, was described in cliché-ridden terms as the cradle of European civilisation being restored to a European destiny once more.

Spain and Portugal joined the EU in 1986, five years after Greece. Their arrival in the EU reinforced the importance of countries where meritocracy in politics often took second place to the operation of patronage networks, enabling public sector jobs, subsidies and the collection of taxes sometimes to be decided on a discretionary basis. Both EU analysts and decision-makers tended to side-step the structural challenges and identify another success for the EU as an entity guaranteeing the success of transitions from authoritarian rule to a bright democratic future.

Spain, the largest new member, resembled the EU in one important respect. It also had an opaque multi-tiered system of government which in time was seen as a drain on resources and a barrier to realising developmental goals. In ascending order of importance, political power in Spain was distributed between local councils, provincial councils, regional governments and the central state. The baroque edifice, designed to promote consensus among different political contenders after the demise of the harsh and divisive Franco dictatorship in 1975, appeared to diminish many of the deep-seated territorial tensions present in Spanish politics. But Spanish decentralisation enabled a previous blight on politics, regional bosses or *caciques,* to make a comeback. Local elites, not confined to any specific party, established partnerships with the financial sector and the property industry to finance gargantuan housing and infrastructure projects. Not only were politicians able to benefit in terms of obtaining lucrative appointments for themselves and those in their circle, but the construction boom became a major source for financing the political parties. Perhaps an even larger chasm emerged in Spain between the general interest and the agenda of the 'partyocracy' than in Greece. This is because the decentralised nature of the political system made it far harder for any central body to control the excesses taking place in Spain's semi-federal state composed of seventeen 'autonomous regions'.

Policies of low-quality infrastructure growth without any genuine development were pursued by successive finance ministers, Rodrigo Rato from 1996 to 2004 belonging to the centre-right Popular Party, and Pedro Solbes from 2004 to 2009 belonging to the Socialists.[48] Some regions like Valencia, which by 2012 had amassed gigantic debts, were run like private fiefdoms. Massive spending occurred on what turned out to be wasteful prestige projects incapable of promoting long-term economic growth.[49] By 2012, Valencia was unable to pay municipal employees or providers of healthcare services and was relying on emergency lines of credit from Madrid. Other regions were better run but in too many places local political bosses, both on the right and left, amassed considerable informal power. From 1999 when Spain became part of the eurozone, there was mounting evidence that a dysfunctional political class was extracting huge rents from society, along with favoured economic interests. The multi-level administrative system and a closed list system of proportional representation enabled the parties to capture much of the state and upgrade a form of oligarchical politics that had sparked off periodic waves of unrest when systematically practised between 1873 and 1923. Property laws were systematically abused. Parliament barely stirred itself when the property boom collapsed in 2011.

Cesar Molinas, one of the few political analysts to take a strong interest in the abuse of power, wrote in 2012 that the financial crisis was treated as if it was a natural phenomenon like an earthquake or tsunami for which nobody was really therefore responsible.[50] He called for a more performance-orientated state where officials were recruited on a meritocratic basis and red tape was drastically cut back, but it looks as if a desperate struggle will need to occur in order to force on to the retreat entrenched forms of crony capital-ism involving the local state, functionaries and favoured business people. They have often operated in an unholy alliance against genuinely independent economic activity in the private sector: it takes far longer to surmount the obstacles needed to launch a business in Spain than in most other EU states.[51]

In Portugal, structural and cohesion funds from the EU were channelled into prestigious infrastructure projects whose long-term value for economic development was never made clear. The country continued to stagnate, held back by a cumbersome public administration and, arguably, one of the most unsatisfactory state education systems in the Western world.[52] State-run utility companies found room for an army of relatives and allies of politicians who were also prominent in semi-private banks. The bloated salaries which were provided through the exercise of such nepotism ensured that Portugal had one of the highest levels of income inequality in the developed world.[53] The excessive behaviour of political families contributed to the bankruptcy of the Portuguese state which in May 2011 required an emergency bail-out from the European Central Bank in order to keep public services going. In 2011, the head of the Portuguese Bar Association, Marinho Pinto, considered that none of the competing parties (which included two on the far left, enjoying around 20 per cent of the vote) was really interested in tackling corruption.[54] Ironi-cally, the deadline had just passed for the 'Lisbon Agenda', the blueprint for growth in high-tech industries in specialised areas with well-paid jobs, a growth strategy named after the city in which the strategy had been signed in 2000. Yet Portugal, in 2011, had been forced to slap tolls on some of its motorways, perhaps the most visible symbols of EU-sponsored growth, and soon they emptied of traffic as motorists clogged up the older pre-accession roads.[55] It was a metaphor for the acute limitations of growth based on the piecemeal transfer of funds from Brussels with rapid spending deadlines and no coherent strategy for utilising the money wisely in ways that would generate worthwhile results in the long term.

Many Southern Europeans, traditionally at the mercy of unimpressive national elites, had given enthusiastic approval to the concept of European integration because of the hope that their voices would count in ways that they never had with national power structures. But instead, the Brussels institutions entered into a partnership with many of these same elites, leaving ordinary citizens as powerless as before. There were no impediments preventing a former party colleague of José Socrates chairing meetings, in 2009, of the EU's anti-crime watchdog, Eurojust, which was investigating an alleged corruption case that was linked to Portugal's then Prime Minister. Socrates had been Environment Minister in the late 1990s when he allowed the construction of a shopping mall known as 'Freeport' on protected land, allegedly in return for kickbacks.[56] José da Mota, a governmental colleague of Socrates's at that time, went on to become head of Eurojust in 2007 and resigned two years later after having been suspended for allegedly trying to stop the corruption probe into the Portuguese Prime Minister.[57]

Portugal has not had a balanced budget for over thirty years. But it was permitted to join the single currency at its foundation by Brussels even though its adoption made many Portuguese industries uncompetitive. Consumers found that foodstuffs and other essential goods were marked up in price several times over. Yet unless they belonged to influential professional associations or militant unions, their wages stayed the same, especially if they were low-skilled. EU decision-makers had failed to exercise any kind of responsible guardianship by restraining Portuguese elites from a poorly thought-out gamble that quickly exposed Portugal to severe economic disadvantages. But this is not surprising because the major EU preoccupation of the 1990s, the creation of the single currency, was driven forward by blind faith rather than any rational calculation among its own chief architects.

Unrepresentative parliament

The European Parliament, briefly emboldened by having taken resolute action against abuses inside the Commission, slumped back into torpor despite acquiring some increased powers as a result of the Maastricht Treaty. Pauline Green, the politician who had arguably displayed the chief decisiveness in insisting on a clear-out at the top, was gone from the EP by the end of 1999, having encountered strong hostility especially from the Mediterranean left to her remaining head of the Socialist group. Each of the political groupings in the EP displayed remarkable equanimity about the sweeping statutory powers that the European Central Bank was given by the drafters of the Maastricht Treaty. There was the same nonchalance from Parliament after 2009 when the ECB would take measures that far exceeded its mandate in order to maintain tottering financial sectors in several eurozone members and keep cash flowing in the economy.

Some economists observed with horror that the needs of the well-connected financial sector came before those of pensioners and savers as well as those expected to take swingeing reductions in income to pay for the crisis.[58] Yet there was no revolt from the European Parliament, where much more interest has been shown in the powers in the realm of Foreign Affairs and Security acquired under the 2009 Lisbon Treaty. Baroness Ashton, the first High Representative for Foreign Affairs and Security, has been far more closely monitored by the EP than either Jean-Claude Trichet or his successor Mario Draghi, as head of the ECB. Her work of establishing an EU diplomatic service is far more interesting to MEPs than the tortuous workings of the ECB even though the impact, on ordinary Europeans, of the EU acquiring a diplomatic arm is negligible compared with the effects of the financial crisis.

Romano Prodi, Commission President from 1999 to 2004, was aware that the credibility of his own institution had been badly damaged by the downfall of the previous college of commissioners. Upon assuming office, the former Italian Prime Minister promised that there would be 'zero tolerance' of fraud.[59] But no new start was evident. In response to increases in the EU's powers over legislation, the number of Brussels-based consultancy firms mushroomed in the 1990s, with top lobbyists earning, by 2010, a salary far higher than that of the Commission President.[60] Lobby firms have gone to great lengths to influence the EU's network of over 1000 'expert groups' to whom the Commission regularly turns in order to generate ideas for the first drafts of new legislation. The stakes are high since 'the smallest of changes to EU legislation' are potentially capable of 'altering profit margins by millions of euros'.[61] By 2012 worried MEPs demanded action when it emerged that lobbyists were joining expert groups by claiming they were there in 'a personal capacity' when they were representing third parties.[62]

Officials in political party offices are also increasingly being wined and dined so as to influence the thinking of parliamentary groups on specific laws.[63] But small economic interests which cannot afford such a public relations armoury, perhaps not surprisingly, often suffer from EU law-making. A classic example may be the alternative medicine sector, a trade which the EU decided needed to be regulated after centuries of being largely overlooked by member states. A law licensing products was passed in 2004 which included numerous restrictions on existing products and which required firms to find funds for compliance. According to Daniel Hannan MEP, this law illustrated why Parliament and the Commission were seen as high-handed and willing prisoners of corporate interests by millions of Europeans:

> the ban suits the big pharmaceutical corporations, who lobbied openly and enthusiastically for its adoption. The large chains will be able to afford the compliance costs. Smaller herbalists will not, and many will go out of business, leaving the mega-firms with something close to a monopoly ... Such a ban would never have got through the national legislatures. MPs would have

been deluged, as MEPs were, by letters from thousands of constituents who felt that their health was being imperilled. In a national parliament, this would almost certainly have been enough to block the proposal; but the EU was designed more or less explicitly to withstand public opinion. Lobbyists understood from the outset that their best chance was to push through in Brussels what no democratic parliament would accept.[64]

Strong loyalty to the EP as an institution has been conspicuous by its absence in many countries. A survey of 32,268 people in Britain who were polled online between 29 May and 4 June 2009 revealed that 35 per cent were voting to express views on Britain's relations with Europe, 30 per cent to express their views on the state of British politics, but only 23 per cent to influence the composition of the European Parliament.[65] Overall in 2009, the Europe-wide turnout at EP elections continued on the downward trajectory it had been on for several decades, down from 45 to 43 per cent.[66]

The lowering of the exorbitant charges for cross-Europe phone calls proved to be an EU initiative that brought benefits for millions. But such breakthroughs for the citizen were infrequent. The main EU priority continued to be its own headlong expansion in terms of national members and the powers it exercised over them.

The twenty-year period from 1950 to 1970 when, except for Japan, the EU had been the world's fastest growing economic region had been replaced by decades of stagnation. While eurozone nations had contributed 20 per cent of global GDP growth during the 1970s, that share was now well below 10 per cent given the new importance of the emerging Asian economies.[67] Not for the first time, the power-brokers of the EU took solace by seeking to expand their prerogatives at the expense of national members.

The drive for centralised power after 2000

In December 2001, the Laeken European Council launched a decade of constitution-building. Appropriately, it was Belgium, seeking to subsume its own state failures with militant backing for EU integration, which launched the Convention on the Future of Europe. The Belgian presidency obtained agreement for bold visionary thinking. An in-depth review of the EU's governance soon led on to proposals to try and give coherence to the Union's complex constitutional order, its 'incredibly layered, incoherent and incomprehensible morass of treaties'.[68] The treaties that had been enacted in less than two decades, the Single European Act (1986), the Treaty of Maastricht (1992), the Treaty of Amsterdam (1997) and the Treaty of Nice (2000), were to be formalised by a Constitution which would define the EU's competencies. A new constitutional settlement would aim to define the balance of power between national democracies and the main institutions of the EU.[69]

The individual to drive forward such a task was also waiting in the wings:

Valéry Giscard d'Estaing, the principal *éminence grise* of radical integration, emerged almost supernaturally as head of the Convention on the European Constitution. The selection procedure that catapulted him to the forefront of European affairs, after twenty-two years out of frontline politics, was a cloudy one. But his approach was immediately clear from the opening session on 28 February 2002: the agenda was to be controlled by a thirteen-member 'Presidium' chosen by himself.[70] Giscard successfully ensured that French would be the working language, which further undermined the Convention's representative character according to one of the dissenting members of the Convention, the British Labour MP Gisela Stuart.[71] Giscard successfully minimised the influence of the ten new member states which were due to join the EU in 2004. He also caused eyebrows to be raised by demanding a salary equivalent to that of the EU Commission President, as well as generous personal and office expenses. By comparison, Roman Herzog, a recent German head of state and chair of the Rights Convention, had received only expenses.[72]

Giscard may have been acceptable because he straddled conventional left–right boundaries in a number of respects. There was never any trace of pro-Soviet sympathies in Giscard's behaviour as a leading French minister and later President of France between 1965 and 1981, but this aristocrat who was conservative and aloof in manner enjoyed more success than perhaps any other Western leader in cultivating ties with the Soviets even during tense periods in the Cold War. He refused to follow the US lead and boycott the 1980 Moscow Olympics as a gesture of protest over the invasion of Afghanistan. He had a liking for pursuing secret diplomacy with Moscow which led his successor François Mitterrand to dub him Brezhnev's 'little telegraph messenger'.[73] Perhaps he had good reason at least in domestic politics since there is evidence that his reasonableness persuaded the Soviets to have a restraining influence on the French Communist Party in its twilight years of influence.[74]

Behind the Convention scenes, fierce tussles erupted which pitted rival pro-integration leaders against one another. The Commission President, Romano Prodi, championed the 'Community method' which enabled the Commission to play a balancing role in interpreting the interests of all members, not just the most sizeable ones. He pointedly remarked at the 2002 launch that he wanted a 'European democracy' rather than a structure based on 'the laws of the few largest, strongest or most senior members'.[75] But Giscard could not be expected to identify with such a vision. His aim was for the European Council to supersede the Commission and be the seedbed for a future government of Europe. He had been the one who had introduced the Council as a pillar in the architecture of the EU by holding regular summits of the leaders of member states from the mid-1970s onwards. He saw the Council as confirming the confederal vision that many within the French elite possessed for the EU. Top decision-makers would give leadership on problematic issues and drive the integration agenda forward with the Commission slipping into the background.[76] Germany preferred a more quasi-federal approach in which the Commission retained central influence. But Joschka Fischer acceded to Giscard's desire to have a 'President of Europe' appointed by the Council; besides, in a confederal Europe the largest members would be the ones that counted, and German influence was bound to be considerable.[77]

To boost the credibility of such a managed exercise, Giscard gave civil society actors cameo roles in the Convention. But the engagement with civil society was selective, not to say spurious, and was 'heavily tilted towards organisations from within the Brussels ringroad'.[78]

Giuliano Amato, one of the Convention's vice-presidents, may have been anxious to stress the importance of 'the support of civil society in legitimising the final outcome of the convention's work'.[79] But soon it became impossible to disguise that participants were selected from client groups, many of them maintained largely by Commission funding. In the plenary sessions where they spoke up, they were unabashed in their support for expanding EU power: 'the working group on citizens and institutions called for "the government of the Union to be in the hands of the Commission, which alone was capable of representing the common interests of its citizens"'.[80]

At the Convention's start, Giscard had stated that even the EU's existing powers, contained in the body of laws known as the *acquis communautaire*, could be reviewed, but they turned out to be untouchable.[81] No debate was permitted about giving the Parliament the power to censure individual commissioners or to initiate legislation; proponents of greater democratic accountability were told that the EP was not ready to exercise such responsibilities.[82] As the member of the Presidium meant to represent national parliaments, Gisela Stuart observed that 'the consensus reached was only among those who shared a particular view of what the Constitution was supposed to achieve'.[83] Having started out with definite hopes that the Convention's work could make an enlarged European Union operate more efficiently with its workings more open and accountable, her outlook changed. The exercise, to her, became one to enable unrepresentative elites to strengthen their influence even further at the expense of democracy. She wrote in 2003:

> Not once in the sixteen months I spent on the Convention, did representatives question whether deeper integration is what the people of Europe want, whether it serves their best interest or whether it provides the best basis for a sustainable structure for an expanding Union ... None of the existing policies were questioned.[84]

Tellingly, she related that even the members of Giscard's hand-picked Presidium were not allowed to take his draft constitution away for study. Stuart relates that it was given to her and her colleagues 'in sealed brown envelopes' for a limited period of study.[85] She and eight other Convention members challenged the draft document when it was finally published. They pointed out, in a minority report, that the document did not bring the Union closer to its citizens, give an acceptable role to national parliaments, make the division of responsibilities more transparent, or encourage the institutions to behave less bureaucratically. They complained that the draft constitution was 'never drafted through normal democratic methods', Giscard refusing to allow votes. They demanded 'a new draft from a much more representative convention, democratic in content and democratic in procedures'.[86] For a time, it appeared that members like Spain and the Netherlands might refuse to support the Constitution. But on 29 October 2004, EU leaders met in Rome to initial it in the room where the original Treaty of Rome was signed.

The French and Dutch say no

A survey conducted in April 2002 reported that only 28 per cent of European citizens were actually aware of the Convention, a fact confirmed by a later Eurobarometer survey.[87] Giscard and his constitution-makers were wrapped up in their own work of destiny. Little heed was shown to the report of the European Employment task force under the former Dutch Prime Minister Wim Kok that was published in 2003. Entitled 'Jobs, Jobs, Jobs, Creating More Employment in Europe', it issued a stark warning that 'unless the member states step up their efforts, it is looking increasingly unlikely that the over-arching goal of 2010 (the Lisbon Agenda on competitiveness), will be attainable'.[88] Instead, Giscard seemed more wrapped up in the longer sweep of history. At one stage in the Convention, he told the Presidium that 'this is what you have to do if you want the people to build statues of you on horseback in the villages you all come from'.[89] But in what turned out to be an ill-omen, Giscard lost his own mayoral seat in the French rural fastness in which he dwelt shortly before the Constitution was placed before French voters for ratification in the referendum of 29 May 2005. President Chirac may have felt that he had no alternative to allowing a popular vote after Tony Blair had promised one in April 2004, proclaiming 'let the people speak'.[90]

A vigorous debate ensued in the French campaign with 420,000 copies of the Constitution being printed and distributed.[91] The debate focused not just around a lacklustre President Chirac and his colourless Prime Minister Jean-Pierre Raffarin, presiding over 10 per cent unemployment, but extended to forthright criticism of a haughty and unconstrained political class. It was difficult to conceal the fact that by boldly stepping up European integration, the form of government which the French showed strong signs of being dissatisfied with grew even less accountable. Daniel Hannan, the British MEP who was an active campaigner on the 'no' side, brushed aside claims that Europe had not really been a concern of voters:

To claim that the French are voting on the wrong issue is to underestimate their perspicacity. If you feel that administration is already too remote, you are hardly going to want to transfer powers to even more distant institutions. If you have had enough of unelected commissars and *énarques* in Paris, you don't want to be pushed around by another set of commissars and *énarques* in Brussels.[92]

In a turnout of 70 per cent, one of the highest in any French referendum in the past fifty years, 54.8 per cent of voters rejected the proposed constitution. Three days later, on 1 June 2005, it was rejected again in the Netherlands where 61.6 per cent voted against on a 63.3 per cent turnout. Dutch anxieties had arisen about the single currency being managed to suit the concerns of Franco-German state and economic elites. The Netherlands had also been engaged in a reassessment of its previously strong pro-EU orientation ever since the assassination, in 2002, of Pim Fortuyn, a politician who had argued that the EU was damaging the cohesion of Dutch society. Both countries had seen a deep split between elites with cosmopolitan outlooks and citizens who still operated within firmly national boundaries in their everyday lives. Such cleavages were not at all evident (at least then) in Spain where, on 20 February 2005, 76.2 per cent of voters had backed the Constitution on a 42.3 per cent turnout. Spain was one of the main EU beneficiaries, as was Luxembourg, where there was a 56.5 per cent vote in favour on 10 July 2005.[93]

The people have no right to be wrong

The rejection of the next decisive stage in European integration by two leading founder members of the EU was an undoubted bombshell. For a time the ratification process seemed dead and Britain was just one of several countries to hastily cancel its referendum. This might have been the ideal moment to take stock and level with citizens about how best to reconcile national democracy with European centralisation of decision-making. But the determination among the true believers in the European political elite to persist in the face of major popular rejection was unstoppable.

The European Parliament's President, Josip Borrell, and the leader of the Popular Party, Hans-Geert Pöttering, both called for ratification to continue. The leader of the Alliance of Liberals and Democrats (ALDE), Britain's Graham Watson, even proposed holding a super- or pan-European referendum to be preceded by governments patiently explaining the meaning of Europe to their presumably uninformed electorates, sparking 'a truly European debate', the key, as he saw it, to swinging opinion firmly behind the Constitution.[94] In January 2006, the EP's Constitutional Affairs Committee approved the Constitution, and MEPs passed a resolution (by 386 to 125) calling for it to be ratified by 2009 at the latest.[95] Germany was the holder of the European presidency in the first half of 2007 and Chancellor Merkel made it clear that she saw reviving the treaty as the best way to drag the EU out of its rut. In a letter to the other heads of state and government, leaked to the *Daily Telegraph,* she proposed keeping the substance of the failed Constitution while utilising 'necessary presentational changes' to persuade the public that all that was at stake was 'merely' revision of the existing treaties.[96]

The draft Lisbon Treaty which was agreed in 2007 was viewed as the same as the Constitution by the Swedish Council on Legislation (Lagrådet) – the Swedish expert body on constitutional matters.[97] But in Britain the Labour government took a different attitude. Tony Blair and his successor, Gordon Brown, argued that the constitutional features had been removed, what was left was a modest treaty and therefore another referendum was unnecessary. Labour rejected the advice of Blair's chief European adviser, Roger Liddle, who in a 2005 BBC interview called on Blair to be open about the drive to give Europe a political identity:

> In the past, pro-Europeans have talked about Europe as though it is some sort of economic free trade area that doesn't threaten our sovereignty ... I think we have got to be much more honest and open with people, that Europe always has been a political project.[98]

Labour preferred obfuscation. Between 1997 and 2010, there had been no less than twelve Europe Ministers, a sign that European affairs was not a policy issue where Labour required real expertise. Even the Europhile *Financial Times* was astonished by Labour's stance on the Lisbon Treaty and it backed the call for a referendum.[99]

Blair's argument that there 'was no major constitution issue that had to be dealt with' falls apart on inspecting the treaty. He had failed to prevent the policy area covering policing and crime from being included in the jurisdiction of the European Court of Justice. Similarly, he had failed to prevent the European Public Prosecutor from acquiring new powers to initiate criminal investigations; and in the foreign policy field, the government gave up its veto in many areas.[100]

Irish and Czech insurgencies quelled

By contrast Ireland, under its Constitution, was required to hold a referendum on any matter which involved a transfer of sovereignty. Constitutional experts concluded that it was impossible to deny this was the case with regard to the Lisbon Treaty. In different ways, the draining of power from national parliaments was stepped up. The judicial power of the ECJ was vastly expanded, enabling it to adjudicate over the newly installed Charter of Fundamental Rights (approved by the European Council in Nice in 2000). This widened the scope of European justice, enabling its practitioners to re-design the societies of member states in particular respects.[101] The EP, still shorn of many of the key functions of a normal legislature, was nevertheless given the right, under the treaty, to initiate future revision of the treaty itself.[102]

On 12 June 2008, the Lisbon Treaty was voted down in Ireland on a 53 per cent turnout by 53.2 per cent to 46.42 per cent of the votes. A majority had responded to the effective campaign against the Lisbon Treaty mounted by the businessman Declan Ganley, the founder of the Libertas movement. Far from campaigning to exit the EU, he wished to dilute the concentration of power in the hands of secretive and non-elected structures, enabling ordinary citizens to influence its affairs.[103] But arguably, the referendum was lost due to the complacency of the government, which mounted an unimpressive campaign on behalf of the Lisbon Treaty; Brian Cowen, Ireland's Prime Minister, even admitted in 2008 that he had neglected to read the document. Charlie McCreevy, Ireland's EU Competition Commissioner, declared that 'no sane and sensible person' would attempt to read such 'an impenetrable' document.[104]

Shortly before the 2008 Irish referendum, Bernard Kouchner, the French Foreign Minister, delivered an unusually outspoken warning, stating that 'it would be very, very, troubling ... that we could not count on the Irish, who themselves have counted a lot on Europe's money'.[105] The pressure continued after a verdict that was seen as incomprehensible; leading politicians stated that Ireland must not be allowed to hold up the march of European integration and that the referendum needed to be repeated so that the Lisbon Treaty could be ratified. A ritual ensued whereby the impression was given that after tough negotiations, Dublin had won important concessions. Concerns that the treaty would allow the EU to 'meddle in Irish taxation, abortion issues, workers' rights and neutrality' were allayed.[106] France's Europe Minister put what was essentially a role-playing exercise in perspective when he remarked: 'From the French point of view, there are no difficulties with these guarantees since they only repeat and clarify the content of the treaties, without adding anything nor taking anything away.'[107]

An unpopular government stood aside from campaigning for the referendum held in October 2009 and supposedly non-political pro-Lisbon groups were urged to promote the virtues of the treaty. The 'yes' side was able to outspend the 'no' side by ten to one. The European Commission tossed aside any claims of being neutral in the contest over two differing visions for Europe and its officials spoke frequently on the Irish media in support of the 'yes' side, despite having no mandate to intervene in the politics of EU member states.[108]

Ireland went back on its earlier popular decision and approved the Lisbon Treaty on 2 October 2009 by 67.1 per cent to 32.9 per cent on a 59 per cent turnout. The country was then heading into a deep recession and any sense of national self-reliance had receded. But Charlie McCreevy, the country's outgoing EU Commissioner, had claimed in June 2009 that voters in most other EU countries would also have voted no to the treaty (as the Irish had done in 2009), if only they had been given a say. He added that many EU leaders were glad they had no legal obligation to hold referendums on the treaty in their own countries.[109]

There had been open alarm and scorn at the top of the European elite about small nations, not just Ireland, being capable of disrupting the European project. The Czech Republic was due to assume the EU presidency at the start of 2009 and its Eurosceptic head of state, Václav Klaus, would confirm fears about his reliability by welcoming the Irish 'no' vote'. In October 2008, according to the Belgian newspaper *De Standaard*, the EU legal services had been investigating whether or not it would be possible to extend Sarkozy's presidency beyond December of that year because Barroso wanted 'continuity'.[110] He was then busy campaigning for a second term as Commission President and Sarkozy's backing was instrumental for this to be realised. At a press conference on 16 October, Sarkozy had said: 'We cannot work like this, changing every six months on such important subjects.'[111]

Tensions spilled over at a meeting between President Klaus and senior MEPs at Prague Castle on 5 December 2008. The leader of the European Greens, Daniel Cohn-Bendit, assailed Klaus for refusing to fly the European flag and for his ties to Declan Ganley, a well-known Irish opponent of the Lisbon Treaty. Despite being a guest in the Czech President's official residence, Cohn-Bendit said: 'How can you meet a person whose funding is unclear? You are not supposed to meet him in your function. It is a man whose finances come from problematic sources.'[112] Sarkozy later called it 'an outrage' that Klaus discouraged the flying of the European flag in the Czech Republic and the Irish Foreign Minister condemned him for having agreed to be the chief guest in Dublin of a dinner organised by Ganley.[113] There was no precedent for European politicians complaining in this way about the actions of the head of state of an EU member, actions which did not contravene any democratic rules.

The Czech Republic only signed the Lisbon Treaty on 13 November 2009 which enabled it to finally come into force on 1 December of that year. Two new important positions were created as a result of this new leap forward for the integration process. A President of the European Council was elected by the heads of government with a thirty-month term, renewable once. Herman Van Rompuy, a former Belgian Prime Minister and long-term backer of monetary and political union, was chosen. He coordinated the work of the European Council, reported to the European Parliament, and represented the EU at various international gatherings. He was meant to work closely with Baroness Cathy Ashton, a Briton appointed to be High Commissioner for Foreign Affairs and Security and supposed to build up the EU's authority in these areas of fresh responsibility. Revealingly, the core EU states could only agree on relative political lightweights for these pivotal jobs. The monolingual Ashton, who had never been elected to any public office, struggled to establish her credibility in the increasingly crowded EU organisational labyrinth. Her efforts to establish an EU diplomatic service met with resistance and the Commission, as well as the foreign ministers of major governments, were keen to marginalise her. It looked as if after tenacious efforts at bestowing a constitutional personality on the EU, the need to defend bureaucratic bailiwicks once again took precedence over consolidating the EU's authority.

Low standards in the crisis era

The politics of patronage continued to dominate Europe-wide politics despite the need to demonstrate professionalism and responsibility in the face of grim economic challenges. In February 2010, Barroso appointed his former Chief of Staff, João Vale de Almeida, to become the EU's Head of Mission in Washington. Under the Lisbon Treaty, diplomatic posts were meant to be Ashton's prerogative, but the detailed rules of procedure would not be in place until April. Sweden's Foreign Minister publicly complained about what he saw as sharp practice, but Barroso brushed it off. According to one EU official, this 'power-grab' meant that 'In the future, if the US wants to send a message to the EU, it will go through Almeida because it knows he has a special relationship with Barroso. Ashton will be left out.'[114]

If the new powers had made the EU chiefs more dependent on voters' approval, it is unlikely that such underhand tactics would have been practised so openly. Günther Verheugen, Barroso's outgoing Industry Commissioner, arguably would also have been more circumspect when he founded a lobbying firm whose website promised clients 'expertise and vast experience in the area of EU policy' as well as 'the best strategy' to deal with European institutions. Verheugen neglected to seek the Commission's permission to set up his 'European Experience Company'.[115] Such a step was required to be looked into by an ethical committee according to the Commission's code of conduct and eventually permission was obtained as long as the lobbying did not extend to areas of the Commission where Verheugen and a close colleague had wielded influence.[116]

Unhelpful publicity, shining a light on the high-handed ways of senior EU officials, continued to surface in what was supposedly a new era in European governance. Remarkably, it emerged in early 2012 that the Secretary-General of the European Court of Auditors used public funds to hire lawyers and to sue the EU's anti-fraud office (Olaf) over an inquiry into alleged irregularities about the manner in which he hired security guards. Eduardo Ruiz García lost the case, but the EU paid for his legal costs and no action was taken against him.[117]

But at least the European Parliament took resolute action when three MEPs, each of whom had held high office in their countries, were ensnared by a newspaper investigating the extent to which lobbyists had a hold over certain European parliamentarians. On 20 March 2011, the *Sunday Times* in London revealed its investigation into what became known as the 'cash-for-laws' scandal. Three MEPs, Adrian Severin and Zoran Thaler, former Foreign Ministers of Romania and Slovenia respectively, and Ernst Strasser, a former Interior Minister in Austria, were secretly filmed agreeing to propose amendments to EU laws believing they would be paid for this work with a €100,000 (£87,300) annual salary, a consultancy fee or both.[118] Except for Severin who grimly retained his seat after being disowned by the European Socialists, the other two quickly stood down in the face of outraged public opinion. In July 2012 Severin would be charged with siphoning €436,000 from the EU budget by state prosecutors in Romania.[119]

Democracy has not fared well during the years in which the EU's role has expanded. The transfer of authority from national parliaments to bureaucratic and judicial power centres in the EU has accelerated. During the recent years of permanent economic crisis, it has been a select number of countries which have come to dominate the affairs of the eurozone. No representative forum at European or national level is able to properly oversee EU decisions which have an increasing impact on the everyday lives of 500 million citizens in the EU. Most elections are nowadays greeted with apprehension by high EU officials. The voters are seen as unpredictable and indeed capable of behaving irrationally. The palpable sense of relief when elections, like the ones in France in the spring of 2012, are over and normal EU business can resume is not a healthy trait. It shows that the relationship between the EU authorities and those they govern has become a strained one, marred increasingly by mutual suspicion and fear.

Disenchantment with the operation of democracy is by no means confined to EU states. But it has become a pronounced feature in an increasing number of long-established democracies. This is shown by plunging voter turnout, the inability of the major parties to renew themselves through recruitment, and the domination of the political process by people drawn from a narrow stratum of life and who have few active links with society.

Parties find it increasingly difficult to be elected for more than one consecutive term and often can only prolong their tenure in office by forming unlikely coalitions with erstwhile rivals. No single explanation exists for the increasingly ineffectual character of democratic party government. But one thing is clear: it is virtually impossible for parties to promote EU policies and benefit electorally. EU agricultural, justice and social affairs policies generate incomprehension and hostility as do the sweeping ways in which the EU is seen to exercise its regulatory powers. The EU's fabled democratic deficit is acknowledged as a problem by many Eurocrats. But there is no desire to give voters a greater role in influencing EU powers, nor do the successive treaty changes ever reveal any desire to reduce the scope of these powers.

Defenders of the EU's political record point to the north Mediterranean states which joined in the 1980s after experiencing dictatorships of longer or shorter duration. Shaky democratic transitions, in countries with internal problems hampering the consolidation of democracy, blossomed after EU entry. It became an article of faith that the involvement of the EU in the affairs of formerly authoritarian states was a crucial factor promoting political stability and expanding freedoms. The linkage between European integration and democratic consolidation appeared to apply also for the ten states, previously under communist rule, which joined the EU between 2004 and 2007. Europe had been largely under authoritarian rule in the first decades of the EU's existence and tyranny had nearly disappeared from the continent when the EU celebrated its 50th anniversary in 2007.

It was strange that an organisation which had frowned upon real popular oversight of its own actions should be seen as such an effective recruiting sergeant for democracy. More than once it has been said that the EU would be unable to comply with the democratic rules that it had drawn up for new members to meet, if it had decided to submit its own application for EU membership.

By 2011, with Greece, Spain and Portugal experiencing acute economic difficulties as members of the eurozone, their own democratic health was in decline. Old problems which had given rise to authoritarian rule appeared to be resurfacing. The irresponsible behaviour of privileged political elites, sharp disputes between central power and the regions, and the failure to pursue policies meant to promote long-term development were responsible for a sharp increase in political volatility. In the 1970s and 1980s, popular endorsement at elections for pro-EU parties in the new democracies had been seen as a dramatic vindication of the European project. But a preference for a post-democratic formula to centrally manage the economic crisis appeared to have emerged a generation later. In the autumn of 2011, EU power brokers did not hesitate to orchestrate the speedy departure of democratically elected governments (of both right and left) in Italy and Greece, substituting them with technocratic formations. In Greece in 2012, two general elections were held in rapid succession, the main purpose being to obtain a working majority for policies of deep economic and social cuts. Long years of austerity appear to lie ahead for countries where the economic decisions will be taken in Brussels and Frankfurt instead of their home capitals.

It is hard to make a compelling case for democratic government if policies on taxation, budget deficits and the level of unemployment, social welfare and healthcare are largely removed from national parliaments. A novel and disturbing situation will surely arise if only certain EU countries actually enjoy genuine democratic oversight over these matters due to having avoided the worst effects of being in a troubled currency union.

Conclusion

In Eastern Europe before 1989, there were successive revolts in countries which felt they were damaged because they lacked a voice through being trapped as satellites in the communist bloc. Whatever legitimacy the EU still possesses, it is unlikely to save it from similar protests if countries on the margins of the eurozone consider themselves ill-used by institutions like the ECB and more senior member states. Already, after only a few years of full EU membership, democratic forms of government are experiencing a sharp challenge in former communist states like Hungary and Romania. It is hard to see how democracy can flourish across the EU if the relationship between powerful institutions and those whom they effectively rule over continue to deteriorate. If the EU only becomes more responsive to popular feelings after full-scale unrest occurs in one or more states where the 'European Dream' has died, it may well be too late. EU leaders appear to be unaware of the transience of power. Previous European empires such as Austria-Hungary and the Soviet Union were gripped by even higher levels of arrogance and complacency. There is still some time left for the EU to rehabilitate democracy and make it a factor in its practical decision-making. But this will involve a degree of fresh thinking and purposeful innovation which is not normally present in the type of leviathan that the EU has turned into.

Notes

1 See Martin Wolf, 'Draghi alone cannot save the euro', *Financial Times*, 12 September 2012; David McWilliams, 'An anorexic on a drip is not a healthy patient', *Sunday Business Post*, 9 September 2011; and Open Europe, 'Draghi's incomplete vision for the future', 12 September 2012.

2 Craig Murray, 'The day democracy died in Europe', Craig Murray Blog, 11 November 2011: www.craigmurray.org.uk.

3 O'Neill, *The Struggle*, p. 386, quoting BBC Monitoring, International Reports, 2 June 2005.

4 *Daily Telegraph*, 3 June 2005.

5 Mark Tran, 'Tory heavyweights join Blair for launch of Britain in Europe campaign', *Guardian*, 14 October 1999.

6 BBC News, 'Timeline: British beef ban', 8 March 2006.

7 Booker and North, *The Great Deception*, p. 447.

8 Brooks, 'The technocratic nightmare'.

9 See Ernst Haas, *The Uniting of Europe, Political, Social and Economic Forces 1950–1957* (Stanford, CA: Stanford University Press, 1958).

10 See Majone, *Europe as the Would-be World Power*, p. 26.

11 Daniel Hannan, 'The EU is an antidote to democratic governments, argues President Barroso', *Daily Telegraph*, 8 October 2010.

12 Hannan, 'The EU is an antidote'.

13 Bonde, *Mamma Mia*, p. 54.

14 Bonde, *Mamma Mia*, p. 84.

15 Open Europe, 'Get Günter', 11 December 2006.
16 *EUObserver*, 17 October 2006; Open Europe, 'Get Günter'.
17 Booker and North, *The Great Deception*, p. 422.
18 Tomás Břicháček, 'Grand ideas and empty jargon', *Presseurop*, 15 March 2013.
19 Booker and North, *The Great Deception*, p. 271.
20 Grant, *Delors, Inside the House*, p. 19.
21 Shore, *Building Politics*, p. 179.
22 Roy Denman, *Missed Chances: Britain and Europe in the Twentieth Century* (London: Cassell, 1996), pp. 277–8.
23 John Mole, *Mind Your Manners: Managing Culture Clash in the Single European Market* (London: Nicholas Brealey, 1992), p. 19.
24 Grant, *Delors, Inside the House*, pp. 102–3.
25 Shore, *Building Politics*, p. 190; Haller, *European Integration*, p. 73.
26 Shore, *Building Politics*, p. 190.
27 A.C. Bramwell, '*Dans le couloire*: the political culture of the EEC Commission', *International Journal of Moral and Social Studies*, 2, 1, pp. 63–80.
28 Grant, *Delors, Inside the House*, p. 93.
29 Open Europe, 'The weird and wonderful (?) world of the European Parliament', 19 May 2009.
30 Vaubel, *The European Institutions*, p. 24.
31 Bonde, *Mamma Mia*, p. 83.
32 Gilbert, *European Integration*, pp. 190–1.
33 Bonde, *Mamma Mia*, pp. 10–11.
34 Bonde, *Mamma Mia*, p. 10.
35 Bonde, *Mamma Mia*, pp. 10–11.
36 *Daily Telegraph*, 20 January 2012.
37 'Europe court rules against ex-French PM', BBC News, 11 July 2006.
38 Gillingham, *European Integration 1950–2003*, p. 322.
39 Daniel Hannan, 'Non-sense', *Spectator*, 23 April 2005.
40 Gillingham, *European Integration 1950–2003*, p. 323.
41 See Suzanne Mulcahy, *Money Politics and Power – Risks of Corruption in Europe* (Berlin: Transparency International, 2012), pp. 14, 54.
42 Mead, 'Will German politicians wreck Europe'.
43 Honor Mahony, 'National stereotyping – the eurozone's other story', *EUObserver*, 22 February 2011
44 Nikos Tsafos, 'Are we all Greeks now?', *Greek Default Watch*, 24 April 2011.
45 See Richard Clogg, *Greece 1981–89: The Populist Decade* (London: Palgrave, 1993).
46 Tsafos, 'Are we all Greeks now?'
47 For the trans-party nature of the clientelistic state, see Christos Lyrintzis, *Greek Politics in the Era of Economic Crisis: Re-assessing Causes and Effects*, London: Hellenic Observatory papers on Greece and Southeast Europe, 44, 2011.
48 Sebastian Royo, 'Reform betrayed? Zapatero and continuity in economic policy', in Bonnie N. Field (ed.), *Spain's 'Second Transition': The Socialist Government of José Luis Zapatero* (London: Routledge, 2011), p. 64.
49 Julien Toyer and Carlos Ruano, 'Valencia, a cruel reflection of Spain's economic woes', Reuters, 2 May 2012.
50 Cesar Molina, 'Las élitas extractivas: una téoria de la clase política española', *El Pais*, 9 September 2012 is a rare example of a scholarly, engaged and at times uninhibited profile of the venal power structures that have established themselves in

Spain. A top press outlet has only given such a critical appraisal prominence after several years of economic and political crisis (so far peaceful). Much of the information from the preceding two paragraphs is drawn from this article.

51 Open Europe, 'Opening Pandora's Box?', 15 March 2011.

52 Charles Forelle, 'A nation of drop-outs shakes Europe', *Wall Street Journal*, 25 March 2011.

53 For its very low ranking in the EU, see António Barreto, 'Social change in Portugal', in António Costa Pinto (ed.), *Contemporary Portugal: Politics, Society and Culture* (Boulder, CO: Columbia University Press, 2011), p. 212, n. 46.

54 *Visão*, 11 January 2011.

55 'Toll and trouble', *Portuguese News*, 14 January 2012.

56 Valentina Pop, 'Eurojust chief quits over power abuse scandal', *EUObserver*, 17 December 2009.

57 Pop, 'Eurojust chief quits over power abuse scandal'.

58 See Daron Acemoglu and Simon Johnson, 'Captured Europe', Project Syndicate, 20 March 2012.

59 Bonde, *Mamma Mia*, p. 18.

60 Andrew Willis, 'Senior lobbyists profit from expanding EU', *EUObserver*, 17 September 2010.

61 Willis, 'Senior lobbyists'.

62 Nikolaj Nielsen, 'MEPs threaten to block Commission funding over transparency', *EUObserver*, 5 September 2012.

63 Willis, 'Senior lobbyists'.

64 Daniel Hannan, 'EU bans herbal remedies: another victory for corporate interests', *Daily Telegraph* (Daniel Hannan's blog), 30 December 2010.

65 Open Europe, ' Euro election results reflect … views on Europe', 12 June 2009.

66 Open Europe, ' Euro election results reflect'.

67 Liam Halligan, 'Eurozone burns money while the banks fiddle their balance sheets', *Sunday Telegraph*, 22 January 2012.

68 K. Kiljunen, *The European Constitution in the Making* (CEPS, Brussels, 2004), p. 44, quoted by O'Neill, *The Struggle*, p. 76.

69 Gisela Stuart, *The Making of Europe's Constitution* (London: Fabian Society, 2004), p. 26.

70 Booker and North, *The Great Deception*, pp. 483–4.

71 O'Neill, *The Struggle*, p. 94.

72 O'Neill, *The Struggle*, p. 94.

73 Friend, *The Linchpin*, p. 62.

74 Friend, *The Linchpin*, p. 61.

75 Booker and North, *The Great Deception*, p. 484.

76 O'Neill, *The Struggle*, p. 169.

77 Booker and North, *The Great Deception*, p. 460.

78 O'Neill, *The Struggle*, p. 89.

79 Charlemagne, 'A rigged dialogue with society', *Economist*, 21 October 2004.

80 Charlemagne, 'A rigged dialogue with society'.

81 Stuart, *The Making of Europe's Constitution*, p. 16.

82 Stuart, *The Making of Europe's Constitution*, p. 16.

83 Stuart, *The Making of Europe's Constitution*, p. 25.

84 Stuart, *The Making of Europe's Constitution*, p. 3.

85 Booker and North, *The Great Deception*, p. 497.

86 'Alternative Report: the Europe of Democracies, in the report from the presidium of the convention to the president of the European Council', Brussels: The European Convention, 18 July 2003, CONV 851/03.
87 S. Kurpas, 'The Convention on the future of Europe – complex but not unknown', CEPS Commentaries, p. 1, quoted by O'Neill, *The Struggle*, pp. 91–2.
88 Kevin Featherstone and Dimitris Papadimitriou, *Limits of Europeanization: Reform Capacity and Policy Conflicts in Greece* (London: Palgrave, 2008), p. 121; see also Menon, *Europe: The State of the Union*, pp. 154–5.
89 Stuart, *The Making of Europe's Constitution*, p. 57.
90 Haller, *European Integration*, p. 2.
91 Haller, *European Integration*, p. 5.
92 Hannan, 'Non-sense'.
93 Haller, *European Integration*, pp. 5–7.
94 European Information Service, European Report, 4 June 2005, quoted by O'Neill, *The Struggle*, p. 388.
95 O'Neill, *The Struggle*, p. 396.
96 *Daily Telegraph*, 27 April 2007, quoted by O'Neill, *The Struggle*, p. 414.
97 Open Europe, 'Swedish legal opinion: Lisbon Treaty same as Constitution', 23 June 2008.
98 BBC News, 7 March 2005.
99 Editorial, *Financial Times*, 15 January 2008.
100 Open Europe, 'The line between fact and fiction', 16 April 2010.
101 Ambrose Evans-Pritchard, 'Does the EU club have a future?', *Daily Telegraph*, 14 September 2009.
102 Andrew Duff, *Saving the European Union* (London: Shoehorn, 2009), p. 44.
103 Bruce Arnold, *The Fight For Democracy (A Series of Interviews with Declan Ganley)* (Dublin: Killynon House Books, 2009), p. 49.
104 *Daily Mail*, 3 September 2009.
105 Honor Mahony, 'France warns Ireland on EU treaty "No" vote', *EUObserver*, 10 June 2008.
106 *Wall Street Journal*, 26 June 2009.
107 Open Europe, 'Ni plus ni moins', 22 June 2009.
108 Open Europe, 'Desperate times', 24 August 2009.
109 Open Europe, 'Ireland you are not alone', 26 June 2009.
110 *De Standaard*, 23 October 2008, quoted by Open Europe, 'Sarko puts in for overtime', 28 October 2008.
111 Open Europe, 'Sarko puts in for overtime'.
112 Open Europe, 'Does Danny the Red need help?', 8 December 2008.
113 *The Parliament* (Brussels), 17 December 2008; Bruce Arnold, 'Brash Martin shows he has yet to master the art of protocol', *Irish Independent*, 18 November 2008.
114 Andrew Rettman, 'Sweden complains about EU appointment to US', *EUObserver*, 22 February 2010.
115 Open Europe, 'Time to get serious about Commissioners' code of conduct', 20 September 2010.
116 *EUObserver*, 21 January 2011.
117 Valentina Pop, 'EU auditor used public funds to hamper anti-fraud inquiry', *EUObserver*, 27 April 2012.
118 Open Europe, 'Is the European Parliament reformable?', 21 March 2011.
119 *EUObserver*, 17 July 2012.

6

Return to European strife
via monetary union

The currency union is our common destiny. It is a question, no more or less, of the preservation of the European idea. That is our historical task: for if the euro fails, then Europe fails.[1]

Angela Merkel, June 2010

I cannot remember that European policy makers have seen anything coming throughout the euro crisis. The general rule is that they do not see problems coming.[2]

Paul de Grauwe, London School of Economics; former Commission adviser

Costly monetary delusions

The momentum behind European integration efforts sprang from the need to replace Franco-German rivalry with a spirit of practical cooperation. Their bilateral relations became the crucial pivot determining the shape and extent of European cooperation. But there was a failure to synchronise their effort behind a coherent strategy. French introspection and opportunism too often became a drag on integration efforts. By the time Germany felt prepared to take a more prominent role, widening economic differences meant it was difficult to reconcile the core interests of both states. Initiatives increasingly had a predominantly political character. Thus the single currency was overtly designed to lock a newly united Germany into a common monetary union in which it would act in concert with countries possessing less powerful economies rather than dominate them outright.

However the post-1999 currency union is by far the costliest mistake in the history of the European integration process. It was the culmination of a growing tendency by central planners and Europhile politicians to take decisions over the heads of citizens, ones that benefited a small group of vested interests and had the potential to disadvantage millions of others.

The formation of a single currency was portrayed as a seminal event. It was supposed to be the culmination of a series of top-down efforts to forge an embryo European state, one shaped around deepening economic integration. But it turned out to be a policy error as monumental as any which could be associated with imprudent national democracies. By the end of its first decade in existence, the eurozone had shown itself to be a collection of different currencies pretending to be a cohesive monetary union. Its political architects had shrunk from placing a banking union and fiscal convergence at the centre of the plan because of the likely resistance to a central regulator deciding borrowing and spending policies. The struggle to achieve democracy in some countries had revolved around such basic economic decisions being decided by citizens through their elected representatives. Accordingly, a so-called transfer union with shared liabilities in return for surrendering key economic sovereignty to a pan-European structure remained off the table.

Within the eurozone, in key respects states lost control over important financial decisions. Provided that the ECB gives permission, national central banks can provide the domestic banking system with liquidity but beyond that their powers are limited. They have no control over interest rates and cannot use unconventional monetary policy tools such as the large-scale purchase of government bonds, known as quantitative easing (QE). Lacking control of monetary policy, most central banks can do little to protect their economies from exogenous shocks. But as was becoming clear even before the crisis erupted, the ECB also lacked powers possessed by national banks in pre-euro times. Political constraints meant that it could not restore market confidence in troubled economies by authorising QE.[3]

In the single currency era, the power of individual states to destabilise others if crises occurred affecting financial institutions with trans-national holdings across the eurozone was reinforced. Such practical dangers, however, failed to have any sobering effect on leaders encouraged by organs of opinion like the *Financial Times* to see themselves as Europe's visionaries. Political manoeuvring concealed the tawdry reality behind the hype: the membership rules were interpreted liberally so that countries with weak and unstable economies could join.

The currency union brought together countries that were not compatible economically. It was essentially a political exercise drive by decision-makers who often had a shaky grasp of economics. When countries such as Ireland, Greece and Spain joined the euro, their interest rates immediately dropped to near-German levels, in some cases from double-digit figures. A sense of euphoria ensued on realising that such low interest rates need no longer lead to a sharp depreciation of their currencies. Unprecedented levels of cross-national investment occurred with the banks of the peripheral eurozone countries being favoured destinations for the savings and investments of North Europeans.

It was presumed that, as long as a few basic rules in good housekeeping were followed, the euro could act as a security blanket, preventing shocks arising from any economic policy failings in member states. For just over a decade, there were few regrets about the abolition of the currency exchange rate, the standard mechanism for balancing out differences between national economies. A 'Stability Pact', supposedly committing members to budgetary restraint, was an inadequate substitute. By 2004, it was being flouted by France and Germany, the very nations responsible for the single currency's existence.

Short of a fiscal union, it is hard to see just what mechanism could have replaced floating exchange rates so as to enable countries with economic imbalances to correct them. Accordingly when weak and often imprudently managed economies descended into crisis, it was assumed by the elites in the European Union, and indeed by most commentators, that the entire eurozone was in jeopardy. National financial systems faced contagion because of the degree to which banks and other financial bodies had become interlinked.

Disastrous precedent: the 2010 Greek bail-out

The crisis first revealed itself outside the eurozone in Iceland. The collapse of the giant US investment bank Lehman Brothers led to the withdrawal of credit worldwide in the autumn of 2008. Iceland's over-leveraged banks were soon revealed to be insolvent and the government moved rapidly to close them down. In the eurozone, Greece was the first to succumb to the suddenly much harsher lending conditions. But it was decades of profligate budgetary practices that exposed its devastating economic weaknesses.

In May 2010, the EU agreed to bail out Greece. At the same time (and along with the IMF) a €440 billion rescue facility was agreed for any other countries in the eurozone facing sovereign debt problems. The letter and the spirit of the EU treaties did not allow for the bail-out fund which was known as the European Finance Stability Facility (EFSF). Indeed, as late as March 2010, Angela Merkel had said, 'We have a Treaty under which there is no possibility of paying to bailout States in difficulty.'[4]

EU leaders justified the bail-out by invoking Article 122 of the EU treaties which states:

> Where a member state is in difficulties or is seriously threatened with difficulties caused by natural disasters or exceptional occurrences beyond its control, the Council, on a proposal from the Commission, may grant, under certain conditions, Union financial assistance to the member state.[5]

This was a breathtaking manipulation of EU statutes and it would merely be the first of many as EU efforts failed to tame the crisis. The crisis had arisen from human actions which, in the case of Greece, had been well known to leading EU decision-makers who previously had merely winked at them.

By using a legal clause designed for earthquakes or potentially extreme unforeseen circumstances, the EU ensured that all twenty-seven members would have to cover the default if the receiving country was unable to pay back the loan. Thus British taxpayers would be liable for about 13 per cent of any losses (corresponding to the UK's share of the EU budget).[6] The burden was far tougher for Slovakia which had joined in 2009. It merely exposed the hollowness of 'talk of pan-European solidarity' when a poor but fiscally well behaved new member was required to bail out a much richer one.[7]

Just three years after the May 2010 bail-out, the IMF finalised a report entitled 'Greece: Ex Post Evaluation of Exceptional Access Under the 2010 Stand-By Arrangement'[8] in which it conceded that it had been ill-conceived to collude with the EU-led strategy of piling more debt on to Greece:

> The Fund approved an exceptionally large loan to Greece under a stand-by agreement in May 2010 despite having considerable misgivings about Greece's debt sustainability. The decision required the Fund to depart from its established rules on exceptional access.[9]

Only with difficulty had the EU overcome its reluctance about allowing any external actors to contribute to managing its internal economic affairs. The IMF had been included in a 'troika' also comprising the European Commission and the ECB to steer the eurozone through its crisis. Since its creation in 1944, its standard approach to indebted countries that had sought its assistance was to advocate a restructuring package in which the debt was rescheduled and steps were taken to stimulate economic growth and lower unemployment. Debt restructuring would eventually occur in 2012. But this was only after the principal banks of core EU states had extracted much of their exposed capital from Greece and indeed other parts of the eurozone periphery. The 2013 IMF report put it in a laconic way: 'the delay provided a window for private creditors to reduce exposures and shift debt into official hands. This shift occurred on a significant scale and left the official sector on the hook.'[10]

The EU dressed up a stance that benefited a key insider interest – namely some of the leading banks of core members France and Germany – by insisting that the lack of confidence in the eurozone caused by debt restructuring would cause capital flight and threaten national economies with meltdown and the currency union with a messy dissolution. A policy that was sold as 'help for Greece' was a set of improvised measures that artificially propped up the balance sheets of Greek banks, enabling an orderly withdrawal of funds to occur.[11] In the process, the destruction of a large part of the Greek economy would take place.

The troika declared in 2010 that Greece's economy would contract by 2.6 per cent that year before recovering with growth of 1.1 per cent in 2011, and 2.1 per cent in 2012. But what happened amounted to a virtual depression for

Greece. Far from growing, Greek GDP contracted a further 7.1 per cent in 2011 and 6.4 per cent in 2012, the troika misjudging the scale of economic decline over three years by 12 per cent of GDP. The total economic decline Greece suffered would be around 25 per cent.[12]

A draconian austerity policy on top of a 5 per cent interest rate on a loan whose primary beneficiary would be the Greek banks and their West European investors greatly intensified a recession that (at the time of writing in 2013) is now in its sixth consecutive year. According to an editorial in the *New York Times*, a day after the report was leaked, the IMF was publicly admitting that 'it should have known that the agreement would leave Greece with far more debt than it could have ever hoped to pay back. It also ... underestimated the damage that government spending cuts and tax increases would do to the Greek economy.'[13]

No systemic crisis

As well as admitting its own failings, the 2013 IMF report pointed to a damaging absence of coordination between the main EU players, particularly the Commission and the ECB. Indeed, after the launch of the policy for Greece which had been given the Orwellian title 'expansionary fiscal contraction', the leading EU crisis managers denied that there was any euro crisis at all. Rather, in the eyes of Merkel, Trichet, the head of the ECB and Jean-Claude Juncker, the head of Ecofin, the body of EU finance ministers, it was simply a debt crisis in some eurozone countries. There was an adamant failure to recognise that without a common currency, Greece's problems would have been unlikely to spill over into Spain and Italy.[14]

An acknowledgement that the crisis was a systemic one that arose from a monetary experiment whose defects had been exacerbated by low-grade political oversight would have meant harsh realities had to be confronted rather than covered up. Simply too much was at stake in terms of careers and reputations. The single currency project had been kind to those pulling the strings in the eurozone; it had given them status, power that placed them beyond the control of mercurial electorates, and convinced some of them that they were making history despite the gathering storm clouds. Rarely if ever did anyone pause to ask what benefits had been given to other citizens, especially groups such as small business people, savers or low-income earners without powerful advocates at the heart of the EU able to champion their interests.

Instead, there was a tendency to clutch at any straws that could enable the seriousness of the situation to be downplayed. Olli Rehn, the Commissioner for Economic Affairs, offered a telling example in a speech to the Brookings Institution, a Washington-based think tank, on 14 April 2011: 'While I cannot yet say "Mission accomplished", I am increasingly confident that we are entering into the endgame of the crisis management phase.'[15] Portugal had just been given a bail-out, indicating the expanding scale of the crisis. But Rehn saw it differently: 'we are quite confident that with the Portuguese programme, we will have contained the problem'. He also believed that 'Spain has decoupled from the other three countries', even though recent ECB interest rate increases had worsened its outlook. Overall, he told his American audience: 'The euro's critics are wrong to claim that [the crisis] will lead to its failure or break-up. The euro will not only survive but is coming out of the crisis stronger than before.'

But it was futile to insist that the crisis was nearly over before it had even really started in earnest. The interest rates (or yields) on the bonds which governments needed to sell in order to raise funding increased for a growing number of countries. Paralysis reigned at the top of the ECB until Trichet's mandate was completed in the autumn of 2011. Recession conditions spread beyond the countries facing a full financial emergency, leaving Germany the only one with strong economic indicators. There were no plans to restore growth and competitiveness elsewhere and thus put in place the conditions that might enable infirm parts of the currency union to recover.

Protecting the financial sector at all costs

In December 2011, to avoid banking meltdown in the periphery spreading to the core, the new ECB head, Mario Draghi, placed the eurozone's banking sector on an ECB life-support machine. Central banks released gigantic amounts of funds – totalling by March 2012 one trillion euros – to enable banks to buy high-yield government bonds: Long-Term Re-Financing Operation (LTRO) was the name for this scheme. The rules prevented the ECB from practising what had already become widely known as quantitative easing. Under LTRO, central banks were instructed to pile debt liabilities on to their national taxpayers, especially in the more solvent core of the eurozone. But under existing rules, only elected governments were permitted to carry out such fiscal transfers; instead, legal niceties were cast aside and byzantine methods were used by the unelected monetary authority to promote conditions that could extend the life of the single currency.[16]

Markets were not impressed by the claims that the LTRO operation would enable the peripheral economies to regain health. Ailing banks had been required to lodge their better-quality collateral with the ECB, thus diluting the quality of their remaining balance sheet. By mid-2012, Spain and Italy were finding it difficult to finance their spending owing to the soaring cost of their government bonds. In September 2012, the ECB announced that it would purchase, if necessary, unlimited quantities of sovereign bonds from struggling eurozone member states. In an even more inventive interpretation of the rules, Draghi insisted that bond-buying was simply a by-product arising from the ECB carrying out its mandate of preserving a single monetary policy –

restoring a sense of economic interdependence in the currency union by trying to reduce the differences in government bond yields members were faced with merely came within the central bank's legal and political mandate.[17]

Outright Market Transactions (OMT), as the new departure from ECB orthodoxy was known, was meant to offer a two-year breathing space to put strategic reforms in place in distressed eurozone countries. But a short-tem gambit cannot blossom into a long-term agenda for recovery unless the EU is able to devise a growth-orientated strategy for the crisis-ridden parts of the eurozone. Instead, submission to austerity measures supervised by the troika of the ECB, Commission and IMF was to be a condition for obtaining access to OMT funding.[18]

The handling of Greece showed the level of confusion that continued to reign at the top of the EU. In February 2012, Luc Frieden, Luxembourg's Foreign Minister, had publicly warned that despite the accelerating contraction of the Greek economy, Greece had no choice but to persist with draconian austerity measures: 'If the Greek people or the Greek political elite do not apply all of these conditions, I think they exclude themselves from the eurozone.'[19] He even suggested that a return to the drachma 'might be something which would allow Greece also to get a new start, to create an economy that can create jobs'. But by September, a far more powerful figure, Chancellor Merkel, had adopted a very different position. Athens must be stopped from leaving the eurozone at all costs even if it meant massaging the figures in the forthcoming troika report on its performance in reducing state costs.[20] Greece's problems were to be put on ice until after the following year's Bundestag elections. Such inconsistency, after it seemed Greece was on the verge of being bundled out of the eurozone, showed the problem of designing and delivering on reforms meant to restore the eurozone to at least a precarious level of health.

The EFSF launched in May 2010, the LTRO in December 2011, and now in the autumn of 2012 the OMT were efforts to shield the banks from the effects of a monetary union involving disparate states in which the irresponsibility of many financial institutions had not been checked by those regulating the eurozone's financial affairs. The language of political union and economic governance for the eurozone used by Merkel and Draghi (despite his lack of any kind of political mandate) masked the fact that EU decision-makers had no viable strategy for reviving stricken economies.

The financial sector had not become a protected zone of the eurozone overnight. Ever since the passing of the Single European Act in 1986, its perceived needs had come to shape the concerns of EU decision-makers to an increasing degree. But with the arrival of monetary union, the concerns of this politically well-connected sector became uppermost. It was perhaps unavoidable given the extent to which the euro was not merely a technical monetary arrangement, but, in the words of Olli Rehn, 'the core political project of the EU'.[21]

The EU's twenty-first-century Maginot Line

For Merkel and Sarkozy, preserving the financial architecture of the eurozone became as big an article of faith as defending pre-1940 France had been by erecting a supposedly impenetrable Maginot Line. An expensive, protective shield would need to be thrown around banks, even if they were at the point of expiry through having overloaded their own bank balances with debt. There was no shortage of financial analysts who argued that a far less charitable stance towards many of Europe's banks was essential for the future viability of the regional economy. EU decision-makers were frequently reminded of the long-term irresponsibility of this protected sector. In the words of the US economist, James K. Galbraith: 'the European banks leveraged up to buy toxic American mortgages and when those collapsed they started dumping their weak sovereign bonds to buy strong ones, driving up yields and eventually forcing the whole European periphery into crisis. Greece was merely the first domino in the line.'[22]

Afterwards, financial chiefs pleaded surprise – 'no one could have known!' – and often blamed their clients for recklessness and cheating. They were not only listened to but extended a lifeline because of the widely held assumption that the eurozone's own survival was bound up with theirs. It became an article of faith that the banking sector needed to be shored up to prevent the financial convergence, a primary goal of EMU, from spreading contagion across the eurozone.

In the case of Ireland, this involved guaranteeing 'the assets and liabilities of some of the worst banks in the history of modern banking in the name of EU banking stability', which were to receive 'the largesse of the Troika as a result'.[23] In November 2010, the Irish government was coerced into the repayment at 100 per cent interest of unsecured and unguaranteed bondholders in bust banks. This crippling debt was imposed on the Irish Exchequer by the European Central Bank, outside the terms of the financial programme arranged days earlier with the EU and the IMF.

The economist Colm McCarthy has written: 'the ECB does not enjoy explicit powers to dictate the terms on which bust banks are to be resolved. It appears, however, to have assumed such powers, under the presidency of Jean-Claude Trichet, before and during the negotiation which led to the November 2010 rescue.' The terms were imposed against the advice of the IMF and in light of correspondence which the ECB has been determined to keep undisclosed.[24]

The main beneficiaries of Greek bail-out money have not been the country's economy but French and German banks. JP Morgan bank estimates that only €15 billion of €410 billion total aid to Greece went into the domestic economy; by far the bulk went to the nation's main creditors. Frances Coppola, an independent banking analyst, has argued that 'purchases of that debt were also effectively a rescue of the banks that were overexposed to Greek debt'.[25]

The 2013 IMF report criticising its own acquiescence in the EU-led approach to the Greek crisis had been leaked on 6 June, the day figures were released in Athens showing that 62 per cent of the country's under-25s were out of work. It clearly indicated that a poorly conceived austerity strategy had worsened the plight of Greece. Olli Rehn's spokesman, Simon O'Connor, brushed aside the criticism, observing that 'an assessment by some IMF staff does not reflect an official view'.[26] But on 7 June, his boss lashed out at IMF chief Christine Lagarde for apparently repudiating the common front with the EU: 'I don't think it's fair and just for the IMF to wash its hands and throw the dirty water on the Europeans.'[27] (Shortly afterwards, the head of the EU's bail-out fund, Klaus Regling, declared that the IMF should not play a role in the longer term in eurozone rescue packages.[28])

In the case of Germany alone, an estimated $353 billion (€270 billion) returned from the five crisis countries – Greece, Ireland, Portugal, Italy and Spain – in 2010 and 2011, a retreat to safety made possible by a policy of rein-forcing debt-ridden banks with EU taxpayers' money.[29] With inconvenient candour, the IMF report had lent powerful legitimacy to the claim that bereft of a strategy for the crisis, top EU decision-makers had made it their priority to defend well-placed interests irrespective of the colossal human damage that would be caused, eventually far beyond Greece itself.

In the case of Portugal, the main beneficiaries of the €78 billion bail-out which it obtained in May 2011 have been the Spanish banks which dominate its financial sector. (The ECB was prepared to accept Portuguese government debt as collateral for its loans to banks, even when it was downgraded to junk status, the decision breaking its own rules on credit quality.[30]) As for Ireland, the banks most exposed to its financial malaise are British, though closely followed by German ones.

Greece, along with Portugal and Ireland, has endured cuts in public spending of intensifying severity, leading to fears that depression conditions will be the norm for many years ahead. Opinion polls and the reaction of the media show huge indignation in Germany about Greek irresponsibility. But arguably much of it is misplaced. Reckless lending by German and French banks detonated the crisis of the eurozone. These favoured parts of the financial sector carried heavy responsibilities but they avoided retribution. Instead, they received trillions of euros in bail-out money. In a co-authored article, Simon Johnson, a former senior official at the IMF, expressed wonder-ment in the spring of 2012 that:

> many of the losses that bankers should have faced are being shouldered by the public sector, including through various forms of direct support and the extraordinary and risky actions of the European Central Bank. The extent of subsidies in this sector is stunning and, under current policies, will only

increase over time – thereby primarily supporting the lifestyles of the top 1 per cent of people in very rich countries.[31]

Banks in the eurozone, subject to a covert rescue, often have close links to the state administration and to the political world. This is nowhere truer than in France where retired mandarins sit on their boards and advise them on political strategy.[32] Insider arrangements link elite financiers and Eurocrats, and both see the value in the kinds of enhanced centralisation which Barroso was demanding in the autumn of 2012.

In Germany, at least away from the ailing Landesbanken in the country's federal regions, there is rather more transparency. But Coppola has argued that 'all the hard work that Germans put in to repair their economy after reunification is going to waste as their taxes and their savings are used to bail out banks, whether indirectly via sovereign bailouts or directly through infusions of capital'.[33]

Amidst the top-level squabbling about how to manage the crisis, common ground appears to have been found about the need to ringfence the banks. These favoured interests escaped pressure to open their books and, where necessary, acknowledge the scale of their huge losses and be wound up. Instead light-touch stress tests carried out by the ECB on a range of banks in mid-2010 were described as 'comprehensive and rigorous'. The exercise 'confirms the resilience of EU and euro area banking systems to major economic and financial shocks [and] ... represents an important step forward in supporting the stability of the EU and euro area banking sectors'. Within a few months, several of the Irish banks stress tested were shown to be toxic institutions but the air of serenity endured for a second set one year later, considered more rigorous and which focused on the Spanish banks. This exercise was hailed as 'an important tool to enhance transparency in the EU banking system. It provides for the disclosure of all the information that is relevant for the market to assess the resilience of the institutions in the context of an adverse scenario.'[34]

Many of these banks, from early 2012 onwards, were allowed to gorge themselves on ECB money to enable them to appear viable. Constantin Gurdgiev, a Dublin-based economic analyst, warned that 'by stuffing the banks with sovereign debt, European politicians and regulators are making the inevitable default much more financially dangerous'.[35]

The Icelandic exception

High priests of the European project had in the past recognised that it often advanced through crisis. Decision-makers after 2009 grew used to finding artful technocratic solutions that offered a temporary reprieve rather than concluding that the systemic problems thrown up by a half-baked monetary system required a thoroughgoing reappraisal. The lessons of Iceland were studiously ignored in Brussels and Frankfurt. Cheap credit had led to chronic mismanagement of the banking sector which collapsed in 2008. Instead of propping up the banks, the state let them go. Well over 70 per cent of businesses quickly became insolvent. But the banking system was cleaned up and the worst offenders prosecuted. By 2012, with the eurozone facing gathering storms, Iceland had 'a set of relatively clean bank balance sheets, a falling unemployment rate, an increase in economic output, and a national sense that the economy and the society is healing'.[36] In September 2012, the IMF released figures that anticipated a growth rate of 2.6 per cent for Iceland while that for the euro area was −0.3 per cent.[37]

The Icelandic government's return to international debt markets in June 2011 saw its bond offering subscribed twice over.[38] Iceland had resisted public overtures from the EU Commission's Olli Rehn to seek salvation in the EU and accept its approach to crisis. He promised that arrangements could be made for it to join as early as 2011 but it would mean adopting the euro as its currency.[39] Arguably, the retention of its own currency gave it vital breathing space. Iceland was able to sign up to an IMF programme that was focused on growth and which enabled the Reykjavik authorities, and not some neo-imperial troika, to decide where and how cuts were to be made.

Onwards to post-democracy

In 2010, José Manuel Barroso, the President of the Commission, had publicly warned that democracy was at stake unless austerity was embraced: 'Look, if they do not carry out these austerity packages, these countries could virtually disappear in the way that we know them as democracies. They've got no choice, this is it.'[40] But his insistence that citizens carry a crushing debt burden which, in most cases, had never been their responsibility perhaps was a stronger indication that a large part of the EU was itself clearly entering a post-democratic phase.

In his September 2012 'State of the Union' speech, Barroso once again invoked democracy, but his objective was 'deeper and genuine economic and monetary union' under a new treaty.[41] It would result in a new radical transfer of sovereignty to central institutions like the ECB but with no greater democratic oversight over its actions than was previously the case. Designing new machinery for the EU that gives ever tighter control to a swarm of political insiders is like a drug which the top EU decision-makers increasingly crave. It is not hard to see why. EU institutions which are beyond the voters' reach give politicians a span of influence and power that they could not hope to have in conventional democracies. Normally, they are out after one term (two at the most). But someone like Barroso can stay at the helm of the European Commission for a decade and even dream of a third term in charge (or else of switching to be the head of NATO). Guido Westerwelle, the German Foreign Minister, whose Free Democrat Party is fighting for its very survival, can busy himself with a commission of EU notables looking into 'the Future of Europe'. The report released in September 2012 advocated a European army and treaty changes arranged simply on the basis of qualified majority voting. A diplomat quoted by *Der Spiegel* remarked afterwards that the report 'is unimportant for the future of Europe, but is very important for the future of Westerwelle'.[42]

The genuine visionaries animated by a borderless Europe began with Monnet and Schuman and seem to have expired with the retirement of Jacques Delors and Helmut Kohl in the 1990s. The integration agenda in the last twenty years has increasingly been directed by the requirements of political expediency, a characteristic that has also shaped the management of the current crisis in specific ways.

Much of the initial enthusiasm for the euro had sprung from the anticipated gains for what are now seen as peripheral members. Debtor nations which had bought their sovereign debt before their eurozone membership could sell it more cheaply thanks to the low interest rate set for the currency. This financial cushion enabled them to postpone structural reform because of the ability 'to borrow a lifestyle [which] they were not generating'.[43]

It has been hard for many of the *dramatis personae* to conceal the way in which their own personal agendas shape their approach to the ordeal of the euro. Nicolas Sarkozy, who was one of the key crisis managers until mid-2012, seemed driven by the view that France needed to count in all circumstances. This made him team up with Angela Merkel, a politician for whom he had no noticeable affinity, in order to pursue a debt-busting strategy based on rigid austerity that appeared to draw France away from its natural partners in the rest of the eurozone's Latin bloc where it had strong banking and financial links.[44] France has a current account deficit as opposed to Germany's surplus and has steadily lost competitiveness against Germany. Arguably, the strategy of taking short-term measures to increase liquidity in the financial sector, rather than opting for a recapitalisation and restructuring of the banks, was not in the interests of the French economy. Plenty of analysts believed that 'kicking the can down the road' increased the likelihood that France would eventually come under the degree of pressure from the markets that confronted Spain and Italy in 2012. But the image of Franco-German coordination in the crisis played to the authority which, in the semi-monarchical Fifth Republic, French Presidents normally crave.

Germany was much more mindful of democratic procedures and the rule of law. Prominent past and serving Federal presidents, Roman Herzog and Christian Wulff, expressed dismay in public about the risks to democracy posed by the ECB being seen to exceed its mandate and the EU's treaties being viewed as expendable if they got in the way of particular crisis solutions.[45] Successive rulings by the German Constitutional Court on expanding EU powers received even more attention; in 2009, ruling on the Lisbon Treaty, it concluded that German constitutional law enjoyed supremacy over EU law as a permanent principle; in 2011 another ruling, this time on the bail-out machinery, stated that the Bundestag must not surrender its budgetary powers to a supra-national body on a permanent basis.[46]

Franco-German electoral timetables and the crisis

In France, no such checks and balances were visible. The temptation to override the rules of the EU in order to arrive at a solution which would convey decisive leadership was a constant temptation not just confined to Sarkozy and his neo-Gaullists. At different stages in the crisis, both Merkel and Sarkozy presented the other eurozone states with ready-made solutions worked out by their officials and with the Commission having scant input. Jean-Claude Juncker, who was supposed to coordinate policy among eurozone finance ministers, expressed public disgruntlement about Franco-German neo-imperialism on 1 May 2012.[47] By now Sarkozy was in the last stages of his re-election bid. In March, when a brief respite occurred over Greece, he had disingenuously proclaimed a breakthrough: 'How happy I am that a solution to the Greek crisis, which has weighed on the economic and financial situation in Europe and the world for months, has been found. Today the problem is solved.'[48]

Instead of edging Greece out of the eurozone, Germany and its allies had decided to impose heavy losses on holders of Greek bonds in order to reduce the Greek debt from around €350 billion to what was seen as a more sustainable €200 billion.[49] Economic activity was collapsing due to the impact of austerity which meant that Greece's volume of debts was inexorably rising. Numerous leading economists had looked at Greece's alarming economic figures and the impact of the EU's 'solution' known as 'expansionary fiscal contraction' and concluded that without a write-down of a substantial part of the country's debt, it had little viable economic future.[50]

Hitherto, senior EU decision-makers had blamed Greek hesitancy in swallowing the harsh economic medicine for the continuing crisis and, as seen, there were high-level calls for Greece to consider leaving the eurozone. This would have amounted to *de facto* expulsion and could have had an unwelcome impact on the forthcoming German elections. So such punitive rhetoric was cut back in mid-2012.

Hardly noticed at the time was the dire impact on Cypriot banks. They were already struggling due to the collapse of the Greek economy. Now they found themselves among the biggest casualties of this partial default due to the sheer scale of their remaining investments in Greece.

A more alert and less opportunistic set of decision-makers might have seen the need to recapitalise Cypriot banks as part of the March 2012 Greek deal in order to prevent a fresh emergency on the eurozone's exposed southern flank.[51] In the summer of 2012, the Cypriot authorities had approached Brussels with this objective in mind. Cyprus would actually hold the EU presidency in the second half of 2012. But negotiations on a possible EU bail-out were frozen until a general election in Cyprus in February 2013. There were warnings from financial experts that Cyprus had the potential to spark another phase of the eurozone crisis.[52] But Cyprus and more systemic aspects of European crisis management were being placed on hold with repercussions that few could have imagined when the mishandling of Cyprus detonated, arguably creating the worst stage of the eurozone crisis in March 2013.[53]

From mid-2012 at least, Chancellor Merkel had been shaping policy on the Greek crisis around her own looming re-election battle, regardless of the fact that such a stratagem had not saved Sarkozy from defeat. But she was a more complex and skilful crisis manager. Her low-key and patient approach was a foil to Sarkozy's histrionics and quixotic style. She endured taunts from Silvio Berlusconi and, more importantly, obtained crucial endorsement from her chief domestic rival, the SPD, for her policy of ensuring that eurozone members lived within their means to try and bring sovereign debt levels down. The fiscal compact which enshrined the austerity approach went through several versions in 2011–12. Merkel combined an appetite for personal power with an ability to occasionally speak for the European general interest (even though for much of the time it seemed that only German industry benefited from her advocacy of a deflationary approach).

Occasionally, to appease the populist tabloids like the influential *Bild*, she singled out weaker eurozone members as culprits for the crisis. To a major domestic opponent like the SPD's Sigmar Gabriel, such playing to the gallery was 'gambling away the European idea'.[54] Commentators, some in Germany, most beyond its borders, appealed to Merkel to speak with candour to German citizens about the origins of the crisis. Merkel insisted that Germany had a sound model. In a speech to her party in 2010, she made a point of defending Germany's export-led model, which many say has contributed to the euro's problems, adding: 'We will not allow ourselves to be punished for something that we do well. We'll not allow ourselves to be whipped because we export good products, made in Germany, all around the world.'[55] Candid discussion about the feasibility of a single currency experiment involving a country with Germany's industrial prowess and a swarm of others unable, in virtually any scenario imaginable, to come anywhere near it in terms of economic efficiency remained off the table.

What was far less often heard was the claim that Germany had achieved its enviable position not just because of the productivity of its labour force or frugality of its savers but because for much of the time, ECB strategy appeared designed to reinforce Germany's advantages.

Little public self-examination was evident about the readiness of German banks and investment companies to underwrite debt in the Mediterranean eurozone area over a prolonged period. Successive German governments had encouraged such a stance, presumably because the domestic economy appeared to be thriving as a result of high demand for German manufactured products from debtor members. German banks continued to be informed that the sovereign debt of eurozone members could be carried on their books risk-free. This assessment continued to be accepted even after 2008 as these countries grew steadily less creditworthy.[56] Martin Wolf, a leading columnist on the *Financial Times*, was in no doubt that creditor nations like Germany played a big role in bringing the crisis to a head. He expressed dismay about the unwillingness in Germany 'to recognise the link between the external surpluses of core countries and the financial fragility of the periphery'. Instead 'the focus remains overwhelmingly on fiscal indiscipline'.[57]

There was no lack of evidence that Merkel's Finance Minister, Wolfgang Schäuble, was pursuing his own personal agenda during the marathon crisis. Born in 1943 and confined to a wheelchair after an assassination attempt in 1990, he made no secret of his ardent desire to drive Europe towards economic governance of which the fiscal compact was merely the first step.[58] Greece scarcely featured in his vision and in the spring of 2012, he appeared ready to jettison Greece from the eurozone unless politicians and voters accepted the austerity formula laid down by the troika. This willingness to reconfigure the eurozone to preserve wider integration objectives had already brought an indignant response from Michel Rocard, a former French Prime Minister now sitting in the European Parliament. He believed that excluding states was entirely ruled out by the eurozone's founding treaties and warned Germany against being 'prepared to destabilise the zone and common currency to meet its own policy ends'.[59]

By the autumn of 2012, the evidence was clear that Merkel had had second thoughts on Greece. The survival of semi-orderly life and even the stability of the Eastern Mediterranean appeared capable of being jeopardised by any precipitate moves. The bill for Germany arising from a Greek exit from the eurozone was estimated at no less than €62 billion. She accepted advice that Greece should be extended more money in the short term to meet its costs, but later transfers would be reduced.[60] The prospects for Greece looked bleak, especially when it was revealed that the budget gap was higher than the previously assumed €30 billion.[61] But the troika's report on its prospects, due in October, was postponed until the end of the year. It also meant that President Obama would not be diverted from campaigning for re-election by a new stage of the eurozone crisis. If luck was on Merkel's side, she could face her own election battle without the trauma of an impending Greek exit.

Merkel proved herself to be a cool-headed political manager able to balance interests and opinions across the German and indeed a large part of the European scene. But she lacked the imagination to see that the organisation of the monetary union itself was defective and that the case for an overhaul, reducing the chronic imbalances between the few creditor nations and the growing number of indebted and ailing ones, was increasingly harder to refute. She was fortunate that the European Parliament showed no inclination to play a strong role as a forum where not only the merits of different approaches to the crisis were argued out, but a more rational approach was championed.

Europe's money men rescued by the new rules

The ever-widening democratic deficit was revealed by the increasing assertiveness of Mario Draghi, soon after becoming head of the ECB in November 2011. The decision to throw cheap loans at eurozone banks was his signal that he thought the crisis entitled the ECB to interpret its mandate in sweeping ways. Re-distributing economic risks and rewards throughout the eurozone, from the winter of 2011 onwards, occurred with only a veneer of democratic oversight. Arguably, the ECB was bidding to become a new and unassailable force in the EU landscape approaching the first anniversary of his appointment.[62] This began to be the verdict after Barroso announced in September 2012 that the ECB would be given responsibility for supervising 6,000 banks across the eurozone. It would be able to revoke banking licences, fine banks up to 10 per cent of their revenues, remove members of their boards and, crucially, coordinate future bail-outs of failing banks using taxpayer funds.[63] There was no note of circumspection about the ECB's successive low-grade inspection of banks after the crisis had started and how they had probably saddled European taxpayers with a bill of many hundreds of billions of euros.

Given the chronic democratic deficit in the EU, there appears to be little chance that financiers who presided over irresponsible banking will be hauled before any assembly in the eurozone to explain their actions. In the mid-1930s, congressional hearings in America brought to light the frauds and abuses that contributed to the Wall Street crash of 1929. A smart and determined former assistant district attorney from New York, Ferdinand Pecora, electrified Depression-era America with his relentless and expert grilling of bankers and regulators in hearings fully open to the public.[64] Banks were forced, under threat of criminal prosecution, to disclose their full balance sheets. Those beyond repair were broken up. Retail and investment banking were separated, root-and-branch, by the Glass-Steagall Act. Nobody in the EU hierarchy appears capable of playing the role that this fearless and highly effective son of a Sicilian shoemaker performed, helping to bring the curtain down on an era of banking excess. The European Court of Justice, thrilled by its role in preparing the judicial framework for political union, shows no sign of ending its subservience to those carrying out integration by autocratic means.

After examining the contrasting approaches to banking excesses, the British financial journalist Liam Halligan reckoned that Europe's political leaders 'are cowed by the money-men, caught between awe and financial dependence. Many Western banks remain beyond full-audit. Those guilty of serious "white collar crime" have sailed away, their riches intact, leaving nothing in their wake but financial and human destruction.'[65]

In Ireland, the reality of a parliament with few inquisitorial powers and very lax legal sanctions towards white-collar crime meant that senior bank officials remained beyond the reach of the law despite shocking revelations about their conduct at the start of the country's financial crisis in 2008. Leaked tape conversations, published in 2013, indicated that bank chiefs in Dublin had duped the government so that huge sums were injected into the failing Anglo-Irish Bank on the basis that its problems merely stemmed from temporary illiquidity.[66] The bankers had mocked German savers and one had disparagingly sung 'Deutschland über alles'; Chancellor Merkel, in response, said that such revelations damaged democracy and conceded that the disrespectful tone towards the wider society appeared to be a common problem in the banking community – in Ireland, Germany and elsewhere.[67]

Plans for a banking union and a 'super regulator' in charge of all savings, and 'deeper and genuine economic and monetary union', all possibly confirmed by yet another treaty, dominated EU discussions at senior level from the autumn of 2012 onwards. In response to calls from France, Italy and Spain in June 2012, Merkel accepted that the European Stability Mechanism (ESM), the eurozone's bail-out fund, could 'have the possibility to recapitalize banks directly'.[68] But this was going too far for a cross-section of opinion in the Bundestag.[69] It soon became clear that Germany, historically committed to common rules of European integration binding on all, was lukewarm about fiscal integration.

A meaningful banking union appeared pointless without a common supervisor, a centrally funded deposit insurance scheme, and a taxpayer-friendly and jointly funded resolution scheme in the face of banking difficulties.[70] But by the end of 2012, it was apparent that Merkel was unhappy about a single banking supervisor (originally her own idea), about giving a key oversight role to the ECB, and even about the idea of including all of Germany's banks in the scheme.[71] It almost seemed that Germany wished to direct Europe's financial affairs through a model that primarily benefited Germany irrespective of the damage being done to a mounting list of eurozone countries unable to insulate themselves from the crisis.[72]

In March 2013, the Netherlands admitted that it would be joining the ranks of countries not abiding by the EU's target of keeping budget deficits under 3 per cent of GDP. Olli Rehn said that the penalties supposed to be applied on countries with a deficit overshoot would be withheld because the long-term prospects of the Netherlands appeared good and its government was taking 'effective action'.[73]

It was the Dutch government which, in September 2011, actually proposed that highly indebted states be put into 'guardianship', with spending decisions seized from the elected government and placed under the direct control of a European commissioner.[74] It had grown less hawkish as its own troubles mounted and it expected and received leniency from the rule-setters presumably because of its adherence to the 'no turning back' approach to managing the crisis. Such double standards are obviously nothing new in the wider sweep of European history, despite the EU's claim to offer a fresh start in terms of the continent's governance: Giovanni Giolitti, the Italian politician whose corrupt liberal regime was swept aside by Mussolini in 1922, had observed: 'laws are applied to enemies, but only interpreted as regards friends'.[75]

In the year of the euro's launch, a British journalist had observed that Brussels lacked an administrative culture in which there were agreed rules: 'what is cronyism in one country is legitimate use of patronage in another and such practices have seeped into the hybrid Brussels bureaucracy'.[76] The post-2009 crisis had shown the continued addiction to discretionary approaches to issues of fateful importance for the future of millions of Europeans. Banks have been given successive clean bills of health in stress tests which in the early phases of the crisis were plainly bogus or unprofessional. In mid-2011, the European Commission stress tested Spain's banks, and declared that the government had more than enough resources to cover any liquidity needs.[77] But a year later it was publicly acknowledged that many of the same banks were riddled with toxic assets requiring another massive EU rescue.[78] In fact it soon emerged that more than half of the large and medium-sized banks in Spain are partially or wholly dependent on state support. Only Spain's three largest banks were both fully independent and well capitalised.[79] Yet according to the editor of one of Spain's leading daily newspapers, *El Mundo*, Prime Minister Mariano Rajoy texted his Finance Minister Luis de Guindos, who was engaged in tense bail-out negotiations in Brussels:

Resist, we are the 4th power of the EZ [eurozone]. Spain is not Uganda.

A follow-up message has been translated as:

We are powerful, and if they don't give in, the whole thing will go down. It will cost Europe 500 billion if Spain goes bust, and then another 700 billion if Italy goes bust.[80]

Such behaviour by a top-level leader suggests that EU decision-makers do not belong on any superior moral plane politically. Stripping away the lofty rhetoric about solidarity and enhanced unity, infighting and low blows are not hard to detect. This is how it was in 1931 when Germany signed a trade agreement with Austria. From pure pique, France deployed her economic muscle to bring down the largest Austrian bank, the Wiener Kreditanstalt, in May of that year. It led to a German banking crisis and perhaps more than anything paved the way for the rise of Adolf Hitler.[81]

The European right persists with corporatism

It is hard to see how supervisory control of banks could work when big countries demanded and expected preferential treatment in their hour of difficulty. This has been a longstanding practice in the EU and it is arguably the determination of successive ECB leaders, Trichet and Draghi, to safeguard particular sectoral and national interests which helps to explain why the ECB approach to the crisis has been erratic for so much of the time. However, the case for overhauling failing institutions at the centre of monetary Europe lacks decisive backing among the major state players in the eurozone. Their politicians are locked into the prototype European semi-state to varying degrees; politicians who believe it is the central institutions which need to be subject to a searching cost–benefit analysis, and not national economies and taxpayers, are often dismissed in withering terms.

Italy's unelected Prime Minister Mario Monti blundered while on a visit to Germany in August 2012 by seeming to instruct national governments to ignore their parliaments. Speaking to *Der Spiegel*, Monti said, 'If governments allow themselves to be completely bound by the decisions of their parliaments without maintaining some room for manoeuvre in international negotiations, then a break-up of Europe will be more likely than closer integration.' Invariably for Eurocrats it is the actions of national players rather than the actions or inactions of those in charge of the European institutions which imperil the continent's future. Even an ardent integrationist like Foreign Minister Westerwelle felt obliged to state that 'parliamentary control over European policy is out of any discussion. We need to reinforce, not weaken, democratic legitimacy in Europe.'[82]

Such weariness with already much-diminished parliamentary sovereignty only revived memories of pre-war corporatists like the Belgian Hendrik de Man who believed that corporate planning at European level, completely sidestepping national parliaments, was the only viable course for the future (see Chapter 2). Within a month, Monti had identified a fresh menace, anti-Euro populism; in September 2012, he called for heads of government to convene to discuss how to contain mounting signs of disunity and populism in the region.[83] This smacked of the desire to institute a Holy Alliance against nationalism of the kind Europe had witnessed between the defeat of Napoleon and the 1848 revolutions.

Leading technocrats, by their statements and repeated variations of centralising proposals for European governance, see voters only getting in the way of their schemes. Not a few have scant connections with voters or party activists in the seventeen eurozone states. Believing that electorates are disqualified from being able to properly evaluate key issues on which Europe's progress depends places them in dangerous company.[84] Communist leaderships in the pre-1989 'People's Democracies' of Europe repeatedly demonstrated that the people could not be relied upon to express an independent judgement about the supposed progress being carried out in their name.

Wilful technocrats like Monti, Draghi and Barroso have been able to unveil bold plans for tight managerial control of European affairs owing to the failure of the major wings of European democratic politics to preserve intellectual creativity and maintain firm links with the active producers in society. The ascendancy of the political right appears increasingly short-lived thanks in part to the elevation of leaders whose agendas often mirror those of the already privileged sectors in society. Sarkozy and Berlusconi proved unable to turn austerity conditions into an opportunity to reform sclerotic public institutions. Britain's David Cameron has proven to be a colourless and irresolute figure from a public relations background who is out of touch with Britain's 'coping classes'.[85] Mariano Rajoy is a sly, provincial politician who, at crucial points since becoming Prime Minister of Spain in November 2011, has shown a dramatic failure to understand the magnitude of his country's economic crisis. His complacency and amateurism may even place at risk the democratic settlement of the past thirty-five years and Spain's own territorial continuation as a single state.[86] When in office much of the European centre-right has shown itself to be prepared to turn a deaf ear to the problems of the middle and lower classes and adapt an un-critical or complacent stance to poorly performing European institutions whether it be the banking industry or the EU itself.[87]

The European left: impotence and collusion

The European left's chances brightened despite the failure of previous Social Democratic attempts to enable the market to successfully co-exist with high levels of taxation, regulation and welfare spending. In the summer of 2012, plenty of attention beyond Germany was given to the memorandum that Jürgen Habermas and other post-Frankfurt School philosophers drew up which called for restoring, at the European level, 'the sovereignty stolen by financial markets'.[88] This would involve moving rapidly ahead with proposals to centralise mutually binding fiscal, economic and welfare policies at the European level after consent had been acquired by consulting citizens through national referenda.

At the age of 85, Habermas was even invited to help draft the manifesto of the German Social Democratic Party for the 2013 federal elections at a time when the party seems prepared to change its eurozone policy by backing collective debt liability in exchange for stricter budgetary oversight. The need to transfer even more authority to those wedded to top-down solutions was cloaked in quasi-Jacobin language. Habermas and emulators like the British economist Will Hutton have been silent about the type of elitist power align-ments that have sprung up within EU structures.[89] They seem to expect that 'more Europe' can lead to a hopeful new paradigm in which progressive politics can flourish once again even though the ones making the decisions are likely to be the same senior bureaucrats and Europhile politicians weighed down by failures in the era of the single currency. Martine Aubry, the daughter of Jacques Delors and a power in France's ruling Socialist Party, is likely to be an influential advocate of maintaining France's social model based on high taxes and a rigid labour market, combined with centralising measures that turn the EU into a transfer union.[90]

But the German public is allergic to the kind of solidarity that involves financing deficits in states disinclined to adopt the labour reforms that a previous SPD Chancellor, Gerhard Schröder, introduced after 2000. It is just one of the awkward facts that lie in the way of Habermas's visionary blueprint. Many Germans already feel they have cause to be wary about transferring a significant chunk of Germany's GDP to the peripheral states indefinitely if the euro is to survive. Arguably, the much stronger dollar is helped to survive as a single currency by sometimes very large annual fiscal transfers from economically stronger to weaker regions.[91] During the era of the single currency, the eurozone's economic divergences have vastly expanded and may soon be poised to overtake those between different parts of the USA.

Ironically, both Habermas and Oskar Lafontaine, the leading SPD figure when the Berlin Wall came down in 1989, were opposed to going down the unification road for their country in the early 1990s. This was not due to the likely cost but because this historic event appeared to be breathing unnecessary life into the dying corpse of the nation-state. 'The Germans,' Lafontaine argued, 'on the basis of their recent history, are virtually pre-destined to be the driving force in the supra-national process of European unification.'[92] According to Lafontaine, the nation-state was simply no longer capable of mastering global problems.[93] But by 2013 he had recanted, joining others on the radical left like the leader of the powerful Communist Party in Portugal, Jeronimo de Sousa, in condemning the euro's impact on large parts of the continent: 'Hopes that the creation of the euro would force rational economic behaviour on all sides were in vain,' according to Lafontaine, adding that the policy of forcing Spain, Portugal and Greece to carry out internal devaluations was a 'catastrophe'.[94]

European integration was already proving to be a boon, not for unionised workers but in very large measure for multinational firms which enjoyed cosy ties both with EU institutions and with the core member states. Much of the European left now finds itself in the paradoxical situation of defending a monetary arrangement whose leading beneficiary has been the distrusted financial sector. It is not hard to make the case that, by contrast, lower-income groups in numerous countries have fared far less well from the introduction of the euro and face gloomy prospects owing to internal devaluation and the accompanying savage economic contraction.

Thomas Pascoe, a British financial analyst, wrote in 2012:

the working classes are enduring appalling deprivations in order to sustain a financial system which benefits the wealthy ... by allowing their assets to remain denominated in 'hard' currency. Instead, the survival of the euro – an arrangement which has produced 25 per cent unemployment in Spain, left public-sector workers unpaid for six month stretches in Greece, and will eventually beggar France – is considered a worthy object of public policy.[95]

Habermas appears to have lost sight of the fact that across much of the continent, European Socialism is now largely in the hands of dedicated careerists, uttering empty phrases about Socialist solidarity in a continental union dominated by economic cartels against which they only mount token resistance. For them, grand projects like the eurozone still have a mesmeric attraction even when mired in crisis. Perhaps the career of the rising German Social Democrat Jörg Asmussen helps to bear this claim out. At the time when the bail-out was imposed on Ireland, he was the most senior official in the German finance ministry advising Wolfgang Schäuble, who played a key role in this event. He himself later played a key role in supervising the austerity-without-growth policy that the troika imposed on Ireland. On 12 April 2012, while in Dublin on one of these inspections, he made a significant admission. He related that 'the main reasoning [behind the bail-out] was to ensure that no negative spillover effects would be created to other Irish banks or to banks in other European countries'.[96] In other words the imperative was to ringfence the badly managed and over-extended banks in core Europe. It was the first time that a leading ECB official had been so candid. In light of such an admission, it is not hard to view the bail-out as one where it is Ireland which was coming to the rescue of the Franco-German axis at that time regulating the workings of the eurozone.

Everyone for himself

The haircuts which junior and senior bondholders were spared in Ireland would be imposed almost with gusto in Cyprus during the financial emergency of March 2013. Not just these investors but shareholders and large depositors in leading banks risked being wiped out under the terms of an EU-imposed deal to avoid bankruptcy. Unlike the Irish case, there were few central European investors in the Cypriot financial sector. Chancellor Merkel actually told parliamentarians in Berlin that to remain in the eurozone, Cyprus had to recognise that it had no future as an offshore financial centre for wealthy Russians and Britons.[97] A PR campaign had accompanied the build-up to the EU-imposed settlement, finalised during the early hours of 25 March, which questioned the integrity of the Cypriot financial model and the clients which it had carried out business with.

Athanasios Orphanides, who had sat on the board of the ECB through being head of his country's central bank for four years, slated his former colleagues: 'I would have expected them to support the European project. I would have expected them to protect the citizens of the smallest and weakest member states against discrimination. We have seen a cavalier attitude towards the expropriation of property and the bullying of a people.' He added that the treatment of Cyprus had made 'a mockery' of EU treaties, indicating that 'in Europe not all people are equal under the law' and he offered the prediction that 'the European project is crashing to earth. This is a fundamental change in the dynamics of Europe towards disintegration and I don't see how this can be reversed.'[98]

Understandably, investors were likely to forsake financial centres on the uncertain edge of the eurozone for core countries, especially the dwindling few with triple A credit ratings. During key moments in the crisis, Cyprus had been characterised as a shady island which deliberately sought out illicit financial business (Pierre Moscovici, the French Finance Minister, branding it 'a casino economy that was on the brink of bankruptcy').[99] However, according to a study published by the Tax Justice Network that examined 70 countries, Germany is currently one of the biggest havens for tax evasion – ranking even above Switzerland, the Cayman Islands, Luxembourg or Jersey.[100] The European Commission had already launched an infringement procedure against Germany due to the hesitancy of its financial authorities in pursuing money laundering. The German police, in a 2013 report, admitted that transactions from Italy, Russia, Ukraine and Belarus were proving increasingly problematic, all of which put claims about Cyprus's delinquency in perspective.

At the height of the Cyprus drama Olli Rehn issued one of his trademark sophoric statements that 'Cyprus and the Cypriot people are a part of the European family. The European Union stands by them and will help to rebuild the Cypriot economy.'[101] But there was too much evidence that it was now a case of everyone for himself. Increasingly, creditor countries were lukewarm about using the bail-out fund (the ESM) to recapitalise troubled banks, according to its chief, Klaus Regling, in March 2013.[102]

Real solidarity was vanishing partly because EMU has resulted in the participating economies having increasingly divergent needs and performances. Disagreement has turned into acrimony over how to narrow the imbalances in ways that do not undermine the cooperative values upon which the EU is supposedly founded.

Tensions between the core and the periphery of the eurozone have often been searing ones, particularly in the case of Greece and Germany, but these have been present also between the creditor countries regarding how tough the austerity measures to be imposed on the 'laggards' of the eurozone should be. In September 2011, Prime Minister Rutte's proposal that highly indebted states be put into 'guardianship' had been co-signed by his leading ministers, and submitted to the Dutch parliament.[103] Finland meanwhile caused ructions with Germany and the Netherlands by seeking a bilateral deal with Greece by which it was promised collateral (gold reserves being mentioned) in return for contributing to the second Greek bail-out.[104] By August 2012, Erkki Tuomioja, Finland's Foreign Minister, was voicing public suspicions about the existence of a 'gang of four' EU insiders – including the European Central Bank's Mario Draghi – whom he accused of trying to ensnare member states into some form of fiscal union: 'I don't trust these people', was his terse view.[105] Such open mistrust does not bode well for rescue efforts. The agreement of all seventeen eurozone members is required to approve aid and if one of the countries breaks ranks, it could torpedo efforts to contain the crisis.[106]

Rivalries also exist between distressed states on the periphery. Some claim that their particular ranking merits more considerate treatment from the ECB even though their problems are approaching, in scale and intensity, those of the first countries to have their financial affairs subject to oversight by the troika. After Spain obtained €100 billion from the EFSF rescue fund to recapitalise the country's stricken banks, Rajoy was quick to claim that he had secured a no-strings-attached rescue from the eurozone. He said it had 'nothing to do' with the procedures imposed on Greece, Ireland and Portugal. But Germany's Wolfgang Schäuble poured cold water on his claims, stating that 'of course there will be a troika' for Spain.[107]

Introspection and caution: Germany sits tight

For a large part of the crisis, pitting Germany against much of the rest of the eurozone, Schäuble has articulated the view that its troubled peripheral states must return to competitiveness through a lengthy dose of austerity. 'Adjustment' programmes based on virtuous northern rules must be applied in ailing parts of the eurozone. Balanced budgets so as to keep the currency sound must be the goal, even at a cost that requires formerly middle-class people in the periphery to seek charity or scrabble in rubbish bins.

Germany's recovery from its post-unification economic difficulties was not, however, just a story of applying sturdy Teutonic virtues. It was aided by an inflationary boom in the rest of Europe and a sympathetic attitude from the ECB regarding interest rates.[108] To be sure, the stoicism and discipline of German society played their own substantial part, but it appears myopic to expect peripheral countries, ones with much greater problems than Germany had, to return to competitiveness through deflation. Collapsing production and falling tax receipts suggests that full-scale depressions may be what awaits them. Biting austerity has had little impact on debt levels in a string of crisis-hit countries. Growth rates posted by the ECB and IMF have been repeatedly exposed as hopelessly unrealistic. It is possible that the return of countries like Ireland to the bond markets will be undermined and that approaching half the countries in the eurozone will topple over into financial crisis.

Proponents of austerity see it as an elixir enabling stricken countries to eventually compete with Germany and a handful of other robust eurozone economies. With its uniquely strong industrial base, Germany is simply not a country capable of being emulated. The euro has given German exporters a very favourable exchange rate, perhaps 40 per cent below what it would be if it still used the Deutschmark.[109] It has also benefited from very low borrowing costs caused by money flowing to Germany as a safe haven.

Germany's perspective on the crisis prevailed until Sarkozy's electoral defeat in May 2012, and was summed up by Angela Merkel's regularly repeated statement that 'there can be no shared burdens without shared controls'.[110] For most of the crisis even the SPD turned its face against Eurobonds which would have been loans raised in common by the members of the eurozone for distribution among member states. Issuing bonds to hoover up debt appeared a dangerous unorthodoxy, indeed a reversal to the monetary debasement of the 1920s. It was conveniently forgotten in many quarters that the mis-investment of bank and pension fund savings in high interest-rated peripheral banks had, in no small measure, led to the post-2008 crisis. But there was implacable opposition to mutualisation of debt or long-term fiscal transfers.

At torrid points in the crisis Merkel has made tactical concessions to stave off a collapse of financial institutions in a growing number of peripheral countries and prevent a bond market run on Italy. Some claim that she has been using political skills (ones in short supply elsewhere in the eurozone) to soften up German opinion towards accepting burden-sharing. But that is likely to be a very difficult high-wire act to perform.

Disgruntlement has grown as the ECB's Mario Draghi has demonstrated his belief that money needs to be used as a tool to achieve desired outcomes such as economic growth. This highly pragmatic view contrasts with the German view of the euro as a common good protected by treaties and laws and not the plaything of a government or even the ECB. In the Bundesbank's view, 'the economy adapts to money, not the other way around'.[111] Draghi's massive bond-buying operation under his Outright Market Transactions (OMT) scheme led Jens Weidmann to make a comparison with Mephisto's money-printing idea in Goethe's novel *Faust*.[112] The Bundesbank's chief representative on the ECB's governing council found himself isolated. Especially with the return to power of the French left, the initiative appeared (at least for a time) to be with those prepared to abandon the remaining rules on which the currency union was based, to avert economic calamity. But given the strong economic cards it holds, a new policy mix based on loosening economic controls in the North to encourage growth in the periphery, as well as radical interventions to prop up threatened national financial systems, requires German participation.

Draghi's audacious bond-buying operation would not have got very far without leading German decision-makers being won over. Merkel and Schäuble were persuaded by the danger that the markets posed to Spain and Italy and by the strategy of releasing support only in return for guarantees of bold reforms. On the day after Draghi announced his plans for what would shortly be known as OMT, Schäuble issued a clear statement of support while Merkel offered more circumspect backing. The Bundesbank by contrast had earlier in the day attacked bond-buying as 'problematic'. Its criticism would not subside even as it became clear that Draghi indeed had majority support on the ECB board and the ear of Germany's two most powerful politicians. On 1 August 2012, the day before the ECB's governing council ratified OMT, Weidmann declared in an interview that: 'We are the largest and most important central bank in the Eurosystem and we have a greater say than many other central banks.'[113] He also had the support of the bulk of the German media, not just tabloids like *Bild* which had believed that Draghi would be an orthodox ECB chief, approvingly describing him in 2011 as 'rather German, even really Prussian'.[114] But Draghi proved to be the more effective politician, who had the negotiating skills to sell his case for a more activist central bank. Gunnar Beck, a German academic, complained about him on account of 'his Goldman Sachs affiliation, his background in Rome's intrigue-ridden corridors of power, his sardonic smile and his "cheap money" policies', believing Draghi to be 'the antithesis of the solidity and conservative integrity postwar Germans came to expect from a central banker'.[115]

This episode sharply illustrates another fault-line: that between domestic politicians, sometimes in the same political camp, who base their approaches to the crisis on national or else European priorities. Schäuble is firmly European in orientation while 'Merkel favours more Europe as long as it benefits her. But as soon as she has any doubts, she tends to favour a little less Europe.'[116] Overall, Germany no longer responds in a Pavlovian fashion to an appeal for it to display European solidarity. This was shown in a September 2012 poll which might signify a powerful change of attitude towards the EU. Commissioned by *Die Welt*, it showed that 49 per cent of Germans think they would be better off without the EU, as against only 32 per cent who think they would suffer.[117] German society, contrary to impressions elsewhere, does not necessarily have strong grounds for being enthusiastic about the euro. Since 1998, shortly before its introduction, Germany's real disposable incomes have risen remarkably little, as has consumption.[118] Many analysts and media pundits fear that whatever the final outcome of the crisis, it will be the turn of the Germans to face their hour of 'adjustment' and pay substantially for any ultimate stabilising of the financial landscape of Europe. By March 2013, there was a new choice for Germans distrustful of the establishment's handling of the marathon euro crisis and who desired the return of the Deutschmark: 26 per cent of voters in one poll that month stated they would consider supporting the Alternative for Germany but it was only expected to make an impact by the time of the European elections of 2014 (it got 4.7 per cent of votes in the Bundestag elections later in 2013, more than pollsters had predicted but not enough to obtain seats).[119]

Centrifugal tensions and splits

German unhappiness about carrying the European periphery is bound to be influenced by the arduous and costly effort to try and make the unification of the country a success. In twenty years, net transfers from west to east have topped €1.6 trillion. That exceeds by far the original estimates of the costs of the union, €60 billion having been allotted to the original fund for German unification. The former East Germany takes in little in taxes and is faced with high pension and unemployment payments.[120] So Germany has a very direct experience of a transfer union at work and it is bound to fuel real doubts about the wisdom of going down a similar path for a large part of the eurozone. Also there are emerging North–South tensions with north-western states relying increasingly on the revenues coming from Bavaria, Baden-Wurttemberg and Hesse. Germany may have become a byword for electoral stability in an increasingly fractious Europe but it is naive to assume that such fault-lines will not be politicised even in the near future.

Draghi should be only too well aware of far worse and longer-term centrifugal tensions in Italy which have shown how territorially fractured this historically poorly performing state has become. Spain was not far into its financial emergency before they erupted there. For thirty-five years it has possessed a costly and complex system of autonomy. This is not altogether dissimilar to the power-sharing formula which was fashionable in the Delors era where a 'Europe of the regions' was promoted to enable sub-national units across the EU to be the service deliverers for EU projects. On Catalonia's national day, 11 September 2012, as many as 1.5 million people demonstrated against encroaching Madrid centralism with many in favour of outright independence. But the main achievement of most of the regions has been to provide an often unproductive and costly extra layer of bureaucracy; Spain's regions share over 200 regional embassies abroad, the Catalan one in New York City being housed in the Rockefeller centre, with the city's most expensive rent.[121]

Sweden, normally an unobtrusive EU member, has criticised proposed plans for a banking union in the eurozone for its possible negative impact on non-members like itself.[122] In Britain, there has been indignation about proposals, first emanating from Nicolas Sarkozy, for a financial transaction tax designed to raise new revenue streams in order to cope with the crisis. This would be combined with much tougher regulation of financial services, measures viewed as a barely concealed attempt to undermine London's role as home for the world's chief financial services industry. The only other European centre in the top ten is Zurich, with Frankfurt and Paris languishing at 16 and 24 respectively in the league.[123] The British Conservative MEP Daniel Hannan has argued that smaller companies would be most adversely affected by these extensions of EU power. Of the one million people in the financial services industry in Britain, half belong to firms with fewer than 200 employees (hedge funds, equity firms). A requirement to comply not just with UK regulations but with EU ones could put many of them out of business.[124]

Hannan claims that major banks and investment companies actually 'crave regulation', knowing the strains it places on their smaller rivals.[125] They have the resources to handle compliance but, more importantly, the political leverage that enables them to avoid onerous compliance. The despised financial services industry happens to be the biggest in Britain but it lacks defenders in Brussels due, in part, to the shrinking degree of British influence to be found at the upper echelons of the EU. A mere seventeen Britons work in the 544-strong Commission's increasingly powerful economics directorate, which assesses EU countries' economic performances and issues policy recommendations. There are no Britons in the cabinet of the Budget Commissioner Olli Rehn.[126] Governments often work hard to insert their co-nationals into strategic parts of the Brussels bureaucracy, knowing that it enables regulations to be shaped in their favour. Not surprisingly, Britain finds itself open to attack as symbolising the speculators and 'pirates' lying off the coast of Europe, responsible for the euro's ills.[127]

By contrast, the quasi-nationalised banks in a major EU player like France have close links with the EU establishment and overt criticism from the media and MEPs of their conduct has been light. Michel Barnier, the Commissioner for the Internal Market, has persisted in endorsing Sarkozy's plans for a financial services tax.[128] EU taxpayers inside and outside the eurozone have already been compelled to rescue European banking mammoths whose greed and recklessness contributed to the post-2008 crisis. This has been done under the disguise of rescuing particular countries which have actually seen very little of the bail-out funds that have been allocated in recent years.

The claim that the EU in its present form can be a long-term guarantor of peace and stability in Europe is not helped by the warfare occurring barely under the surface to obtain economic spheres of influence. Claims about Anglo-Saxon freebooters who need to be cut down to size come as often from the political right in mainland Europe as from the left. Elmer Brok, a veteran MEP representing the German Christian Democrats, regularly offers variations on this theme of 'Anglo-American interests' conspiring against the EU's well-being.[129] Large financial institutions dream of displacing London as the centre where 70 per cent of investment capital in Europe is run from, replacing it instead with a unified euro centre in Frankfurt. Banks, along with trans-European energy and defence corporations, are careful to ensure that policy-makers in Brussels, as well as in national capitals, are wooed to ensure that they have a stake in the outcome of such plans. The decision of ratings agencies to downgrade financial institutions and individual countries during the protracted crisis has produced angry reactions on cultural grounds.

Plans for the kind of regulation causing alarm in Britain were included in the Treaty on Stability, Coordination and Governance in the European Monetary Union which was ratified by twenty-five countries on 2 March 2012. What was popularly known as the Fiscal Pact had been vetoed by Britain when it was being negotiated at the Council of Ministers the previous December. This meant that it was an inter-governmental treaty, not an EU treaty, and thus the intention of using EU institutions like the ECJ to enforce budgetary restrictions of 3 per cent or less could well be problematical. However, an introspective and divided coalition government in Britain, under David Cameron, has not set out an alternative course for the EU, placing less emphasis on an economic strategy effectively based around state capitalism. Both Cameron and his Finance Minister, George Osborne, have favoured the continuation of the euro. This is a currency which, if Britain had participated, as had been the ardent hope of Tony Blair throughout his 1997–2007 premiership, could well have spelled doom for the project. The free-spending ways of Blair's economics supremo Gordon Brown left Britain with huge borrowing costs, ones which would have overwhelmed its finances had it been unable to make the adjustments denied to countries which had surrendered financial controls to the ECB; Britain's borrowing costs would have been far larger in absolute terms than are Greece's. Several times in the crisis, William Hague, the Foreign Secretary, has called the euro 'a burning house with no exits'.[130] Britain has, however, consented to becoming a prominent contributor to the original EFSF (bail-out fund) which, according to Daniel Hannan, means: 'We are, in effect, paying for the privilege of impoverishing our neighbours.'[131]

George Osborne has favoured the creation of a fiscal union in face of growing evidence that the chief advocates of centralism cannot agree on the terms for a fully fledged banking and monetary union. The model of a single ever-closer union appears increasingly unrealisable even for the seventeen members in the eurozone. Eurocrats have tried to conceal the disagreements and doubts about how to repair the monetary union by indulging in frenetic activity in other areas. Thus in November 2012, Radek Sikorski, Poland's Foreign Minister, pushed for an EU civil–military command structure which would coordinate overseas military operations.[132] On 25 February 2013, the relevant committee of the European Parliament voted to restrict bankers' bonuses to a maximum of 100 per cent of their annual salary.[133] This regulation, if implemented, would have a disproportionate impact on the British economy. It is a classic example of the heavy interventionism with a clear ideological goal which happens also to target a country that has arguably tried to play a constructive role in the five-year eurozone crisis rather than profiting from its eruption. However, Britain has been left vulnerable by its failure to promote an alternative vision for the EU. William Hague, the Foreign Secretary, spoke in October 2012 of the need to reject 'more centralisation and uniformity' in favour of an approach 'that allows differing degrees of integration in different areas, done in ways that do not disadvantage those that do not wish to participate in everything, and preserves the things we all value'.[134] But an introspective government assailed by numerous domestic troubles did not persist with this message.

Salvation via more Europe

EU decision-makers at the centre of a marathon economic crisis are increasingly insistent that there is no way out except for a union adopting full political and economic standardisation. Politicians like Merkel are circumspect about the timetable and the scale of the changes; the technocrats who are less preoccupied by electoral matters are most insistent about the need for a decisive leap forward. Thus, in March 2013, the Commission released a paper intended to prepare the ground for further centralising legislation – it would prevent member states from undertaking major tax, labour or financial reforms without running them by the Commission and other governments first.[135]

'More Europe' remains the clarion call. The acute variations in national economic performances and needs fail to stop central planners in their tracks and prompt reflection about the need to link enhanced cooperation with proper democratic arrangements. Instead, economic governance and a single constitutional order exercise perennial fascination despite all that has already been revealed about the perils of uniform solutions since the euro's launch in 1999.

Eurocrats persist in hoping that the peoples of Europe will ultimately agree, in the face of all previous experiences, to persist with building a post-national order. As the German editorialist Berthold Kohler commented in 2012, this 'is to underestimate the strength of their cultures, collective memories, myths and mentalities – the very diversity that belongs to the essence of Europe'.[136] It is hard to point to any successful accomplishments that have arisen from adopting the euro but easy to point to the disadvantages. Germany may have pulled ahead of most of the other eurozone states but both it and the Netherlands have experienced a growth slowdown compared to two other Northern European economies, those of Sweden and Switzerland, which kept their freely floating currencies.[137] The functioning of the euro produced major discrepancies in competitiveness between its core and periphery members. By 2012, Italy's relative unit-labour costs had become 37 per cent higher than in 1998, before the euro's introduction, while for Germany they were 11 per cent lower.

According to Charles Dumas:

> The ... assumption that such imbalances would be evened out by the ready mobility of labor was always flawed: In the absence of a common language, tax structure and social-security entitlements, workers were never likely to cross borders to take up job opportunities in sufficient numbers.[138]

A broken instrument of integration

In calm conditions, the eurozone never displayed the signs of being an optimal currency area and the desperate attempts to salvage it, without changing its structure or size, have created conditions which clearly block recovery. The ECB, operating in tandem with lead players like Germany and France, has forced through measures that leave a disordered economic landscape. Walter Russell Mead has written:

> Interest rates should be low when there is no growth or a depression, and they should be high when economic activity is robust. Europe has now achieved exactly the reverse. Business and consumers in prosperous Germany have extremely low interest rates and can borrow freely. Companies in snake-bit countries like Italy and Greece face very high interest rates, even if their own business is sound and their prospects are good.[139]

Devotees of European supra-nationalism often blame such outcomes on the irresolute manner in which an ideology, supposedly suited for the age Europe finds itself in, has been implemented. They remain adamant that the nation-state is obsolete and show little interest in re-assessing the usefulness of the nation-state as a partner possessing legitimacy and know-how that could work alongside central European bodies. Single currencies are a leap back to the Middle Ages, it is assumed. Only central agencies can mobilise energy and resources to be effective developmental forces. But during the long-running crisis, the response to each new stage has too often been a mixture of clumsiness, deception and arrogance by the central decision-makers. They have eroded the legitimacy of the project by indicating that its sustainability requires ordinary citizens to pay sometimes huge costs (such as small savers in Cyprus in March 2013) even though it was not their negligence or greed that opened up this new crisis front. Cyprus went from being a one-off case requiring singular solutions to being a blueprint for eurozone countries in difficulties where bank depositors, retail and corporate alike, needed to contemplate making big personal sacrifices. Such warnings were then abruptly withdrawn in the face of uproar from the local population in Cyprus on 18 March, and incredulity on the markets a week later, after the head of Ecofin, Jeroen Dijsselbloem, had revived the idea with unwise candour. From his words and those of other top EU officials, such as Alexander Stubb, Finland's Minister for European Affairs and Foreign Trade, it remains apparent that in dangerous times, with harsh decisions unavoidable, it may only be a matter of time before there is a return to the idea of mobilising the people's money in order to save a political project seen as too big to fail.[140]

Despite the official rhetoric and genuinely held beliefs of many backers of the EU cause, the evidence for the indispensability of this particular European colossus has shrunk rather than expanded over time. The EU's emergence as a quasi-federal entity containing over 500 million people has produced meagre results in terms of modernising industry and improving education. The emphasis on green solutions has harmed a worthwhile principle through the doctrinaire form in which it has been pursued. Thus in 2008, the Commission ruled that members would need to access 10 per cent of transport fuel from 'clean' biological products. This mainly involved boosting the production of palm oil. Within a short time, it led to an increase in deforestation in South-East Asia, boosting CO_2 emissions in the process. Food prices rose for poor people as land use was diverted from food production and the burden on taxpayers within the EU was increased because of the heavy investment in a flawed scheme.[141]

EU Structural Funds are one of the primary tools for enabling the EU to keep up with its chief competitors. But only 10 per cent of the earmarked funds for 2007–13 have actually been paid out to date, due to difficulties in many member states of finding money for co-financing projects.[142] Romania, allocated €23.5 billion for 2007–13, had only been able to access 12 per cent of this amount by the end of 2012 (Bulgaria only 34 per cent of its allocation).[143] The consequences have been dire for these Balkan entrants. Sacrifices made by their societies to ensure entry, as subsidies on essential consumer items were phased out and the state retreated from economic activity, were not matched by any sustained growth in living standards after entry. On current projections, Romania and Bulgaria will take centuries before they can hope to ever reach the average living standards presently to be found in the EU. Understandably, France's 2012 proposal that unspent Structural Funds should be used to bail-out the ailing eurozone periphery caused nervousness in some of the new accession states.[144] There is no sign of modifying the intricate rules for getting projects accepted at the level of the Commission (ones based on a French bureaucratic matrix). These rules have kept much of the money tantalisingly out of reach in Brussels and ensured that the second-poorest country in the EU, Romania, has actually been a net contributor to EU funds for most of the time since its 2007 entry.

Clinging to a monetary fetish

EU decision-makers now wish to commit citizens in more centrally placed EU states to an audacious bargain. They argue that the crisis can be mastered, and normal economic conditions eventually restored, if private debts are socialised. This means that the powerful financial sector, which carries a big responsibility for plunging the European project into a deep crisis, is placed on a life-support machine with the help of massive public subsidies. But the call for such social sacrifices is unlikely to have many takers. The threadbare ideology of 'more Europe' does not have a mobilising capacity. It was thought to be unnecessary to evangelise for Europe at the popular level in the 1950s and to start now, in grim economic conditions that can be traced back to the startling blunders made in monetary matters, appears to be an impossible mission. Besides, calls for a merging of national destinies in one Europe are likely to conceal efforts on the part of core players to defend their turf in any new order. It involves a leap of faith to imagine national banking powers being surrendered to Eurocrats who will interpret the broader 'financial good'.

Jeremy Warner has pointed out that 'national banking systems are still seen as an important conduit for the economic and industrial policies of individual sovereign governments'.[145] In France the *Banque de France* may have become technically independent in 1994 but this has been described as a presentational device meant to align with banking practice in Germany and smooth the path for a Franco-German-inspired drive towards EMU.[146] It remains very much an obedient quango of the French state. As for Germany, its banking system has been openly used to ensure the long-term health of its industrial base, something which could not easily be replicated by a European-wide banking union.

Concentrating even more power in a narrow set of elite forces which have shown that, in this crisis, it is their own interests, rather than any general European cause, which motivate them, is likely to prove a recipe for mounting instability. The Nobel Prize winner Joseph Stiglitz is quite sure of this. He believes that 'Institutions which pretend to be democratic, but lack the most fundamental requirement of democracy, i.e. the voters can get rid of them' will become increasingly alienating to citizens.[147] For how long will Europeans allow themselves to be deprived of jobs, savings and the prospects of a normal life in order to prop up unsalvageable banks? Given the record of resistance in Europe to abuses of power, it is hard to imagine that people will consent to be ruled and exploited indefinitely without accountability. Cultural changes in European societies, weakening a sense of citizenship, have not made these societies sufficiently passive to accept new patterns of oligarchical rule. Italy offered the clearest example in the parliamentary elections of February 2013, when nearly 57 per cent of votes went to parties supporting an anti-austerity agenda. Mario Monti, the veteran Eurocrat who had been parachuted into the Prime Minister's job in 2011, obtained less than 10 per cent support for a platform based on wedding Italy to EU orthodoxy with austerity as its central ingredient. The most successful challenger in an inconclusive poll was Beppe Grillo, the counter-cultural figure at the heart of the Five Star movement which obtained 25 per cent of the vote in its first national outing. It was packaged not as a political party but as a civic revolution and it allowed several hundred new figures to burst on to an ossified political scene long dominated by unappetising cartels. The reaction of German leaders was to treat the result as an aberration. Guido Westerwelle, the Foreign Minister, quickly declared: 'The politically responsible people in Rome recognise that Italy needs a continuation of a policy of reform, of consolidation, one which is able to secure the confidence of the citizens and the markets.' The German Economy Minister Philipp Rösler indicated that governments might come and go but there was only one policy for Italy: 'I could have imagined a better outcome for the reformers in Italy. There is however no alternative to the previously adopted path of structural reforms.'[148]

The rhetoric emanating from the top of the European institutions proclaiming that the hour of fiscal convergence is at hand looks completely unreal when confronted with basic facts on the ground. Since Draghi threw his weight behind long-term re-financing in early 2012, there has been a massive sell-off of foreign ownership of Spanish sovereign debts, and a corresponding increase in their ownership by Spanish banks. As Spain followed Greece, Ireland and Portugal into crisis, many foreign lenders rushed towards the exit. A total of €326 billion was pulled from banks in Spain, Portugal, Ireland and Greece in the twelve months that ended on 31 July 2012, according to data compiled by Bloomberg.[149] The flight of deposits from these countries coincides with an increase of about €300 billion held by lenders in seven nations considered to be the core of the eurozone. The result is a fragmentation of credit leading to a two-tiered banking system; according to Alberto Gallo, the London-based head of European credit research at Royal Bank of Scotland Group Plc, 'Capital flight is leading to the disintegration of the eurozone' and an ever-widening divergence between the periphery and the core.[150] Credit is fragmenting along national lines as countries sharing a currency are increasingly unwilling to hold each other's assets.

If the euro limps on into the future thanks to the determination of its architects to keep patching it up, then the eurozone might well replicate the conditions seen in the USA following its disastrous civil war of 1861–65. Its southern portion was plunged into permanent depression and marginalisation while human and financial resources were drawn to the northern core. George Soros has warned of the emergence in the EU of 'a hierarchical system built on debt obligations', one replacing 'a voluntary association of equals'. Instead, 'there will be two classes of states, creditors and debtors, and the creditors will be in charge'.[151] It is uncertain if democracy will survive everywhere given the ascendancy of public officials who were already clear about their preference for burying democracy in its national form and who are evasive or incoherent about what kind of tolerable substitute could work in a borderless Europe. In parts of the USA's Deep South democracy became an empty shell in the century after the civil war but the USA still managed to renew itself by opening up the mid-west and expanding to the Pacific. No such sunlit horizons exist for a post-national Europe unless the dream of its most utopian architects, of Europe becoming the prototype for a world society, is counted.

Conclusion: ignoring some lessons of recent history

The European idea is a modest affair if its continuation depends on the survival of a currency union, of which many have come and gone. This obsession, amounting almost to a fetish, shows how deficient the integration project is in dimensions where it needs to show strength in order to survive and prosper.

It is true that the nation-state finds it difficult to preserve its own strength in a world where it is hard to shut out the forces of globalisation. But in Europe at different stages in modern history the nation-state has recovered from a variety of setbacks. It can tap energies from the wider society in ways that the EU seems incapable of doing.

What form of engagement at elite level shapes the policy moves that are meant to overcome the crisis? The conduct of EU crisis managers remains shrouded in levels of mystery that would almost do justice to the pre-1989 Kremlin. This is a worrying testimony to the quality of the media coverage of EU affairs. Academic analysis also usually shows a studied lack of interest in the contribution to policy-making of individual political and state agendas and those of mobilised interest groups.

No parliament worthy of the name exists where the record of the main decision-makers can be evaluated and where they are required to obtain a mandate for their actions. In the meetings of the Council of Ministers and ECB, full and frank debates, comparable to what can be seen in national parliaments when a country faces tough options, are noticeable by their absence. Of course, the people's role is to remain passive and subordinate. The hope is that they will meekly acquiesce to their fate upon hearing an intellectual like Bernard-Henri Levy warn: 'We no longer have a choice: it is either political union or death.'[152]

It is far from clear how such a union can be accomplished, or can endure, when its central pillar, the currency union, has become a disintegrative force in the thirteen years since it was launched. It has been unable to integrate goods, capital and labour markets across its seventeen members. The way it has been operated has brought about divergence, not convergence, among these states. Indeed, tensions have risen appreciably between different states as the crisis shows no sign of resolution. Fault-lines are starting to appear within several of them, raising doubt that they will be able to survive within their present boundaries. Advocates of Europe-wide economic governance are weighed down by policy failures and the functionaries who would manage such an entity enjoy far closer links to a financial sector complicit in the crisis than to mainstream societies. The European Union has been overtaken by a deep structural crisis much sooner than is the case for most nation-states of similar weight and importance. It has so far played itself out in a peaceful way, but there is no guarantee that this can continue indefinitely if low-grade and often chaotic decisions are taken which drive the EU deeper into trouble.[153]

Otto Schily, a former German Interior Minister, declared in 2009: 'For me Europe is not a given forever. We have the most peaceful time on our continent for centuries. It's the best time we've ever had in Europe and we have to take care of it.'[154] It is Europe's misfortune that such prescient words appeared to have the least powerful impact in Germany itself.

Notes

1 Ben Hall and Quenton Peel, 'Adrift amid a rift', *Financial Times*, 24 June 2010.
2 Andrew Higgins and Liz Alderman, 'Europeans planted seeds of crisis in Cyprus', *New York Times*, 26 March 2013.
3 David Marsh, *Europe's Deadlock* (London: Yale University Press, 2013), p. 33.
4 Open Europe, 'They said it wouldn't happen', 11 May 2010.
5 See The Lisbon Treaty: www.lisbon-treaty.org.
6 Bruno Waterfield, 'EU bail-out built on a lie', *EUObserver*, 10 May 2010.
7 Stefan Auer, *Whose Liberty is it Anyway? Europe at the Crossroads* (Chicago: University of Chicago Press, 2012), p. 65.
8 See International Monetary Fund: www.imf.org/external/pubs/ft/scr/2013/cr13156.pdf.
9 Larry Elliott, Phillip Inman and Helena Smith, 'IMF admits: we failed to realise the damage austerity would do to Greece', *Guardian*, 6 June 2013.
10 Benjamin Fox, 'Democracy is the real victim in the Greek tragedy', *EUObserver*, 12 June 2013.
11 Klaus Kastner, 'IMF is courageous and admits the obvious', Observing Greece, 6 June 2013.
12 Ambrose Evans-Pritchard, 'Olli Rehn should resign for crimes against Greece and against economics', *Daily Telegraph*, 6 June 2013.
13 'The I.M.F. admits mistakes. Will Europe?' *New York Times*, 7 June 2013.
14 Armin Mahler, 'Delusions of the euro zone: the lies that Europe's politicians tell themselves', *Der Spiegel Online*, 30 December 2011.
15 Leigh Phillips, 'Rehn on eurozone rescue: "mission accomplished"', *EUObserver*, 15 April 2011.
16 Jeremy Warner, 'Euroland will pay for this monetary madness', *Daily Telegraph*, 3 March 2012.
17 Brendan Keenan, 'Questions about the future of EU lurk beneath debt-crisis talks', *Irish Independent*, 6 September 2012.
18 Constantin Gurdgiev, 'Latest EBC plan kicks the can further down the road', *Globe and Mail*, 10 September 2012.
19 Ambrose Evans-Pritchard, 'Greek economy spirals down as EU forces final catharsis', *Daily Telegraph*, 14 February 2012.
20 Konstantin von Hammerstein, Christian Reiermann and Christoph Schult, 'Druck-

version – an unexpected U-turn: why Merkel wants to keep Greece in euro zone', *Der Spiegel Online*, 10 September 2012.

21 Leigh Phillips, 'Rehn on eurozone rescue'.

22 James K. Galbraith, 'The crisis in the eurozone', *Salon*, 10 November 2011: www.salon.com.

23 Stephen Kinsella, 'We need to follow Iceland's lead and punish our bankers', *Irish Independent*, 17 September 2012.

24 Colm McCarthy 'Reward isn't the word, Wolfgang, it's restitution', *Sunday Independent* 26 August 2012.

25 Coppola Comment, 'The real bailout', 15 June 2012.

26 Annie Lowrey, ' I.M.F. concedes major missteps in bailout of Greece', *New York Times*, 6 June 2013.

27 Peter Spiegel and Karin Hope, 'EU's Olli Rehn lashes out at IMF criticism of Greek bailout', *Financial Times*, 5 June 2013.

28 *EUObserver*, 14 June 2013.

29 Fox, 'Democracy is the real victim'.

30 Donal O'Donovan and Laura Noonan, 'ECB breaks own rules accepting Portugal's junk debt', *Irish Independent*, 8 July 2011.

31 Acemoglu and Johnson, 'Captured Europe'.

32 Hannan, 'EU regulation is making the next crash inevitable'.

33 Coppola Comment, 'The real bailout'.

34 For both findings, see Constantin Gurdgiev, 'Thou shalt not read into the ECB PRs too much', True Economics, 28 September 2012.

35 Constantin Gurdgiev, 'Europe's policy errors', True Economics, 22 December 2011.

36 Kinsella, 'We need to follow Iceland's lead'.

37 Constantin Gurdgiev, 'Two points of note from today's economic news', True Economics, 28 September 2012.

38 Paul Cullen, 'Iceland: from ruin to role model?', *Irish Times*, 24 September 2011.

39 Honor Mahony, 'Iceland could join EU by 2011', *EUObserver*, 30 January 2009.

40 *Daily Mail*, 15 June 2010.

41 Louise Armistead, 'Debt crisis: Barroso may want political union – but what's in it for the people?', *Daily Telegraph*, 13 September 2012.

42 Quoted by Open Europe, 'Westerwelle's journey into fantasy world', 25 September 2012.

43 Comment by John Livesey following article by Jeremy Warner, 'Only a matter of time before ECB is forced into massive quantitative easing', *Daily Telegraph*, 13 April 2012.

44 See Hall and Peel, 'Adrift amid a rift'.

45 Ambrose Evans-Pritchard, 'Euro bail-out in doubt as "hysteria" sweeps Germany', *Daily Telegraph*, 28 August 2011.

46 Ambrose Evans-Pritchard, 'Only the German people can renounce their sovereignty', *Daily Telegraph*, 12 September 2012.

47 'Juncker: Germany must not suggest it pays for euro zone', Reuters, 1 May 2012.

48 Liam Halligan, 'Forget "economic spring" – Greek outlook is stormy', *Sunday Telegraph*, 11 March 2012.

49 Andrew Lilico, 'How much did the IMF, ECB and EU bailouts harm Greek bond-holders?', *Daily Telegraph*, 19 March 2012.

50 See Malcolm Moore, 'Stiglitz says European austerity plans are a "suicide pact"', *Daily Telegraph*, 17 January 2012.

51 Colm McCarthy, 'Shocking treatment of Cyprus has exposed the eurozone's inherent flaws', *Sunday Independent*, 24 March 2013.
52 Stephen Fidler et al., 'Rifts over Cyprus bailout feed broader fears', *Wall Street Journal*, 25 January 2013.
53 Nicolas Véron, 'Europe's Cyprus blunder and its consequences', Bruegel, 21 March 2013.
54 Kristen Allen, 'Is Merkel gambling away the European idea?', *Der Spiegel*, International Edition, 19 May 2011.
55 Open Europe, 'Everything is at stake', 15 November 2010.
56 Mead, 'Will German politicians wreck Europe'.
57 Martin Wolf, 'There is no sunlit future for the euro', *Financial Times*, 19 October 2011.
58 Finance Minister Schäuble, 'Euro crisis means EU structures must change', *Der Spiegel Online*, 25 June 2012.
59 Michel Rocard, 'The decline and fall of political Europe', Project Syndicate, 26 April 2010.
60 Von Hammerstein et al., 'Druckversion – an unexpected U-turn'.
61 *Der Spiegel*, 25 September 2012.
62 Jana Mittermaier 'New ECB powers: the buck stops where?', *EUObserver*, 18 September 2012.
63 Mittermaier 'New ECB powers'.
64 Liam Halligan, 'Is the US losing patience with the eurozone debacle?' *Sunday Telegraph*, 22 July 2012.
65 Halligan, 'Is the US losing patience'.
66 *EUObserver*, 25 June 2013.
67 *Irish Times*, 28 June 2013.
68 Euro-Area Summit statement, 29 June 2012: www.consilium.europa.eu.
69 Marcus Walker, 'Merkel's bet on Europe's future', *Wall Street Journal*, 23 April 2013.
70 See Jean Pisani-Ferry, André Sapir, Nicolas Verón, and Guntram B. Wolff, 'What kind of European banking union?', *Bruegel Policy Contribution*, issue 12, June 2012.
71 Valentina Pop, 'Banking union: the German way or no way', *EUObserver*, 10 December 2012.
72 Ross Douthat, 'Prisoners of the euro', *New York Times*, 1 June 2013.
73 Walter Russell Mead, 'Dutch flout EU deficit rules', *Via Meadia*, 1 March 2013.
74 Leigh Phillips, 'Netherlands: indebted states must be made "wards" of the commission or leave euro', *EUObserver*, 7 September 2011.
75 www.inspiringwisdomquotes.com.
76 Stephen Castle, 'Europe in disarray as entire Commission quits over report', *Independent*, 16 March 1999.
77 Daniel Hannan, 'Y con el rescate, díganme ¿cómo les va? ("How's that bailout workin' out for ya?")', *Daily Telegraph* (Daniel Hannan's blog), 14 June 2012.
78 Valentina Pop, 'Spain: ECB cash more important than euro-plans', *EUObserver*, 24 May 2012.
79 Coppola Comment, 'The monsters of Spain', 21 June 2012.
80 Andrew Trotman, 'Debt crisis live', *Daily Telegraph*, 11 June 2012.
81 See Brendan Simms, *Europe, The Struggle for Supremacy: 1453 to the Present* (London: Allen Lane, 2013), p. 341.

82 Open Europe, 'You're wrong, Signor Monti: national parliaments are not the problem – they're the solution', 7 August 2012.

83 Reuters, 8 September 2012.

84 Such a post-democratic approach has had prominent defenders in the academic literature on the European Union. Mention can be made of Andrew Moravcsik, a US scholar of European integration. See his article, 'In defence of the "democratic deficit": reassessing legitimacy in the European Union', *Journal of Common Market Studies*, 40, 2002, pp. 603–24.

85 See Ross Clark, 'Cameron's tragic flaw', *Spectator*, 4 April 2012; Mark Pritchard, 'David Cameron's weakness on Europe forced me to resign from Conservative Party job', *Daily Telegraph*, 7 March 2012.

86 See Editorial, *Financial Times*, 28 September 2012.

87 For a critique of conservative failings on both sides of the Atlantic, see Philip Blond, 'Modern Conservatives make plebs of us all', *Financial Times*, 26 September 2012.

88 See Jürgen Habermas, *The Crisis of the European Union: A Response* (Cambridge: Polity Press, 2012).

89 Will Hutton, 'In defence, as in finance, the truth is clear – our future lies in Europe', *Observer*, 16 September 2012.

90 For her opinion of the new French President, see Steve Erlanger, 'The soft middle of François Hollande', *New York Times*, 13 April 2012.

91 See Peter Baldwin, 'Tracing Europe's long road to economic catastrophe', *The New Republic*, 9 March 2012.

92 Heinrich August Winkler, *Germany: The Long Road West, Volume 2: 1933–1990* (Oxford: Oxford University Press, 2007), p. 431.

93 Winkler, *Germany: The Long Road West*, p. 431.

94 *Daily Telegraph*, 5 May 2013.

95 Thomas Pascoe, 'Why the economics of the left benefit the one per cent', *Daily Telegraph*, 1 August 2012.

96 Colm McCarthy, 'Ireland's grievance over ECB tactics is totally justified', *Sunday Independent*, 15 April 2012.

97 Marcus Walker, 'Merkel's bet on Europe's future', *Wall Street Journal*, 23 April 2013.

98 *Financial Times*, 23–24 March 2013.

99 BBC News, 25 March 2013.

100 'Germany, a safe haven for money laundering', *Deutsche Welle*, 30 October 2012.

101 BBC News, 24 March 2013.

102 *Daily Telegraph*, 3 March 2013.

103 Phillips, 'Netherlands'.

104 Andrew Rettman, 'Finland on Greek collateral: "it's not about the money"', *EUObserver*, 31 August 2011.

105 Ambrose Evans-Pritchard, 'Finland prepares for break-up of eurozone', *Daily Telegraph*, 16 August 2012.

106 Sven Böll and Maria Marquart, 'Triumph of right-wing populists: how dangerous is Finland to the euro?' *Der Spiegel Online*, 20 April 2011.

107 Valentina Pop, 'EU monitors heading to Madrid, despite "Men in Black" claims', *EUObserver*, 12 June 2012.

108 Matt Cooper, 'Germany can't make Germans out of us because of euro crisis', *Irish Examiner*, 18 May 2012.

109 Cooper, 'Germany can't make Germans out of us because of euro crisis'.

110 *Daily Telegraph*, 17 September 2012.

111 For a fuller analysis of these contrasting positions see David McWilliams, 'Prepare for titanic struggle as Draghi turns euro into lira', *Irish Independent,* 27 September 2012.

112 Wolfgang Münchau, 'Draghi is devil in Weidmann's euro drama', *Financial Times*, 23 September 2012.

113 Brian Blackstone and Marcus Walker, 'How ECB chief outflanked German foe in fight for euro', *Wall Street Journal*, 2 October 2012.

114 Blackstone and Walker, 'How ECB chief outflanked German foe'.

115 Gunnar Beck, 'Merkel will win – because my fellow Germans dare not speak of national self interest', *Spectator*, 21 September 2013.

116 Michael Sauga, 'Lonely struggle: Wolfgang Schäuble's fight to save Europe', *Der Spiegel*, 17 July 2013.

117 Daniel Hannan, 'Germans are finally losing patience with the euro racket', *Daily Telegraph* (Daniel Hannan's blog), 18 September 2012.

118 Martin Wolf, 'Why exit is an option for Germany', *Financial Times*, 26 September 2012.

119 Valentina Pop, 'New anti-Euro party forms in Germany', *EUObserver,* 12 March 2013.

120 Petra Gerlach-Kristen, 'Unification realities make Germans wary of bailout toll', *Irish Times*, 29 August 2012.

121 'Spain problem solved', Irish Economy, 11 June 2012.

122 Yalman Onaran, 'Deposit flight from Europe banks eroding common currency', Bloomberg News, 19 September 2012.

123 John Redwood, 'London as the world's number one financial centre', 22 February 2012: www.johnredwoodsdiary.com.

124 Hannan, 'EU regulation is making the next crash inevitable'.

125 Hannan, 'EU regulation is making the next crash inevitable'.

126 Stanley Pignal, 'Britons weigh future in Brussels "eurocracy"', *Financial Times*, 29 December 2012.

127 See Jeremy Warner, '"Them and us" mentality now colours eurozone's relations with UK', *Daily Telegraph*, 17 November 2011.

128 'EU Barnier: financial transactions tax is sensible in economic terms', *Wall Street Journal*, 8 February 2012.

129 See Alex Barker and James Wilson, 'Public failure casts a cloud on Europe', *Financial Times*, 15 January 2012.

130 William Hague, 'Euro is a burning building', BBC News, 28 September 2011.

131 Daniel Hannan, 'The EU's latest bailout will fail, as all previous bailouts have failed', *Daily Telegraph*, 27 October 2011.

132 *EUObserver*, 15 November 2012.

133 *EUObserver*, 6 March 2013.

134 Open Europe, 'Hague's first Europe speech moves the Government in the right direction', 23 October 2012.

135 Honor Mahony, 'EU commission prepares ground for far-reaching economic powers', *EUObserver*, 21 March 2013.

136 Open Europe, 'The choice facing Europe: conformity or diversity?', 9 August 2012.

137 Dumas, 'Euro was flawed at birth'.

138 Dumas, 'Euro was flawed at birth'.

139 Walter Russell Mead, 'Eurozone begins to fracture', *Via Meadia*, 4 September 2012.

140 See Steve Erlanger and James Kanter, 'Stricter rules but signs of disarray in Cyprus deal', *New York Times*, 26 March 2013.

141 Walter Russell Mead, 'Another European green fails', *Via Meadia*, 19 October 2012.

142 Open Europe, 'Message to the Commission: denial won't reduce waste', 3 December 2010.

143 *Revista 22*, 8 October 2013: www.revista22.ro.

144 Charles Grant, 'How Hollande should handle Merkel', *Realclearworld*, 16 May 2012.

145 Jeremy Warner, 'Europeans will never accept a federal banking system', *Daily Telegraph*, 26 April 2012.

146 Connolly, *The Rotten Heart of Europe,* p. 363.

147 Joseph, Stiglitz, 'Capturing the ECB', Project Syndicate, 6 February 2012.

148 Open Europe, 'Italian elections: and now for the warnings from around Europe – stay the course, or else', 26 February 2013.

149 Onaran, 'Deposit flight from Europe'.

150 Onaran, 'Deposit flight from Europe'.

151 George Soros, 'The tragedy of the European Union and how to resolve it', *New York Review of Books*, 27 September 2012.

152 Bernard-Henri Levy, 'Federalism or death!', *Presseurop*, 2 October 2012.

153 See Ivan Krastev, 'The European Dis-Union: lessons from the Soviet collapse', *IVM Post*, 109, 2012, pp. 8–9.

154 Tony Barber, 'A void to fill', *Financial Times*, 27 May 2009.

7

A crisis with no end in sight

European Monetary Union was an essentially political project imposed on unenthusiastic, if not unwilling, European citizens by political leaders impatient to speed up the journey towards a united Europe. One of the chief architects of the single currency, Hans Tietmeyer, declared in 1988: 'Like a marriage made in heaven, EMU must last forever because there is no way out. Monetary union is therefore a monetary community of destiny.'[1]

The level of ideological enthusiasm meant to turn the currency union into the economic foundation of a post-national federal state was not matched by the equivalent practicality to accomplish such an audacious feat. The respective competences of the European Central Bank, created to manage the currency union, and other EU pillars were never properly worked out or applied (as the crisis from 2009 starkly revealed). The member states shared a currency and operate a single monetary policy. But fiscal policy – taxation, spending and debt issuance – remained the responsibility of the individual states.

Between 2008 and 2011, it became impossible for EU chiefs to deny that the crisis was a systemic one, not just one bearing down on countries where the level of state or private indebtedness had grown to dangerously high levels. But there was no resolve to modify the architecture of monetary union so as to create one or more coherent entities. A permanent German withdrawal or the temporary withdrawal of countries which needed to become more competitive through external devaluation were seen as outrageous propositions by the guardians of European integration. At each escalation of the crisis, senior bureaucrats like Olli Rehn or José Manuel Barroso insisted that a corner had been turned and a solution was in sight as long as societies embraced aggressive forms of austerity. Such myopia was combined with ever-more audacious efforts to centralise economic decision-making among central planners and pro-integration leaders, the ones responsible for this costly experiment. Far from leading Europe towards deeper integration, it had proven to be a calamitous economic departure, responsible for the most harmful divisions in sixty years of European integration. The refusal of European decision-makers to change course in the face of escalating damage to individual economies and Europe's global economic position was striking. It recalled nationalism in its most unenlightened and inflexible mode and gravely affected the standing of the European project.

The economic rules contained in the EU treaties were constantly set aside in an attempt to prolong the life of the currency union. The Rubicon was crossed in May 2010 with the decision to bail out Greece and other states facing budgetary or private sector difficulties, thanks to the establishment of a permanent bail-out fund paid for by European taxpayers. In the autumn of 2011, the ECB decided to directly finance governments in difficulty with a vast bond-purchasing programme designed to lower their costs and make it easier for countries to borrow. Such aid, in the form of purchases of debt, was a rescue of the banks that were over-exposed to Greek debt. Very little of the funding actually reached governments directly, enabling them to take decisions that might revive moribund economies.

Suspicions mounted that EU institutions, lacking democratic accountability, had been captured by special interests, namely banks and other financial bodies whose influence had steadily expanded at the top of the EU since the mid-1980s. There was no sign of a counter-reaction to uphold any general European interest. The European Parliament has combined with judges and bureaucrats to increase EU powers over the national members during the crisis years while declining to call an inept set of crisis managers to order. Barroso failed to assert the 'Community method' which, in past crises, had enabled the Commission to play a balancing role in interpreting the interests of all members, not just the biggest ones.

The Commission was on the sidelines when, on 16 March 2013, the fateful decision was taken to confiscate a proportion of the savings of depositors in Cypriot banks in order to raise funds to rescue Cyprus. Early in the eurozone crisis, bank deposits had been guaranteed across the eurozone so that citizens would not be compelled to move funds from country to country. Outrage in Cyprus and incredulity across much of the world led to the raid on savings below €100,000 being annulled. But it was now clear that there was influential backing for savers and investors to foot the bill for bank failures. Jeroen Dijsselbloem, the Dutch Finance Minister chairing Ecofin since January 2013, articulated such a view on 25 March. He said that the approach taken in Cyprus could be applied elsewhere so as to avoid taxpayers paying for the misdeeds of bankers. He hastily retracted his claim but, significantly, key eurozone figures would be prepared to endorse it.

Cyprus had tumbled into crisis because Germany and its eurozone allies had decided to impose heavy losses on holders of Greek bonds in 2011–12 as a means of reducing the astronomical scale of the Greek national debt. The alternative course was to push Greece out of the eurozone altogether which it was decided was fraught with danger, especially in light of important elections in France and Germany in 2012–13. But the vulnerability of Cypriot banks, so heavily implicated in the Greek financial sector, was not taken into account. Nor had anything been done when money fleeing eurozone countries already in crisis (like Ireland) flowed into Cyprus during its first few years in the eurozone from 2008.[2]

Instead, Germany in 2013 proclaimed that Cyprus's economic model as a financial hub was obsolete and capital controls were imposed on the island state. These were designed to slow-up a flight of capital but they violated a foundation principle of the post-1958 union, namely that capital should be allowed to flow freely. It had been one of the pillars of European cooperation but it was no longer to apply to Cyprus where the euro would no longer be the same as in the rest of the eurozone area.

Here was perhaps the first evidence that the key eurozone players felt that ailing members could be jettisoned without the experiment itself becoming a casualty. It was a particularly graphic example of how the creation of a flawed and ineptly managed currency union had exacerbated differences within the EU rather than being a driver for enhanced cooperation. The EU's policy chiefs appeared to be making decisions increasingly divorced from the real world. It was one where an escalating number of eurozone countries were staring into a full economic depression. In Spain and Greece, a lost generation of citizens aged under thirty seemed to be doomed to perhaps a lifetime of unemployment unless economic conditions dramatically changed. But the project of preserving the euro had taken on a transcendent quality of its own.

Southern European political elites shrank from embracing bold remedies for the economic crisis. Most were seen as involving an abandonment of the euro or else a temporary suspension for some members, or a breaking up of the currency union into several workable parts. Parties on the right and left which had alternated in office since the restoration of democracy at different stages after 1945 had too much invested in the project of European integration. In Northern Europe, there was greater willingness to think of a post-EMU world since the adjustments appeared to be more manageable for countries relatively insulated from the crisis.

But paralysis reigned and the posture of 'kicking the can down the road', through pursuing competitive austerity and slapping bail-out programmes on countries whose financial health was ruined by eurozone pressures, continued. In addition, a split involving creditor countries increasingly unwilling to support peripheral ones in difficulty became formalised. The latter's problems often (though not always) stemmed from their own imprudence but also from being part of an economic order whose rules were simply not in their own long-term interest.

Germany, and other northern eurozone countries with a similar profile, have, by contrast, done relatively well in the single currency era. This is due to particular virtues but also to the fact that the rules for the eurozone happened to suit the profile of their economies very well. Germany is now strong enough to push its policy preferences on the entire eurozone and dress it up as being in the name of the European cause. The evidence that Germany is striving to acquire European political hegemony through its economic prowess is scanty, however. But it is prepared to use European rhetoric to safeguard particular German economic interests. Protecting the German financial sector (parts of which have been terribly managed) is one such consideration even though propping up a string of insolvent banks may not be in the country's long-term interests. But the short-term and defensive perspective adopted shows that any wider European loyalties are fast receding. Some of Germany's smaller allies are even more introspective: there is no eagerness to revise the architecture of monetary union except in ways that further consolidate the advantages of the northern countries.

The danger cannot be overlooked that a second stage in the history of the EU is opening up where one self-confident and strategically placed country determines its agenda with its own interests very much in mind. France did that under de Gaulle and Germany may be attempting a reprise where a single-minded member is prepared to show inflexibility in signifying the direction in which it wishes European affairs to go. Germany's insistence on a banking union in which a large part of its own banking sector remains aloof from the financial regulator could be an ominous straw in the wind. A parochial German assertiveness offers no way forward for the union and could ultimately badly rebound on Germany itself.

Despite its accumulating woes, the European Union remains a lodestar for adjacent poorer states, or at least for their elites.[3] Croatia became the twenty-eighth member state on 1 July 2013 even though only 39 per cent of Croatians were then in favour of EU membership. In earlier years, there had been a desire to escape from a Balkan periphery to join 'mainstream Europe'. But the allure had faded given the deep economic mess that Slovenia, the most 'central European' of the old Yugoslav republics, toppled into after joining in 2004. Croatians in 2013 have few illusions about the EU being their 'promised land': there is 20 per cent unemployment and more than half of young Croats have no work or prospects of regular jobs. Croatia's economic ties with the rest of the former Yugoslavia are likely to shrivel now that there are no longer free trade links with these countries, and powerful companies from the most dynamic EU states are poised to obtain a stranglehold over much of the Croatian economy. In the worst-case scenario, it could find itself a colony of the lead EU states, a fate that has threatened Romania and Bulgaria since they joined in 2007.[4]

Croatia's elite seemed unfazed that only 21 per cent of the electorate bothered to vote in the elections of April 2013 enabling Croatia to take up its seat allocation in the European Parliament. Joining an entity where the popular will counts for little may be one of the attractions of EU membership. This certainly appears to be the case in regard to Latvia. In July 2013, it was confirmed that the Baltic state would join the euro in January 2014. It did not unduly matter that the latest opinion poll showed that only 22 per cent of Latvians supported this step, with 53 per cent opposed.[5] Latvia stood out – with Bulgaria – as the EU state that had seen worst increase in 'severe material deprivation', with the rate surging from 19 per cent in 2008 to 31 per cent in 2013. The elite had pursued a deflation strategy which had earned it plaudits from top Eurocrats and censure from economists with a global audience alarmed at the devastation caused for such paltry economic gains.[6] But the deflation strategy of the Latvian elite has ensured that the affluent sections of the middle class with foreign currency mortgages have been protected while lower-income groups have borne the brunt of the downturn.

As elites in these two former communist states girded their loins for the rough European voyage, there were simultaneous tremors in a string of older members reeling from the destructive impact of the euro crisis on the fabric of their societies. In Portugal, the summer of 2013 saw deep fissures open up in a ruling coalition implementing troika-directed cuts. The likelihood of Portugal leaving the bail-out programme on schedule in June 2014 receded. Only a new loan with even tougher conditions might stand between the country and outright default. But it is unlikely that any party would take responsibility for increasing the debt which already (in July 2013) stands at 370 per cent of GDP. The political elite has lost whatever legitimacy it once possessed to impose further austerity in what is seen as a futile and masochistic game imposed by outsiders.[7] Portugal appeared at an impasse two years after its bail-out with a mutinous population squaring off against a fractured political elite at a loss about what to do next.

In July 2013, Spain's embattled Prime Minister, Mariano Rajoy, confronted popular outrage over explosive claims by the former treasurer of his party. He appeared to lend credence to persistent media allegations that, over many years, the Popular Party had been financing itself illegally through cash donations from business people whose firms received lucrative public contracts in exchange.[8] The authority that a ruling party requires to impose harsh economic medicine simply does not exist if leading members are so deeply compromised. President Hollande was confronted with a lesser crisis involving his Economics Minister in the spring of 2013, prompting the editor of Spain's *El Mundo* to warn that the fate of his country and of Spain was in the hands of terribly weak leaders who could be pushing their respective nations towards revolution.[9]

Meanwhile, the troika mulled over whether Greece had done enough to merit the next tranche of its latest bail-out. There were various compelling reasons for hesitation. The privatisation programme, designed to earn revenue to pay off debts, was going nowhere due to the lack of interest from international investors who see a country locked in a recessionary spiral. But in the Commission there was a preference for believing that culture is at the root of the problem; a leaked draft report alleged that Greece lacks the 'willingness and capacity' to collect taxes.[10] How an economy still in freefall could meet targets that would have been highly ambitious in more normal circumstances was not addressed.

Increasingly, there was a widespread and growing realisation that not only was the debt burden unsustainable for Greece but that creditors (European taxpayers to the fore) would see little of their money in the future: 'loaning Greece the equivalent of 100% of its GDP to address its excessive debt problems was never going to work out as intended'.[11] Withholding the loan instalment for Greece raised too many uncertainties, especially with market anxieties about the euro on the rise and elections in Germany just a few months away. So the rules were tweaked and the money released even though Greece was falling short of its reform targets.

On 22 September 2013, Angela Merkel became the only leader of a eurozone country to be re-elected since the start of the crisis. 'With me there is no uncertainty' appeared to be her watchword. Her CDU–CSU centre-right bloc was only a few seats short of an outright majority. The campaign focused on the Chancellor as an epitome of caution and common sense. 'We had four good years' she remarked in the aftermath of her victory. No other eurozone leader could dare to make such a claim in 2013 and it showed how introspective the mood in Germany had become. The long election campaign had delayed key decisions on the extent to which Europe would be subject to economic governance. Complicated negotiations between the CDU and potential coalition partners stretched ahead which threatened to put back the timetable for a proposed banking union towards 2016.

It is clear from the statements emanating from Merkel and Schäuble after the election that no conceptually different approach to the eurozone crisis from its lead nation can be expected. Both the CDU and SPD had shown a reluctance for dialogue with voters about the scale of the crisis and the consequences for them. A former senior minister in the first SPD Schröder government remarked at a seminar in July 2013 that 'we have nothing profound to say about Europe to everyday citizens'. Her party and the Greens were bound up with a policy of equivocation: 'We agree with the government on its broad approach [austerity] but we are a bit against it in some of the details' was how she summed up a posture which she feared would cost her party dear electorally.[12]

Policy wonks were firmly in control of SPD strategy while at the European level opaque measures for fiscal coordination were being written by top officials in key national ministries and the European Commission who, all too often, were attentive to the 'interests of their elite clients'. Only a small part of the European political space was taken into consideration. This was shown as social protection measures, enshrined in the Maastricht Treaty, were eroded. Paralysis appeared to reign within the Party of

European Socialists, where in scheduled meetings, leaders of the Euro-left said hello to each other but appeared to have nothing substantial to talk about. SPD officials in Germany – ones prepared to try and sell a transfer union to the public – are cowed by the hostility of the media. Since embracing an unpopular policy at a time of low political fortunes could cost them their jobs, they mainly prefer to stay silent. It is hardly surprising that the left anticipates no revival at the European elections of June 2014. Those who argue for distinctive European policies from the other party formations are voices in the wilderness. Merely saying that 'Europe is important, so therefore you should go out and vote' is self-defeating asserted one regional official where the SPD had enjoyed a rare electoral victory in 2012: 'why should people bother to vote on such a basis. They are not stupid: they will not vote if there is nothing important at stake.'[13]

Whoever governs in a subordinate capacity with the CDU, it is likely that a plural and consensual approach to dealing with the crisis involving input from across the EU will be further eroded. Merkel's approach centres around bilateral or inter-governmental initiatives.[14] These gave her more leverage than working through Community institutions.

There had been undisguised annoyance in Berlin when, in June 2013, the Commission offered France two more years to meet its budget deficit target. On 10 July, Germany rejected the European Commission's model for a single resolution authority in the proposed new banking union. It was nervous about a joint liability European vehicle and used the claim that what was proposed was illegal under existing European treaties to marginalise the Commission's role.[15] Intellectual justification for this approach was provided by the elder statesman of German banking, Otmar Issing. He argued that from the economic reforms of the Lisbon Agenda onwards, centralised policy coordination at EU level had failed; it was inimical to healthy competition between nations and regions which had been a chief basis for European prosperity.[16] But Issing failed to mention that due to its weight Germany had previously been a prime beneficiary of such coordination and had also contributed to failures over the single currency by diluting policies of coordination to suit its own interest. Procrastination over the banking union was merely proving to be a repetition of such a self-centred approach.

Playing up a strategy for tackling Europe's debt crisis increasingly had the hallmarks of a tacky public relations manoeuvre. Effective bank resolution was not on the table. Numerous institutional arrangements had been unfurled and then emptied of content or shelved outright since 2010. A small amount of rescue money would be available at the European level. Probably, just those banks of systemic importance for the EU as a whole would qualify. National co-funding would be obligatory in order to dispel the impression that here was a transfer fund in the making. The evasive language of the key players and the strains within bodies like the ECB and between it and the Commission and lead states inevitably conveys the impression that the funding problems of the banks are massive ones.

The EU will become an entity of secondary importance unless it can re-design itself as a force concerned to identify and defend a European common good. This involves burying the Cold War with national states who view a supra-national Europe as both threatening and unworkable. Reviving economic activity that gives hope to millions trapped in stricken economies is surely the imperative need of the moment. Providing for a generation trauma-tised and dispossessed by war was viewed as a compelling goal by the first architects of European integration. But the current set of elite players appear numb to the social carnage being caused by low-grade policies, often devised at summits which concoct ad hoc solutions late into the night, ones designed to keep a dysfunctional currency union afloat and preserve the vested interests associated with it.

Most of the EU elite signally fail to recognise some ominous parallels with Yugoslavia whose federation collapsed at the start of the 1990s due to the unwillingness of narrow vested interests to renounce some of their privileges, the disappearance of solidarity between component parts of the federation, and a refusal to allow decision-making to be subject to genuine popular scrutiny.

Notes

1 Shore, *Building Politics,* p. 111.
2 Floyd Norris, 'Controls on capital come late to Cyprus', *New York Times*, 31 March 2013.
3 John O'Brennan, 'Will Europe end in Croatia?', Project Syndicate, 30 June 2013.
4 See Tom Gallagher, *Romania and the European Union: How the Weak Vanquished the Strong* (Manchester: Manchester University Press, 2009).
5 *Daily Telegraph*, 9 July 2013.
6 See Paul Krugman, 'Baltic brouhaha', *New York Times*, 1 May 2013; also Martin Wolf, 'Why the Baltic states are no model', *Financial Times*, 30 April 2013.
7 João Ferreira do Amaral's best-selling book *Porque devemos sair do euro* (Why we must leave the euro) has, since its publication in early 2013 by Lua do Papel in Lisbon, crystallised such an attitude.
8 *El Mundo*, 7 July 2013.
9 *Le Figaro*, 2 May 2013.
10 Reuters, 9 July 2013.
11 Brian Carney, 'The coming Greek write-off', *Wall Street Journal*, 9 July 2013.
12 The author attended this seminar.
13 SPD chief from one of Germany's larger cities, speaking at the above seminar.
14 Simon Nixon, 'A reluctant hegemon steps to forefront', *Wall Street Journal*, 8 July 2013.
15 Eurointelligence, Newsbriefing, 11 July 2013.
16 Otmar Issing, 'The risk of European centralization', Project Syndicate, 2 July 2013.

Conclusion: routes away from crisis

In 2013, one envoy from a leading partner of the EU urged EU officials to go to Europe's airports and find out the reasons why so many people are quitting Europe; the need to acquire a reality check on the human dimensions of the crisis is a vital requirement if any early progress is to be made in solving it. The perennial absorption with fresh structural engineering is matched by an incredible numbness towards the alarming social effects of the crisis in a growing number of countries. It is just 'outside their frame of reference' according to the commentator Wolfgang Münchau.[1]

The Irish economist Ray Kinsella simply found it indefensible that, within an economic epoch characterised by intellectual capital and innovation, youth unemployment in the EU should now stand at an average of 25 per cent – and more than double this in some of the peripheral countries which are most in need of the intellectual capital and capabilities of young and often highly skilled Europeans.[2] That was in May 2013. By September, it was revealed that youth unemployment in Greece had risen to around 70 per cent with the economy having sunk by one-quarter in the previous four years.[3] As for the eurozone, its unemployment level had reached 12 per cent and its gross domestic product in the second quarter of 2013 was 3 per cent below its pre-crisis peak.[4]

Short of pouring on to the streets, it is hard to see how populations, confronting an alarming future over subsequent decades, can bring meaningful pressure to bear on decision-makers, who in practical terms rarely show empathy with the plight of the millions of casualties of the crisis. Crisis summits have succeeded one another, involving people with big jobs talking about people with no jobs being 'more flexible'.[5]

One country, Germany, has risen to assume the leadership of the EU. Although currently it enjoys immunity from the pain of much of the rest of the eurozone, the future of the single currency and perhaps of the wider Union itself seems largely to be in its hands. Currently, it insists that its economic model can be emulated by the deficit countries, wrongly believing that its plight at the turn of the century is comparable to the deep crisis many of them are facing. Thus, a morality tale has been preached year after year: painful austerity and structural reforms will enable distressed countries to recover.

But the peripheral eurozone countries lack most of Germany's advantages; and, in the spring of 2013, it turned out that the economic analysis which Merkel and her advisers relied upon to bolster their demand for wholesale austerity was flawed. Harvard professors Kenneth Rogoff and Carmen Reinhart acknowledged major errors in their figures which were meant to prove that debt of 90 per cent above GDP led to a precipitate fall in growth.[6]

But Chancellor Merkel was not for turning. She told German voters in the aftermath of her 2013 election victory that 'what we have done, everyone can do'.[7] This is myopic: it is hard to expect peripheral countries, ones with much greater problems than Germany had, to return to competitiveness through deflation. Collapsing production and falling tax receipts suggest that a series of full-scale depressions may be what awaits them.

For much of the crisis, Germany has wished to direct Europe's financial affairs through a form of eurozone governance that primarily benefits Germany irrespective of the damage being done to a mounting list of eurozone countries unable to insulate themselves from it. This approach lays down that distressed countries must fix their own problems through models worked out and imposed elsewhere. Adjustment programmes, prescribing a lengthy dose of austerity to restore competitiveness, have already been the norm for half a decade. But the national economies subject to these policies have grown increasingly infirm. The approach of 'the troika' is a dangerously high-handed one that runs the risk of reviving deep fractures between European nations and regions. A far less introspective and self-centred German approach is vital if the eurozone is to stand any chance of clambering out of the deep hole it has plunged into.

In the face of short-term measures that amount to muddling through the crisis, there is no influential dynamic insisting that the survival of the integration project requires speedy and decisive moves towards political and economic union. Irrespective of the wisdom of such an approach, the absence of a sense of urgency in tackling the crisis is ominous. Germany wills the end, a coherent and hopefully stable monetary union, without willing the means (a banking union).[8] At the time of writing, the EU's chief decision-makers have been deadlocked over the terms of a banking union for nearly a year. A further extended period of wrangling over what form of central supervision banks should have and how their losses should be allocated appears to stretch ahead. The uncertainty hampers the productive sector, meaning any recovery is likely to be anaemic as under-capitalised and fearful banks are unwilling to lend. Agreeing a plan to nurse back to health a chronically ill banking system is an overdue step. In September 2013, when Mario Draghi asserted in Berlin that a single resolution mechanism was needed to wind up failing banks, a German government spokesperson said that such an idea was legally questionable.[9]

While insisting that European cooperation was important, in practice German decision-makers often preferred a crisis strategy geared towards bolstering their own country's economic interests.

Even with talk of a banking union in the air for over a year, lending is increasingly occurring along national lines. National regulators in 2013 were seeking to impede the transfer of banking funds because of fears that this leakage would further underscore the fragility of the financial industries that they were supervising.[10] Distrust over the impartiality of any super-European regulator is also easy to find. It stems from awareness of how bigger national players have used their weight to influence the opaque rules shaping the single currency before and during its time of crisis.

Still, at the apex of EU decision-making, a greater sense of urgency is badly needed but hardly visible. Holidays, elections and further institution-building continue to be major distractions. Treating what is an emergency with the resolve many think it deserves appears to be alien to the practice and mindset of the lawyers, bureaucrats and accountants who congregate at the top of the various European institutions and also in the Union's lead power.

A search for alibis dominated the first years of the crisis: the problems were temporary ones, or else 'structural' or North American in origin, or sometimes exacerbated by credit agencies or piratical financial speculators. The search for a new centralising framework meant to establish economic governance occurs at a sometimes glacial pace because it has to accommodate the perspectives of the various interest groups entrenched in the EU power structure.

The impression is given of an oligarchy of interests scrambling to stabilise a project that has badly lost its way. A prominent casualty has been the European values that are supposed to provide solidarity for members in difficulty, but that are now increasingly rhetorical ones. In order for such a nadir to be reached, a feel for history has deserted an increasingly pedestrian and provisional set of leaders as this crisis has dragged on. In October 2013, fresh from a trans-European trip to meet academics and policy-makers, the American academic Walter Russell Mead well described the damage to their cherished cause inflicted by low-grade policies:

> It's not just that many Italians now loathe what they see as arrogant German posturing and that many people in the two countries live in completely different mental universes with radically different interpretations of recent history. As I traveled through Europe I felt that both foreign and domestic issues are pulling Europeans away from each other. There was less excitement about the prospect of building a united Europe than I've seen in the past, and more of a sense of nations following their own interests without expecting much support or help from their EU partners.[11]

To prevent such divisions hardening, it goes without saying that discussions about how to overcome the crisis need to extend beyond the various branches of orthodox pro-integration opinion. The views of figures from outside the corporatist European networks who question the narrow priorities and short-term responses to the crisis command respect in the wider global policy community but usually go unheeded in Brussels and Frankfurt. This is just another way in which the integration cause is subverted by those who insist they are its watchful guardians. It would be a sign of maturity if Merkel and other EU leaders emerged from their bunkers and commissioned a cross-section of economists with a global reputation to draw up a report laying out what new approaches could be tried in order to overcome the crisis.

The EU's dismissal of candid appraisals of its crisis strategy just reinforces the absence of a European public sphere. Regarding EU security policy in the 1990s, the historian Brendan Simms wrote that: 'What little discussion that did exist was ill-informed, parochial, fragmented and highly elite-driven.'[12] Such traits characterised the level of discussion on the EU's pre-eminent crisis in the new century. Joschka Fischer, the former German Foreign Minister, believed that 'a lack of vision, courage, and strength of purpose is on display in all European countries but especially so in Berlin (and on the part of government and opposition alike)'.[13]

In mid-2013, when the former head of the IMF's team in Ireland, Professor Ashoka Mody, called for 'a complete rethinking' of the austerity strategy, he was brushed aside as a has-been rather than listened to on account of what he had learnt as a result of direct exposure to one of the biggest emergencies on the periphery of the eurozone. He stated that fiscal overkill is self-defeating, especially if compounded by tight money, and that Ireland should seriously consider scaling back on its fiscal adjustment effort.[14]

A string of leading economists with IMF and World Bank backgrounds, sometimes Nobel Prize winners, have argued that the sting can be taken out of the crisis by reducing interest payments through the restructuring of debt. They believe it is going to happen anyway due to the sheer un-sustainability of debt levels. What is at issue is whether severe political and social upheavals occur in one or more distressed eurozone country first of all. Joschka Fischer has even pinned his hope on 'an unpleasant surprise' that compels the troika to recoil from its disastrous policies: 'it might be Europe's greatest source of hope', he argued in April 2013.[15]

Externally devised and indeed supervised austerity programmes have piled ever larger sums of debt on deficit eurozone countries. These so-called rescue programmes are based on the assumption that through tough housekeeping, countries will be able to generate a fiscal surplus in order to pay off their debts. But as businesses close and tax receipts dry up, the burden of debt becomes unbearable, growing to an ever-larger portion of GDP. In Greece, even at rates of 2 per cent, and with longer maturities, interest payments alone will by 2015 be roughly €7 billion annually, a huge chunk out of a shrunken GDP.[16]

According to Joschka Fischer, writing in the spring of 2013, 'given the debt dynamics, if debt levels remain where they are and growth remains where it is, there is never going to be a reduction in the debt ratio in the foreseeable future. Moving away from austerity at this stage is a sensible course of action.'

Introducing a note of surprise in Germany's torpid election campaign, on 20 August 2013, Wolfgang Schäuble, the German Finance Minister, stated that Greece would need a third bail-out.[17] In key respects, this is necessary in order to find the funds to repay the first two: €20.3 billion must be repaid to the IMF between 2014 and 2016 by a Greece with a shrinking GDP and labour market.[18] Even the lowering of interest rates that Schäuble talked about, along with the lengthening of debt maturities, make the debt repayments of €40 billion due in 2014–15 scarcely attainable. With annual GDP growth of 4.5 per cent, the target might be achievable but the deflationary straitjacket in which the troika placed Greece and other stricken eurozone members conspires against such a benign outcome.[19]

Almost incredibly, re-designing the architecture of a trans-national Europe continues to preoccupy the leading EU decision-makers. Barroso, the Commission chief, is fixated with a federation of European nation-states though meagre details are forthcoming about what new forms of centralisation this will entail.[20] It has become a vast displacement exercise which is only likely to deepen the sense of disconnect between functionaries, their political bosses and millions of ordinary citizens. Leaders possessing the ability and the appeal to accomplish change as fundamental as this are impossible to spot.

Further trans-national initiatives involving the EU's core institutions are only likely to work if they are directed at finding solutions to the contemporary financial crisis. Its origins and duration stem from the very top-down, unrepresentative and often coterie-ridden approaches to policy-making evident over the last strife-torn five years.

Europhile leaders may have pioneered a European unification concept in the 1950s which gave the EU momentum until the end of the Cold War. But crises from that of the Balkans in the early 1990s to the extended financial one have revealed how deep its limitations are in carrying out its own projects or resolving difficulties arising from chronic design faults. The two main guarantors of the eurozone, France and Germany, cannot agree on any form of decisive action beyond a series of quick fixes or else empty rhetorical pronouncements. Their absorption with their own national affairs is hard to conceal and makes the likelihood of any deeper process of integration, involving the abandonment of sovereignty, hard to imagine.

When they issue regular statements calling for progress towards a European order to be speeded up, drab bureaucratic chieftains need to realise how much they are damaging the cause they purport to love. They place a struggling currency, the euro, on the same level as a sacred piece of territory or the well-being of millions of struggling Europeans; but even in the deceptively calm years, it failed to promote the solidarity which a nation normally invokes.

Surveying the EU in late 2013, it is impossible to see any forces which today enjoy the capacity and appeal to promote ever closer union as a credible crisis-busting strategy. The strains of containing a crisis, often through improvised measures which just store up problems further ahead, has instead divided those who previously shared a common vision for the European project. Mutual suspicions have grown too large. The rules were bent by club members in the first decade of the euro's existence to try and give durability to what proved to be a sub-optimal currency. They were then flouted in the half-decade of crisis. The young currency union's traumatic history offers too many ominous lessons: who is to say that if a currency union graduates to being an economic government for the EU, strong or impulsive members will not behave in similar high-handed ways, tossing aside any interest that stands in their way.

The EU can conserve some of its remaining credit if it emphasises practical solutions to the crisis that restore health to stricken economies. There has been no shortage of recommendations but no sign of any deep-seated re-appraisal of the policy of fiscal retrenchment in the EU's inner councils.

In August 2013, two economists, Pierre Pâris and Charles Wyplosz, reviewed what they considered were the options available in order to reduce spiralling debt levels.[21] The present policy was seen as too costly: structural reforms usually take years to have an impact on the economy and the contraction of the economy produced by austerity risks triggering a wholesale depression. The sale of public assets is another initiative often viewed as a solution for enabling governments to reduce high debt levels, but to have such an effect, the sale needs to be accomplished relatively quickly. Inevitably, the true value of the assets is depressed in what can turn into a fire-sale. Besides, a massive administrative effort is needed that is probably beyond the reach of a lot of deficit states.

Debt restructuring might have contained the crisis at the outset but it is increasingly fraught with danger because in each of the crisis countries in the eurozone, public debt has migrated to the books of its commercial banks. The intertwining of public debt and bank assets would 'make sovereign debt restructuring unmanageable without outside help' according to these authors. But the European Stability Mechanism with its 'firepower' of €500 billion is an inadequate rescue service given that the total debt of the current crisis countries – Greece, Ireland, Portugal, Italy and Spain – amounts to some €3,750 billion.

There remains debt restructuring, a transfer of funds from the creditor countries of the eurozone to the heavily indebted ones. The political obstacles to this measure have soared as electorates, facing economic squeezes, have grown fearful of the rhetoric of solidarity. But according to Pâris and Wyplosz the practical constraints are overwhelming. They write:

> Suppose all the other Eurozone countries forgive a quarter of the debts of Greece, Ireland, Portugal, Italy, Spain and France. This represents a write-down for 'forgiven' countries' debt that amounts to about €1200 billion. That is about 30% of the 'forgiving' countries' GDPs.[22]

The option which these authors reluctantly embrace is burying the debt by selling it to the ECB. This could involve the ECB buying bonds of a country perhaps for a value of €100 and exchanging them for a permanent, interest-free loan of €100. Debt monetisation has a bad reputation arising from its link with runaway inflation, but current conditions make this unlikely due to 'the icy state of the credit markets'.[23]

Debt cancellation involves a huge moral hazard but 'it has the advantage that the non-virtuous countries will share the costs in the form of reduced profit transfers from the ECB over the long run'.[24] It is also less debilitating in the long run than financing ongoing deficits in repeated interventions, such as seen over Greece, that produce mounting strains among institutions and nations which normally operate in tandem. But to succeed, rigorous fiscal discipline is needed that has to be centrally coordinated and not based on informal pacts. The disagreements, even among the non-crisis nations, about the methodology and timetable for fiscal union shows just how difficult such a journey is likely to be.

A flawed monetary institution was created by impetuous and economically ill-informed politicians (German ones to the fore) whose flaws have been cruelly exposed in a global economic crisis less than a decade following its inception. Finding a way to emerge from crisis through the retention of the existing model for the single currency is proving daunting. It is impossible to avoid the doleful conclusion that the German electorate, in September 2013, endorsed the cautious, slow-moving approach of their Chancellor, one that is widely disparaged in global economic circles.

There is no agreement about the kind of political and economic union for Europe that will be fit to host its own currency. The restoration to economic health of crisis-hit states is being neglected in the process. A modest expansion in the eurozone economy of 0.3 per cent in the second quarter of 2013 was hailed by defenders of the current policies as a dramatic turning-point after six consecutive quarters of contraction.[25] But it was based on exports to emerging markets and there was no sign of a recovery in consumption needed to make any growth sustainable.[26]

Perhaps it is necessary for decision-makers at European level to modify their ambitions. Plans should be considered for an orderly retreat from the existing model of monetary union. It needs to be revamped in order to enable countries enduring a prolonged slump to enjoy a revival of economic activity. This can take different forms: broad discussions with experts of the kind that the EU has traditionally shunned in favour of a dialogue with true believers

ought to be taking place to identify practical options. Brigid Laffan, perhaps
Ireland's most high-profile Europhile academic, has argued that scholars of
integration need to think more strategically and even factor in negative
scenarios 'ranging from fragmentation to system failure'.[27]

Perhaps some of the grimmest scenarios can still be avoided if EU decision-
makers put aside their campaign to undo the nation-state and treat it instead
as a partner in a common emergency that needs to be overcome. Multi-level
governance failed to promote the solidarity which a nation normally invokes.
The members of the eurozone jockeyed among themselves to derive the
greatest advantage from the currency union and rarely thought in terms of any
greater European cause (whether conceived in supra-national or inter-governmental terms).

The usefulness of the nation-state as a partner possessing greater legitimacy
than the centralised European agencies, and greater know-how also in key
respects, needs to be recognised. In 2013 signs emerged that Britain and
Germany were reaching an informal understanding on the need to repatriate
powers from Brussels to national capitals where they could be far more effectively exercised. Hopefully, the realisation will also eventually grow that
power at national level is less easily grabbed by vested interests than it is in the
opaque corridors of EU power, where any meaningful democratic oversight is
lacking.

From the 1950s, much of Europe has enjoyed a rare span of internal
stability and peace, to which the EU has contributed. At the beginning of this
period, Robert Schuman pointed out that 'Europe will not be created in one
stroke or in one operation, but with concrete achievements that will create a
sound basis from the start.'[28] These achievements have been increasingly
invisible in the past decades even as growing power has been concentrated in
the institutions of the EU. The failure of the currency union needs to prompt a
searching reappraisal of whether the current institutional order is assisting or
hindering European cooperation. This book presents evidence for the
argument that supra-national integration, culminating in a flawed project for
European Monetary Union, is driving the peoples of Europe further apart.
Indeed, unless a correction occurs that gives their views and concerns as much
weight as those enjoyed by insider lobbies and interest groups, then the real
danger exists that the reputation of European cooperation will, in its turn,
suffer the eclipse experienced by political nationalism in the second half of the
last century.

Notes

1 Wolfgang Münchau, 'The dangers of Europe's technocratic busybodies', *Financial Times*, 14 July 2013.
2 Ray Kinsella, 'Should Ireland exit the euro zone?', *Irish Examiner*, 20 May 2013.
3 *Guardian*, 25 September 2013.
4 *Financial Times*, 24 September 2013.
5 Kinsella, 'Should Ireland exit the euro zone?'.
6 Robin Harding, 'Reinhart and Rogoff publish formal correction', *Financial Times*, 8 May 2013.
7 *Guardian*, 25 September 2013.
8 Colm McCarthy, 'Banking reform must be high on the ECB agenda', *Sunday Independent*, 6 October 2013.
9 *Daily Telegraph*, 17 September 2013.
10 Sonia Sirletti and Yalman Onaran, 'Banking Balkanization prevails in Europe on eve of review', Bloomberg News, 23 October 2013.
11 Walter Russell Mead, 'Europe is burning, slowly', *Via Meadia*, 15 October 2013.
12 Simms, *Europe, The Struggle for Supremacy*, p. 517.
13 Joschka Fischer, 'The erosion of Europe', Project Syndicate, 30 April 2013.
14 RTE, Irish Radio, 21 July 2013.
15 Fischer, 'The erosion of Europe'.
16 Costas Lapavitsas, 'Greece doesn't need yet another rescue package – it needs a way out', *Guardian*, 27 August 2013.
17 *EUObserver*, 20 August 2013.
18 Matina Stevis, 'Greek cash shortfall spells problems for euro zone', *Wall Street Journal*, 30 August 2013.
19 Lapavitsas, 'Greece doesn't need yet another rescue package'.
20 Charlemagne, *The Economist*, 30 August 2013.
21 Pierre Pâris and Charles Wyplosz, 'To end the eurozone crisis, bury the debt forever', *Vox*, 6 August 2013: www.voxeu.org/article/end-eurozone-crisis-bury-debt-forever.
22 Pâris and Wyplosz, 'To end the eurozone crisis'.
23 Pâris and Wyplosz, 'To end the eurozone crisis'.
24 Pâris and Wyplosz, 'To end the eurozone crisis'.
25 Jeroen Dijsselbloem, Olli Rehn, Jörg Asmussen, Klaus Regling and Werner Hoyer, 'Europe's crisis response is showing results', *Wall Street Journal*, 9 October 2013.
26 Simon Tilford, 'A eurozone recovery? Think again', *Realclearworld*, 5 October 2013.
27 Laffan, 'No easy options on horizon'.
28 Willis, *France, Germany and the New Europe*, p. 47.

Bibliography

Newspapers and periodicals

American Spectator
City Journal
Daily Telegraph
Der Spiegel, International Edition
Die Welt
Economist
El Mundo
El Pais
EUObserver
Eurointelligence Daily Briefing
Financial Times
Forbes Magazine
Globe and Mail
Greek Default Watch
Guardian
Independent
Irish Examiner
Irish Independent
Irish Times
IVM Post
Le Figaro
London Review of Books
National Interest
New Republic
New York Review of Books
Open Europe
New Statesman
New York Times
Open Democracy
Portuguese News
Presseurop
Realclearworld
Revista 22
Scotsman

Slate
Spectator
Sunday Business Post
Sunday Independent
The Atlantic
Wall Street Journal

Blogs analysing the crisis of the single currency

Coppola Comment, www.coppolacomment.blogspot.com
Irish Economy, www.irisheconomy.ie
Observing Greece, www.klauskastner.blogspot.com
Open Europe, www.openeuropeblog.blogspot.co.uk
Project Syndicate, www.project-syndicate.org
True Economics, www.trueeconomics.blogspot.com

Authored books, journal articles, reports

Acemoglu, Daron and Johnson, Simon, 'Captured Europe', Project Syndicate, 20 March 2012.

Alderman, Liz and Craig, Susanne, 'Sovereign debt turns sour in euro zone', *New York Times*, 10 November 2011.

Allen, Kristen, 'Is Merkel gambling away the European idea?', *Der Spiegel*, International Edition, 19 May 2011.

Andersen, S.S. and Eliassen, K.A., 'European Community lobbying', *European Journal of Political Research*, 20, 2, 1996.

Andreasen, Marta, *Brussels Laid Bare* (Devon: St Edwards Press, 2009).

Armistead, Louise, 'Germany is "playing with fire" on Greece, warns finance minister', *Daily Telegraph*, 16 February 2012.

Armistead, Louise, 'Debt crisis: Barroso may want political union – but what's in it for the people?', *Daily Telegraph*, 13 September 2012.

Arnold, Bruce, 'Brash Martin shows he has yet to master the art of protocol', *Irish Independent*, 18 November 2008.

Arnold, Bruce, *The Fight For Democracy (A Series of Interviews with Declan Ganley)* (Dublin: Killynon House Books, 2009).

Atkins, Ralph, 'Convergence in reverse', *Financial Times*, 4 September 2012.

Auer, Stefan, *Whose Liberty is it Anyway? Europe at the Crossroads* (Chicago: University of Chicago Press, 2012).

Baldwin, Peter, 'Tracing Europe's long road to economic catastrophe', *The New Republic*, 9 March 2012.

Ball, Martin, North, Richard, Oulds, Robert and Rotherham, Lee, *Propaganda: How the EU Uses Education and Academia to Sell Integration* (London: Bruges Group, 2004).

Balzli, Beat, 'Greek debt crisis: how Goldman Sachs helped Greece to mask its true debt', *Der Spiegel Online*, 2 August 2010.

Banks, Martin, 'EU triples its financial contribution to Euronews', *The Parliament*, 13 January 2011: www.theparliament.com.

Barber, Tony, 'A void to fill', *Financial Times*, 27 May 2009.

Barker, Alex and Wilson, James, 'Public failure casts a cloud on Europe', *Financial Times*, 15 January 2012.

Barreto, António, 'Social change in Portugal', in António Costa Pinto (ed.), *Contemporary Portugal: Politics, Society and Culture* (Boulder, CO: Columbia University Press, 2011).

Batzoglu, Ferry, Ertel, Manfred, Hoges, Clemens and Hoyng, Hans, 'Generations of pork: how Greece's elite ruined the country', *Der Spiegel*, International Edition, 7 July 2011.

Beck, Gunnar, 'Merkel will win – because my fellow Germans dare not speak of national self interest', *Spectator*, 21 September 2013.

Beck, Ulrich and Giddens, Anthony, 'If the EU were abolished, we would have less control over our affairs', *Guardian*, 4 October 2005.

Bellamy, Richard, 'Democracy without democracy? Can the EU's democratic "outputs" be separated from the democratic "inputs" provided by competitive parties and majority rule?', in Peter Mair and Jacques Thomassen (eds), *Political Representation and European Union Governance* (London: Routledge, 2011).

Bini Smaghi, Lorenzo, *Morire di Austerita* (Milan: Il Mulino, 2013).

Bittner, Jochen, Finkenzeller, Karen and Jungclaussen, Frederick, 'Europe's seven deadly sins: 2', *Presseurop*, 15 December 2011.

Blackstone, Brian and Walker, Marcus, 'How ECB chief outflanked German foe in fight for euro', *Wall Street Journal*, 2 October 2012.

Blond, Phillip, 'Modern Conservatives make plebs of us all', *Financial Times*, 26 September 2012.

Böll, Sven and Marquart, Maria, 'Triumph of right-wing populists: how dangerous is Finland to the euro?', *Der Spiegel Online*, 20 April 2011.

Böll, Sven, Reiermann, Christian, Sauga, Michael and Wiegrefe, Klaus, 'Euro struggles can be traced to origins of common currency', *Der Spiegel Online*, 7–8 May 2012.

Bonde, Jens-Peter, *Mamma Mia: On 25 Years of Fighting for Openness in the EU* (Copenhagen: Forlaget Vindrose/Notat, n.d.).

Booker, Christopher and North, Richard, *The Great Deception: Can the European Union Survive?* (London: Continuum, 2006).

Bramwell, A.C., '*Dans le couloire*: the political culture of the EEC Commission', *International Journal of Moral and Social Studies*, 2, 1, 1987.

Břicháček, Tomás, 'Grand ideas and empty jargon', *Presseurop*, 15 March 2013.

Brooks, David, 'The technocratic nightmare', *New York Times*, 17 November 2011.

Buchan, David, 'Tilt in the balance of power', *Financial Times*, 13 December 1994.

Bush, Evelyn and Simi, Peter, 'European farmers and their protests', in Doug Imig and Sidney Tarrow (eds), *Contentious Europeans: Protest Politics in an Emerging Polity* (Lanham, MD: Rowman and Littlefield, 2001).

Campanella, Edoardo, 'Europe's crisis of tongues', Project Syndicate, 10 August, 2012.

Carney, Brian, 'The coming Greek write-off', *Wall Street Journal*, 9 July 2013.

Castle, Stephen, 'Europe in disarray as entire Commission quits over report', *Independent*, 16 March 1999.

Charlemagne, 'A rigged dialogue with society', *Economist*, 21 October 2004.

Charlemagne, 'Ask a silly question', *Economist*, 21 February 2008.

Charlemagne, 'France's minister sees a neocon plot', *Economist*, 26 June 2008.

Charlemagne, 'The divisiveness pact', *Economist*, 10 March 2011.

Charlemagne, 'Back to school', *Economist*, 31 August 2013.

Ciechanowicz, Artur and Sadowski, Rafal, 'The future of the Franco-German tandem', Warsaw: Centre for Eastern Studies, 11 July 2012: www.osw.waw.pl.

Clark, Ross, 'Cameron's tragic flaw', *Spectator*, 4 April 2012.

Clark, Simon and Priestley, Julian, *Europe's Parliament* (London: John Harper Publications, 2012).

Clogg, Richard, *Greece 1981–89: The Populist Decade* (London: Palgrave, 1993).

Cole, John, *As It Seemed To Me – Political Memoirs* (London: Weidenfeld and Nicolson, 1995).

Connolly, Bernard, *The Rotten Heart of Europe* (London: Faber, 1995).

Cooper, Matt, 'Germany can't make Germans out of us because of euro crisis', *Irish Examiner*, 18 May 2012.

Crook, Clive, 'In Cyprus, Europe sets a new standard for stupidity', Bloomberg News, 19 March 2013.

Cullen, Paul, 'Iceland: from ruin to role model?', *Irish Times*, 24 September 2011.

Dellepiane Avellaneda, Sebastian and Hardiman, Niamh, 'The European context of Ireland's economic crisis', *The Economic and Social Review*, 41, 4, Winter 2010.

Denman, Roy, *Missed Chances: Britain and Europe in the Twentieth Century* (London: Cassell, 1996).

Diamandouros, P. Nikiforos, 'European Ombudsman speech', Brussels, 17 November 2005: www.ombudsman.europa.eu.

Dijsselbloem, Jeroen, Rehn, Olli, Asmussen, Jörg, Regling, Klaus and Hoyer, Werner, 'Europe's crisis response is showing results', *Wall Street Journal*, 9 October 2013.

Dodge, Peter, *Beyond Marxism: The Faith and Works of Hendrik de Man* (The Hague: Martinus Nijhoff, 1966).

Douthat, Ross, 'Prisoners of the euro', *New York Times*, 1 June 2013.

Duchêne, François, *Jean Monnet: The First Statesman of Interdependence* (New York: WW Norton, 1994).

Duff, Andrew, *Saving the European Union* (London: Shoehorn, 2009).

Dumas, Charles, 'Euro was flawed at birth and should break apart now', Bloomberg News, 1 April 2012.

Dyson, Kenneth, *The Politics of the Euro-Zone: Stability or Breakdown?* (Oxford: Oxford University Press, 1999).

Dyson, Kenneth, 'The first decade: credibility, identity and institutional fuzziness', in Kenneth Dyson (ed.), *The Euro at Ten: Europeanisation, Power and Convergence* (Oxford: Oxford University Press, 2008).

Elliott, Larry, Inman, Phillip and Smith, Helena, 'IMF admits: we failed to realise the damage austerity would do to Greece', *Guardian*, 6 June 2013.

Erhard, Ludwig, *Prosperity Through Competition* (London: Thames and Hudson, 1958).

Erlanger, Steve, 'The soft middle of François Hollande', *New York Times*, 13 April 2012.

Erlanger, Steve and Kanter, James, 'Stricter rules but signs of disarray in Cyprus deal', *New York Times*, 26 March 2013.

Esman, Abigail R., 'Will the new Turkey become the model for a new Europe?', *Forbes Magazine*, 12 February 2011.

Evans-Pritchard, Ambrose, 'Does the EU club have a future?', *Daily Telegraph*, 14 September 2009.

Evans-Pritchard, Ambrose, 'Europe, free speech, and the sinister repression of the rating agencies', *Daily Telegraph*, 7 July 2011.

Evans-Pritchard, Ambrose, 'Euro bail-out in doubt as "hysteria" sweeps Germany', *Daily Telegraph*, 28 August 2011.

Evans-Pritchard, Ambrose, 'Merkel's Teutonic summit enshrines Hooverism in EU treaty law', *Daily Telegraph*, 12 December 2011.

Evans-Pritchard, Ambrose, 'Greek economy spirals down as EU forces final catharsis', *Daily Telegraph*, 14 February 2012.

Evans-Pritchard, Ambrose, 'Europe's nuclear brinkmanship with Greece is a lethal game', *Daily Telegraph*, 10 May 2012.

Evans-Pritchard, Ambrose, 'Finland prepares for break-up of eurozone', *Daily Telegraph*, 16 August 2012.

Evans-Pritchard, Ambrose, 'Only the German people can renounce their sovereignty', *Daily Telegraph*, 12 September 2012.

Evans-Pritchard, Ambrose, 'Olli Rehn should resign for crimes against Greece and against economics', *Daily Telegraph*, 6 June 2013.

Evans-Pritchard, Ambrose and Armistead, Louise, 'IMF slashes global growth over euro woes', *Daily Telegraph*, 20 January 2012.

Featherstone, Kevin, 'The Greek sovereign debt crisis and EMU: a failing state in a skewed regime', *Journal of Common Market Studies*, 49, 2, March 2011.

Featherstone, Kevin and Papadimitriou, Dimitris, *Limits of Europeanization: Reform Capacity and Policy Conflicts in Greece* (Basingstoke: Palgrave, 2008).

Feldstein, Martin, 'EMU and international conflict', *Foreign Affairs*, 76, 6, November–December 1987.

Ferreira do Amaral, João, *Porque devemos sair do euro* (Lisbon: Lua do Papel, 2013).

Fidler, Stephen, Steinhauser, Gabriele and Stevis, Metina, 'Rifts over Cyprus bailout feed broader fears', *Wall Street Journal*, 25 January 2013.

Fischer, Joschka, *From Confederation to Federation: Thoughts on the Finality of European Integration* (London: The Federal Trust, 2000).

Fischer, Joschka, 'The erosion of Europe', Project Syndicate, 30 April 2013.

Flamini, Roland, 'Judicial reach: the ever-expanding European Court of Justice', *World Affairs Journal*, November/December 2012.

Fontaine, Paschal, *A Citizen's Europe* (Luxemburg: OOPEC, 1993).

Forelle, Charles, 'A nation of drop-outs shakes Europe', *Wall Street Journal*, 25 March 2011.

Forster, Anthony, *Euroscepticism in Contemporary British Politics: Opposition to Europe in the Conservative and Labour Parties Since 1945* (London: Routledge, 2002).

Fox, Benjamin, 'Democracy is the real victim in the Greek tragedy', *EUObserver*, 12 June 2013.

Fransen, Frederic J., *The Supranational Politics of Jean Monnet: Ideas and Origins of the European Community* (Westport, CT: Greenwood Press, 2001).

Friend, Julius W., *The Linchpin: French-German Relations, 1950–1990* (Washington, DC: Praeger, 1991).

Friend, Julius W., *Unequal Partners: French-German Relations 1989–2000* (Washington, DC: Praeger, 2001).

Galbraith, James K., 'The crisis in the eurozone', *Salon*, 10 November 2011: www.salon.com.

Gallagher, Tom, *Romania and the European Union: How the Weak Vanquished the Strong* (Manchester: Manchester University Press, 2009).

Gallagher, Tom, *Journey Without Maps: Ireland and the EU during the European Financial Crisis* (Brussels and London: New Directions, 2012).

Gerlach-Kristen, Petra, 'Unification realities make Germans wary of bailout toll', *Irish Times*, 29 August 2012.

Gersemann, Olaf, 'Top ten reasons why the euro was a dumb idea', *Die Welt*, 29 November 2011.

Gilbert, Mark, *European Integration: A Concise History* (Plymouth, UK: Rowman and Littlefield, 2011).

Gillingham, John, *European Integration 1950–2003* (Cambridge: Cambridge University Press, 2003).

Glenny, Misha, 'The real Greek tragedy – its rapacious oligarchs', *Financial Times*, 8 November 2011.

Godley, Wynne, 'Maastricht and all that', *London Review of Books*, 8 October 1992.

Granitsas, Alkman, 'Merkel sees hope as Greeks protest cuts', *Wall Street Journal*, 10 October 2012.

Grant, Charles, *Delors, Inside the House that Jacques Built* (London: Nicolas Brealey, 1994).

Grant, Charles, 'How Hollande should handle Merkel', *Realclearworld*, 16 May 2012.

Gurdgiev, Constantin, 'Europe's policy errors', True Economics, 22 December 2011.

Gurdgiev, Constantin, 'Euro area crisis – no growth in sight', True Economics, 21 May 2012.

Gurdgiev, Constantin, 'Latest EBC plan kicks the can further down the road', *Globe and Mail*, 10 September 2012.

Gurdgiev, Constantin, 'Thou shalt not read into the ECB PRs too much', True Economics, 28 September 2012.

Gurdgiev, Constantin, 'Two points of note from today's economic news', True Economics, 28 September 2012,

Haas, Ernst, *The Uniting of Europe, Political Social and Economic Forces 1950–1957* (Stanford, CA: Stanford University Press, 1958).

Habermas, Jürgen, *The Crisis of the European Union: A Response* (Cambridge: Polity, 2012).

Hackmann, Friedrich and Schnapper, Dominique, *The Integration of Immigrants in European Societies* (Stuttgart: Lucius & Lucius, 2003).

Hader, Leon, 'The rest won't overwhelm the west', *Realclearworld*, 1 July 2011.

Hall, Ben and Peel, Quentin, 'Adrift amid a rift', *Financial Times*, 24 June 2010.

Haller, Max, *European Integration as an Elite Process: The Failure of a Dream?* (London: Routledge, 2008).

Halligan, Liam, 'Eurozone burns money while the banks fiddle their balance sheets', *Sunday Telegraph*, 22 January 2012.

Halligan, Liam, 'Forget "economic spring" – Greek outlook is stormy', *Sunday Telegraph*, 11 March 2012.

Halligan, Liam, 'Is the US losing patience with the eurozone debacle?', *Sunday Telegraph*, 22 July 2012.

Hannan, Daniel, 'Non-sense', *Spectator*, 23 April 2005.

Hannan, Daniel, 'The EU is an antidote to democratic governments, argues President Barroso', *Daily Telegraph*, 8 October 2010.

Hannan, Daniel, 'EU bans herbal remedies: another victory for corporate interests', *Daily Telegraph* (Daniel Hannan's blog), 30 December 2010.

Hannan, Daniel, 'The EU's latest bailout will fail, as all previous bailouts have failed', *Daily Telegraph*, 27 October 2011.

Hannan, Daniel, 'If Nicolas Sarkozy thinks the FT is a free market newspaper, God help France', *Daily Telegraph*, 16 April 2012.

Hannan, Daniel, 'Y con el rescate, díganme ¿cómo les va? ("How's that bailout workin' out for ya?")', *Daily Telegraph* (Daniel Hannan's blog), 14 June 2012.

Hannan, Daniel, 'EU regulation is making the next crash inevitable', *Daily Telegraph*

(Daniel Hannan's blog), 14 September 2012.

Hannan, Daniel, 'Germans are finally losing patience with the euro racket', *Daily Telegraph* (Daniel Hannan's blog), 18 September 2012.

Harding, Gareth, 'Fish tale at European Commission', United Press International, 2 May 2002.

Harding, Robin, 'Reinhart and Rogoff publish formal correction', *Financial Times*, 8 May 2013.

Hartwich, Oliver Marc, 'Germany proves clumsy with foreign matter', *Australian*, 21 October 2010.

Heisbourg, François, *La fin du rêve européen* (Paris: Stock, 2013).

Higgins, Andrew and Alderman, Liz, 'Europeans planted seeds of crisis in Cyprus', *New York Times*, 26 March 2013.

Holmes, Martin, *From Single Market to Single Currency: Evaluating Europe's Economic Experiment* (London: Bruges Group, 1995).

Holmes, Martin, *Franco–German Friendship and the Destination of Federalism* (London: Bruges Group, 1999).

Hutton, Will, 'In defence, as in finance, the truth is clear – our future lies in Europe', *Observer*, 16 September 2012.

Irving, Ronald, *Adenauer* (London: Pearson, 2002).

Issing, Otmar, 'The risk of European centralization', Project Syndicate, 2 July 2013.

Jay, Douglas, *Chance and Fortune* (London: Hutchinson, 1980).

Jenkins, Roy, *European Diary, 1977–1981* (London: Collins, 1989).

Johansson, Jan A., 'Euronews: channel of propaganda', *EUD, Alliance for a Europe of Democracies*, 18 January 2011. www.eudemocrats.org/eud/news.php?uid=296.

Kaiser, Wolfram, 'Plus ça change? Diachronic change in networks in European governance', in Wolfram Kaiser, Brigitte Leucht and Michael Gehler, *Transatlantic Networks in European Integration: Governing Europe 1948–1983* (Basingstoke: Palgrave, 2010).

Kaldor, Nicholas, 'The dynamic effects of the Common Market', *New Statesman*, 12 March 1971.

Kastner, Klaus, 'Prof Ralf Dahrendorf – a visionary', Observing Greece, 27 April 2013.

Kastner, Klaus, 'IMF is courageous and admits the obvious', Observing Greece, 6 June 2013.

Kazan, Olga, 'Thousands of Greek police join anti-austerity protests as June unemployment hits 24.4 percent', *Washington Post*, 6 September 2012.

Keenan, Brendan, 'Questions about the future of EU lurk beneath debt-crisis talks', *Irish Independent*, 6 September 2012.

Keohane, Robert and Hoffman, Stanley, 'Institutional change in Europe in the 1980s', in Robert Keohane and Stanley Hoffman, *The New European Community: Decision-Making and Institutional Change* (Oxford: Westview Press, 1991).

Kiljunen, K. *The European Constitution in the Making* (CEPS: Brussels, 2004).

Kinsella, Ray, 'Should Ireland exit the euro zone?', *Irish Examiner*, 20 May 2013.

Kinsella, Stephen, 'Five years after crash, what have we learned?', *Irish Independent*, 20 August 2012.

Kinsella, Stephen, 'We need to follow Iceland's lead and punish our bankers', *Irish Independent*, 17 September 2012.

Krastev, Ivan, 'The European Dis-Union: lessons from the Soviet collapse', *IVM Post*, 109, 2012.

Krugman, Paul, 'Baltic brouhaha', *New York Times*, 1 May 2013.

Laffan, Brigid, 'No easy options on horizon as crisis raises spectre of euro area fragmentation', *Irish Times*, 5 September 2013.

Lamy, Pascal, 'European leaders must lead from the front', World Trade Organization, Geneva, 21 June 2013: www.wto.org.

Lanchester, John, 'Once Greece goes', *London Review of Books*, 8 July 2011.

Lapavitsas, Costas, 'Greece doesn't need yet another rescue package – it needs a way out', *Guardian*, 27 August 2013.

Lederer, Edith M., 'EU confident Europe will overcome crisis', *Jakarta Post*, 18 May 2012.

Leonard, Mark, *Why Europe Will Run the 21st Century* (London: Fourth Estate, 2005).

Leucht, Brigitte, 'Expertise and the creation of a constitutional order for a core Europe: transatlantic policy networks in the Schuman Plan negotiation', in Wolfram Kaiser, Brigitte Leucht and Michael Gehler, *Transatlantic Networks in Regional Integration: Governing Europe 1945–1983* (Basingstoke: Palgrave, 2010).

Levy, Bernard-Henri, 'Federalism or death!', *Presseurop*, 2 October 2012.

Lilico, Andrew, 'How much did the IMF, ECB and EU bailouts harm Greek bondholders?', *Daily Telegraph*, 19 March 2012.

Linz, Juan J., *Robert Michels, Political Sociology, and the Future of Democracy* (New Brunswick: Transaction Publishers, 2006)

Lloyd, John, 'The beautiful folly of the European experiment', Reuters, 18 November 2011.

Lowrey, Annie, 'I.M.F. concedes major missteps in bailout of Greece', *New York Times*, 6 June 2013.

Ludlow, Peter, 'The European Commission', in Robert Keohane and Stanley Hoffman (eds), *The New European Community: Decision-Making and Institutional Change* (Oxford: Westview Press, 1991).

Lyrintzis, Christos, *Greek Politics in the Era of Economic Crisis: Re-assessing Causes and Effects*, London: Hellenic Observatory papers on Greece and Southeast Europe, 44, 2011.

McCarthy, Colm, 'Sarkozy's grandstanding on our corporation tax misses the point', *Sunday Independent*, 16 January 2011.

McCarthy, Colm, 'Ireland's grievance over ECB tactics is totally justified', *Sunday Independent*, 15 April 2012.

McCarthy, Colm, 'Reward isn't the word, Wolfgang, it's restitution', *Sunday Independent*, 26 August 2012.

McCarthy, Colm, 'Shocking treatment of Cyprus has exposed the eurozone's inherent flaws', *Sunday Independent*, 24 March 2013.

McCarthy, Colm, 'Banking reform must be high on the ECB agenda', *Sunday Independent*, 6 October 2013.

McCarthy, Patrick, 'Of Richeliu, Adenauer and sundry others', in Patrick McCarthy (ed.), *France-Germany in the Twenty-First Century* (London: Palgrave, 2001).

McDonald, Charlotte, 'Are Greeks the hardest workers in Europe?', BBC News, 26 February 2012.

McGurk, Tom, 'Who will hoist the Jolly Roger?', *Sunday Business Post*, 17 April 2011.

MacSharry, Ray and White, Padraic, *The Making of the Celtic Tiger: The Inside Story of Ireland's Boom Economy* (Cork: Mercier Press, 2000).

McWilliams, David, 'We're being played for fools', *Sunday Business Post*, 24 April 2011.

McWilliams, David, 'An anorexic on a drip is not a healthy patient', *Sunday Business Post*, 9 September 2011.

McWilliams, David, 'Germany is too strong – a Yes vote just solidifies this', *Sunday Independent*, 8 March 2012.

McWilliams, David, 'Prepare for titanic struggle as Draghi turns euro into lira', *Irish Independent*, 27 September 2012.

Mahler, Armin, 'Delusions of the euro zone: the lies that Europe's politicians tell themselves', *Der Spiegel Online*, 30 December 2011.

Mahony, Honor, 'Call for EU anti-fraud office to investigate MEPs' expenses', *EUObserver*, 21 February 2008.

Mahony, Honor, 'France warns Ireland on EU treaty "No" vote', *EUObserver*, 10 June 2008.

Mahony, Honor, 'Iceland could join EU by 2011', *EUObserver*, 30 January 2009.

Mahony, Honor, 'National stereotyping – the eurozone's other story', *EUObserver*, 22 February 2011.

Mahony, Honor, 'EU commission prepares ground for far-reaching economic powers', *EUObserver*, 21 March 2013.

Majone, Giandomenico, *Europe as the Would-be World Power: The EU at Fifty* (Cambridge: Cambridge University Press, 2009).

Marsh, David, *The Euro: The Politics of the New Global Currency* (London and New Haven: Yale University Press, 2009).

Marsh, David, 'Faltering ambitions and unrequited hopes: the battle for the euro intensifies', in Nathaniel Copsey and Tim Haughton (eds), *JCMS Annual Review of the European Union 2010*, 49.

Marsh, David, *The Euro: The Battle for the New Global Currency* (London: and New Haven: Yale University Press, 2011).

Marsh, David, *Europe's Deadlock* (London: Yale University Press, 2013).

Mead, Walter Russell, 'Will German politicians wreck Europe to save their own skins?', *Via Meadia*, 28 January 2012: www.blogs.the-american-interest.com/wrm.

Mead, Walter Russell, 'Eurozone begins to fracture', *Via Meadia*, 4 September 2012.

Mead, Walter Russell, 'Another European green fail', *Via Meadia*, 19 October 2012.

Mead, Walter Russell, 'Dutch flout EU deficit rules', *Via Meadia*, 1 March 2013.

Mead, Walter Russell, 'Europe is burning, slowly', *Via Meadia*, 15 October 2013.

Menon, Anand, 'France and the ICG of 1996', *Journal of European Public Policy*, 3, 2, June 1996.

Menon, Anand, *Europe: The State of the Union* (London: Atlantic Books, 2008).

Middlemas, Keith, *Orchestrating Europe: The Informal Politics of the European Union* (London: Fontana Press, 1995).

Mierzejewski, Alfred C., *Ludwig Erhard: A Biography* (Chapel Hill and London: University of North Carolina Press, 2004).

Milward, Alan S., *The European Rescue of the Nation-State* (London: Routledge, 1992).

Milward, Alan S., 'Allegiance: the past in the future', *Journal of European Integration History*, 1, 1995.

Mittermaier, Jana, 'New ECB powers: the buck stops where?', *EUObserver*, 18 September 2012.

Mole, John, *Mind Your Manners: Managing Culture Clash in the Single European Market* (London: Nicholas Brealey, 1992).

Molina, Cesar, 'Las élitas extractivas: una téoria de las clase política española', *El Pais*, 9 September 2012.

Molloy, Thomas, 'Half of Irish businesses on verge of collapse, new survey shows', *Irish Independent*, 31 July 2012.

Moore, Charles, 'If Strasbourg has its way, we will all end up as prisoners', *Daily Telegraph*, 12 February 2011.

Moore, Charles, 'The civil servants are the masters now', *Daily Telegraph*, 16 March 2012.

Moore, Malcolm, 'Stiglitz says European austerity plans are a "suicide pact"', *Daily Telegraph*, 17 January 2012.

Moravcsik, Andrew, *Choice for Europe: Social Purpose and State Power from Messina to Maastricht* (Ithaca, NY, and London: Cornell University Press, 1998).

Moravcsik, Andrew, 'In defence of the "democratic deficit": reassessing legitimacy in the European Union', *Journal of Common Market Studies*, 40, 2002.

Mosse, George L., *The Culture of Western Europe in the 19th and 20th Centuries* (London: John Murray, 1963).

Mudde, Cas and Rovira Kaltwasser, Cristobal, *Populism in Europe and the Americas: Threat or Corrective for Democracy?* (Cambridge: Cambridge University Press, 2012).

Mulcahy, Suzanne, *Money Politics and Power – Risks of Corruption in Europe* (Berlin: Transparency International, 2012).

Mullally, Lorraine, 'Bad news for democracy', *EUObserver*, 30 July 2008.

Münchau, Wolfgang, 'Germany is stuck between a brick and a volte-face', *Financial Times*, 6 February 2012.

Münchau, Wolfgang, 'Draghi is devil in Weidmann's euro drama', *Financial Times*, 23 September 2012.

Münchau, Wolfgang, 'The dangers of Europe's technocratic busybodies', *Financial Times*, 14 July 2013.

Murray, Craig, 'The day democracy died in Europe', Craig Murray Blog, 11 November 2011: www.craigmurray.org.uk.

Nemo, Philippe, 'Europe's endangered soul', *City Journal*, Spring 2010.

Nielsen, Nikolaj, 'Sarkozy threatens to end EU passport-free travel', *EUObserver*, 13 March 2012.

Nielsen, Nikolaj, 'MEPs threaten to block Commission funding over transparency', *EUObserver*, 5 September 2012.

Nixon, Simon, 'A reluctant hegemon steps to forefront', *Wall Street Journal*, 8 July 2013.

Norris, Floyd, 'Controls on capital come late to Cyprus', *New York Times*, 31 March 2013.

Nowak, Wolfgang, 'Germans don't want a Europe of broken promises and big bail-outs', *Daily Telegraph*, 6 September 2011.

O'Brennan, John, 'Will Europe end in Croatia?', Project Syndicate, 30 June 2013.

O'Brien, Dan, 'Interplay of biggest powers pits self-interest against bailout rate', *Irish Times*, 28 May 2011.

O'Donovan, Donal and Noonan, Laura, 'ECB breaks own rules accepting Portugal's junk debt', *Irish Independent*, 8 July 2011.

O'Leary, Jim, 'External surveillance of Irish fiscal policy during the boom', Irish Economy Note, 11 July 2010: www.irisheconomy.ie/Notes/IrishEconomyNote11.pdf.

O'Neill, Sir Con, *Britain's Entry into the European Community: Report on the Negotiations of 1970–1972* (London: Frank Cass Publishers, 2000).

O'Neill, Michael, *The Struggle for the European Constitution: A Past and Future History* (London: Routledge, 2009).

Onaran, Yalman, 'Deposit flight from Europe banks eroding common currency', Bloomberg News, 19 September 2012.

Palliser, Michael DOHB biographical details and interview, 28 April 1999, Churchill

College, Cambridge, archives: www.chu.cam.ac.uk/archives/collections/ ...
Phillips_hayden.pdf.

Pappas, Takis S., 'The causes of the Greek crisis are in Greek politics', *Open Democracy*, 29 November 2010.

Pappas, Takis S., 'Why Greece failed', *Journal of Democracy*, 24, 2, April 2013.

Pâris, Pierre and Wyplosz, Charles, 'To end the eurozone crisis, bury the debt forever', *Vox*, 6 August 2013: www.voxeu.org/article/end-eurozone-crisis-bury-debt-forever.

Parsons, Craig, *A Certain Idea of Europe* (Ithaca, NY, and London: Cornell University Press, 2003).

Pascoe, Thomas, 'Why the economics of the left benefit the one per cent', *Daily Telegraph*, 1 August 2012.

Pels, Dick, 'Hendrik de Man and the ideology of planism', *International Review of Social History*, 32, 3, December 1987.

Phillips, Leigh, 'ECB turned blind eye to predatory lending', *EUObserver*, 8 March 2011.

Phillips, Leigh, 'Rehn on eurozone rescue: "Mission accomplished"', *EUObserver*, 15 April 2011.

Phillips, Leigh, 'EU finance chiefs cool on German plans for Europe', *EUObserver*, 19 September 2011.

Phillips, Leigh, ' Netherlands: indebted states must be made "wards" of the commission or leave euro', *EUObserver*, 7 September 2011.

Pignal, Stanley, 'Britons weigh future in Brussels "eurocracy"', *Financial Times*, 29 December 2012.

Pinto-Duschinsky, Michael, *Bringing Rights Home* (London: Policy Exchange, 2011).

Pisani-Ferry, Jean, Sapir, André, Véron, Nicolas and Wolff, Guntram B., 'What kind of European banking union?', *Bruegel Policy Contribution*, issue 12, June 2012.

Pop, Valentina, 'Eurojust chief quits over power abuse scandal', *EUObserver*, 17 December 2009.

Pop, Valentina, 'Greece scores worst in corruption ranking', *EUObserver*, 17 October 2010.

Pop, Valentina, 'Merkel under fire for "lazy Greeks" remark', *EUObserver*, 19 May 2011.

Pop, Valentina, 'EU auditor used public funds to hamper anti-fraud inquiry', *EUObserver*, 27 April 2012.

Pop, Valentina 'European finances still in bad shape, statistics show', *EUObserver*, 16 May 2012.

Pop, Valentina, 'Spain: ECB cash more important than euro-plans', *EUObserver*, 24 May 2012.

Pop, Valentina, 'EU monitors heading to Madrid, despite "Men in Black" claims', *EUObserver*, 12 June 2012.

Pop, Valentina, 'Banking union: the German way or no way', *EUObserver*, 10 December 2012.

Pop, Valentina, 'New anti-euro party forms in Germany', *EUObserver*, 12 March 2013.

Pop, Valentina, 'Cyprus "business model" was no mystery to EU', *EUObserver*, 23 March 2013.

Pritchard, Mark, 'David Cameron's weakness on Europe forced me to resign from Conservative Party job', *Daily Telegraph*, 7 March 2012.

Rachman, Gideon, 'Europe's zero-sum dilemma', *The National Interest*, May–June 2012.

Redwood, John, 'London as the world's number one financial centre', 22 February 2012:

www.johnredwoodsdiary.com.

Reis, Ricardo, 'The Portuguese slump-crash and the euro crisis', paper delivered at the Brookings Panel on Economic Activity, Washington, DC, 21–22 March 2013.

Rettman, Andrew, 'Sweden complains about EU appointment to US', *EUObserver*, 22 February 2010.

Rettman, Andrew, 'Van Rompuy's "egg" goes down badly at EU summit', *EUObserver*, 24 June 2011.

Rettman, Andrew, 'Finland on Greek collateral: "It's not about the money"', *EUObserver*, 31 August 2011.

Reyes, Oscar, 'EU's flagship climate policy is sinking fast', *EUObserver*, 16 April 2013.

Rocard, Michel, 'The decline and fall of political Europe', Project Syndicate, 26 April 2010.

Ross, George, 'Policy development and the cabinet system in the Delors Commission', Pittsburg: American Enterprise Institute, no date, http://aei.pitt.edu/7234/1/1002484_1.pdf.

Ross, Shane, *The Bankers: How the Bankers Brought Ireland to its Knees* (Dublin: Penguin Ireland, 2009).

Royo, Sebastian, 'Reform betrayed? Zapatero and continuity in economic policy', in Bonnie N. Field (ed.), *Spain's 'Second Transition': The Socialist Government of José Luis Zapatero* (London: Routledge, 2011).

Russell, Jonathan, 'Martin Feldstein: French "don't get" problems at euro's heart', *Daily Telegraph*, 29 December 2011.

Santer, Jacques, 'The euro, instrumental in forging a European identity', *InfoEurope*, No. 8, May 1998.

Sauga, Michael, 'Lonely struggle: Wolfgang Schäuble's fight to save Europe', *Der Spiegel*, 17 July 2013.

Schmitter, Philippe and Bauer, Michael, 'A (modest) proposal for expanding social citizenship in the European Union', *Journal of European Social Policy*, 11, 1, 2001.

Scruton, Roger, 'The nation-state and democracy', *The American Spectator*, 14 February 2007.

Scruton, Roger, *Green Philosophy* (London: Atlantic Books, 2012)

Shore, Cris, *Building Politics: The Cultural Politics of European Integration* (London: Routledge, 2000).

Shore, Peter, *Separate Ways: Britain and Europe* (London: Duckworth, 2000).

Siedentop, Larry, *Democracy in Europe* (London: Penguin, 2001).

Simms, Brendan, *Europe, The Struggle for Supremacy: 1453 to the Present* (London: Allen Lane, 2013).

Sirletti, Sonia and Onaran, Yalman, 'Banking Balkanization prevails in Europe on eve of review', Bloomberg News, 23 October 2013.

Smith, Helena, 'Greek police send crime victims to neo-Nazi "protectors"', *Guardian*, 28 September 2012.

Soros, George, 'The tragedy of the European Union and how to resolve it', *New York Review of Books*, 27 September 2012.

Spiegel, Peter and Hope, Karin, 'EU's Olli Rehn lashes out at IMF criticism of Greek bailout', *Financial Times*, 5 June 2013.

Spinant, Daniela, 'Ombudsman urges committees to look at fish scandal', *EUObserver*, 28 May 2002.

Spinelli, Altiero, *The Eurocrats: Conflict and Crisis in the European Community* (Baltimore: Johns Hopkins University Press, 1966).

Spourdalakis, Michalis, *The Rise of the Greek Socialist Party* (London: Routledge, 1988).

Stephens, Philip, 'Europe's German question', *Financial Times*, 26 March 2010.

Sternhall, Zeev, 'The "anti-materialist" revision of Marxism', *Journal of Contemporary History*, 22, 1987.

Stevis, Matina, 'Greek cash shortfall spells problems for euro zone', *Wall Street Journal*, 30 August 2013.

Stiglitz, Joseph, 'Capturing the ECB', Project Syndicate, 6 February 2012.

Stuart, Gisela, *The Making of Europe's Constitution* (London: Fabian Society, 2004).

Taylor, Paul, 'Over-complex Europe keeps making same mistakes', Reuters, 14 May 2012.

Thompson, Derek, 'Fiscal union cannot save the euro', *The Atlantic*, 28 November 2011.

Tilford, Simon, 'A eurozone recovery? Think again', *Realclearworld*, 5 October 2013.

Toyer, Julien and Ruano, Carlos, 'Valencia, a cruel reflection of Spain's economic woes', Reuters, 2 May 2012.

Tran, Mark, 'Tory heavyweights join Blair for launch of Britain in Europe campaign', *Guardian*, 14 October 1999.

Trotman, Andrew, 'Debt crisis live', *Daily Telegraph*, 11 June 2012.

True, Nicholas, 'European Union', in Lord Howard of Rising (ed.), *Enoch at 100* (London: Biteback, 2012).

Truman, Edwin M., 'Unraveling the euro crisis', speech delivered at the National Economists Club, 26 January 2012, Petersen Institute for International Economics: www.piie,com/publications/paper/paper.cfm?ResearchID=2035.

Tsafos, Nikos, 'Are we all Greeks now?', Greek Default Watch, 24 April 2011.

Tsoukalis, Loukas, *The New European Economy Revisited* (Oxford: Oxford University Press, 1997).

Umbach, Gaby and Wessels, Wolfgang, 'The changing European context of monetary union: "deepening", "widening" and stability', in Kenneth Dyson (ed.), *The Euro at Ten: Europeanization, Power and Convergence* (Oxford: Oxford University Press, 2008).

Vaubel, Roland, *The European Institutions as an Interest Group: The Dynamics of Ever-Closer Union* (London: Institute of Economic Affairs, 2009).

Verney, Susannah, 'Justifying the second enlargement', in Helene Sjursen (ed.), *Questioning Enlargement: Europe in Search of Identity* (London: Routledge, 2006).

Véron, Nicolas, 'Europe's Cyprus blunder and its consequences', Bruegel, 21 March 2013.

Vogel, Toby, 'Principles for EU officials', *European Voice,* 21 June 2012.

von Hammerstein, Konstantin, Reiermann, Christian and Schult, Christoph, 'Druckversion – an unexpected U-turn: why Merkel wants to keep Greece in euro zone', *Der Spiegel Online*, 10 September 2012.

Walker, Marcus, 'Merkel's bet on Europe's future', *Wall Street Journal*, 23 April 2013.

Wall, Stephen, *A Stranger in Europe: Britain and the EU from Thatcher to Blair* (Oxford: Oxford University Press, 2008).

Wallace, William, 'Walter Hallstein: the British perspective', in Wilfried Loth, William Wallace and Bryan Rupert, *Walter Hallstein: The Forgotten European* (London: Croom Helm, 1998).

Warner, Jeremy, '"Them and us" mentality now colours eurozone's relations with UK', *Daily Telegraph*, 17 November 2011.

Warner, Jeremy, 'Euroland will pay for this monetary madness', *Daily Telegraph*, 3 March 2012.

Warner, Jeremy, 'Time to put the doomed euro out of its misery', *Daily Telegraph*, 13 April 2012.

Warner, Jeremy, 'Europeans will never accept a federal banking system', *Daily Telegraph*, 26 April 2012.

Waterfield, Bruno, 'José Manuel Barroso: "What we have is the first non-imperial empire"', *Daily Telegraph*, 11 July 2007.

Waterfield, Bruno, 'EU bail-out built on a lie', *EUObserver*, 10 May 2010.

Waterfield, Bruno, 'Ordinary people were misled over the impact of the euro', *Daily Telegraph*, 27 May 2010.

Waterfield, Bruno, 'House of History cost estimates double to £137 million', *Daily Telegraph*, 3 April 2011.

Weatherill, Stephen, 'The constitutional context of (ever-wider) policy-making', in Erik Jones, Anand Menon and Stephen Weatheril, *The Oxford Handbook of the European Union* (Oxford: Oxford University Press, 2012).

Webber, Douglas, 'Successful and genuine failures: France, Germany, and the others in the history of "multi-speed" European political integration', Fourth Pan-European Conference on EU Politics, Riga, 24 September 2008: http://jhubc.it/ecpr-riga/virtual-paperroom/125.pdf.

Weber, Eugen, *Peasants into Frenchmen: The Modernization of Rural France, 1870–1914* (Stanford, CA: Stanford University Press, 1986).

Weiler, J.H.H., *The Constitution of Europe* (Cambridge: Cambridge University Press, 1999).

Weisenthal, Joe, 'Full text of George Soros speech', *Business Insider*, 4 June 2012.

Weiss, Maurice, 'Interview with Helmut Schmidt and Valéry Giscard d'Estaing', *Der Spiegel Online*, 11 September 2012.

Williams, Charles, *Adenauer: The Father of the New Germany* (London: Little Brown, 2000).

Willis, Andrew, 'Senior lobbyists profit from expanding EU', *EUObserver*, 17 September 2010.

Willis, F. Roy, *France, Germany and the New Europe 1945–1967* (Stanford, CA: Stanford University Press, 1968).

Winand, Pascaline, *Eisenhower, Kennedy and the United States of Europe* (New York: St. Martins Press, 1993).

Winkler, Heinrich August, *Germany: The Long Road West, Volume 2, 1933–1990* (Oxford: Oxford University Press, 2007).

Wise, Peter, 'Portugal: waiting it out', *Financial Times*, 26 May 2013.

Wolf, Martin, 'The "grand bargain" is just a start', *Financial Times*, 29 March 2011.

Wolf, Martin, 'There is no sunlit future for the euro', *Financial Times*, 19 October 2011.

Wolf, Martin, 'Draghi alone cannot save the euro', *Financial Times*, 12 September 2012.

Wolf, Martin, 'Why exit is an option for Germany', *Financial Times*, 26 September 2012.

Wolf, Martin, 'Why the Baltic states are no model', *Financial Times*, 30 April 2013.

Yglesias, Matthew, 'Are Greeks lazy?', *Slate*, 19 December 2011.

Index